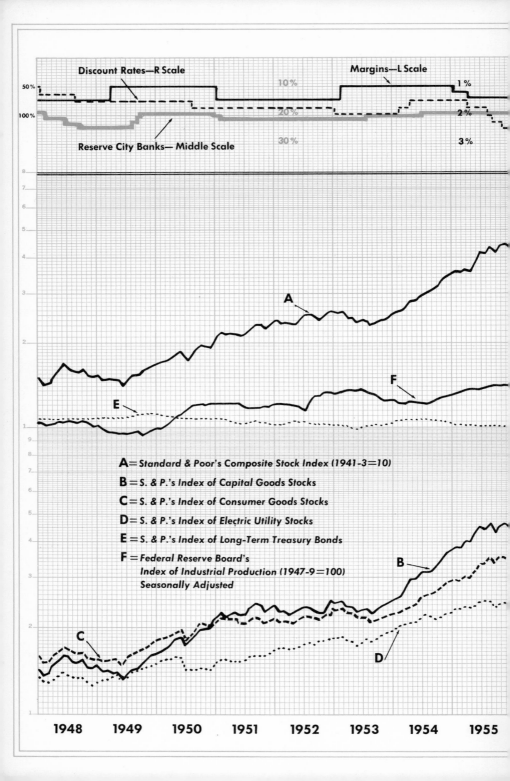

Discount Rates—R Scale

Margins—L Scale

50%

10%

1%

100%

20%

2%

Reserve City Banks— Middle Scale

30%

3%

A

F

E

A = Standard & Poor's Composite Stock Index (1941-3=10)

B = S. & P.'s Index of Capital Goods Stocks

C = S. & P.'s Index of Consumer Goods Stocks

D = S. & P.'s Index of Electric Utility Stocks

E = S. & P.'s Index of Long-Term Treasury Bonds

F = Federal Reserve Board's
Index of Industrial Production (1947-9=100)
Seasonally Adjusted

B

C

D

1948   1949   1950   1951   1952   1953   1954   1955

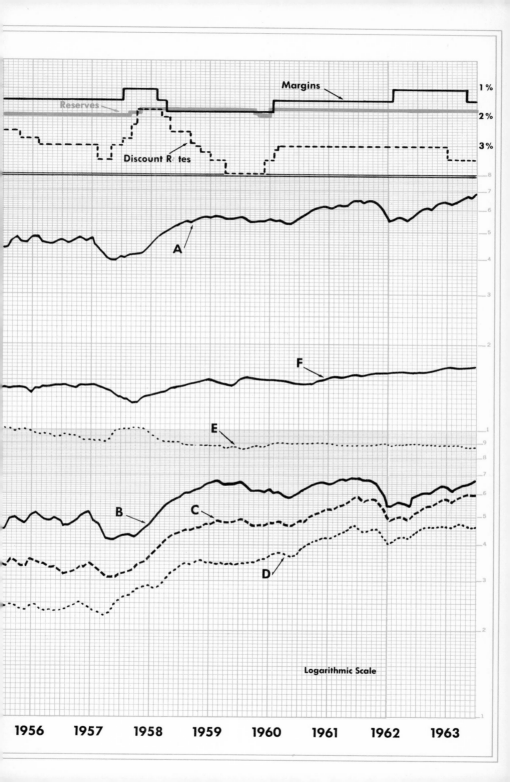

THE

SOPHISTICATED

A GUIDE TO STOCK MARKET PROFITS

Also by BURTON CRANE

Getting and Spending: An Informal Guide to National Economics
A Century of Financial Advertising in *The New York Times*
The Practical Economist

INVESTOR

by Burton Crane

REVISED AND EXPANDED BY

SYLVIA CRANE EISENLOHR

SIMON AND SCHUSTER · NEW YORK

FIRST PRINTING	1959
SECOND PRINTING	1959
THIRD PRINTING	1959
FOURTH PRINTING	1959
FIFTH PRINTING	1960
SIXTH PRINTING	1960
SEVENTH PRINTING	1960
EIGHTH PRINTING	1961
NINTH PRINTING	1961
TENTH PRINTING	1963

Revised Edition, EIGHTH PRINTING

LIBRARY OF CONGRESS CATALOG CARD NUMBER: 59-7267
MANUFACTURED IN THE UNITED STATES OF AMERICA

To Esther

Contents

Foreword

WHEN I *was about to begin my sophomore year at college, I told my father, the author of this book, that I wanted to elect an economics course so that I could understand his* New York Times *stock-market column.*

"Don't do that," he advised with some heat. "You won't get anything out of it but the prejudices of your professor. You might as well have my prejudices. I will give you the economics course."

It was a leisurely course, spread over a decade or so. The Crane Lectures were given during motor trips or on the golf course or at the dinner table. There was no syllabus. At one time, when my father was a New York Times *correspondent in Tokyo, I was a free-lance correspondent for a string of trade and business papers in the U.S. and elsewhere, and the course was tailored to my many requests for advice on how to handle certain stories. Much later, when my father was back in New York, I had a job as a researcher for* Time Magazine's *business section and I confronted for the first time the problem of covering Wall Street—among many other business topics. I brought home a lot of questions, and the pace of the lectures picked up.*

Late in 1962, when Burton Crane began work on the second edition of The Sophisticated Investor, *he had been an invalid for six months. Although he had been unable to write his daily* New York Times *column, he had worked on financial articles whenever he felt well enough, dictating to me or to my mother from his hospital bed and using a tape recorder after he was allowed to go home. Discussing his work with him, I found there was still plenty to learn.*

When my father died in February 1963, only a few pages had been completely rewritten, but his penciled reminders to himself on almost every page indicated quite clearly the extent of the overhaul operation he had envisioned.

9

My initial reaction, on learning that I was to complete the revision, was panic. Then, feeling somewhat (but not much) steadier after rereading the book, I decided it needed some clarification for the readers for whom it was originally intended.

"My main target," Burton Crane had written in the foreword to the first edition, "is the man or woman who draws a good salary and has a few thousand dollars for investment or speculation. I am not really thinking about the people who have to live entirely on the income from their investments. Neither am I worrying about those unlucky persons in the top-income tax brackets. They can hire experts to worry for them. . . .

"I am writing this book for an imaginary character named Alistair Brythwyte. Alistair has a commuting-train and cocktail-party knowledge of the stock market. He knows a good many things about it and almost half of them are true. . . .

"How about Barbara Brythwyte, who knows nothing but has stopped being proud of that fact? At the end of the book, just before the Index, I have placed a Glossary. Not all the useful definitions are there—some are carried in the text—but I think Barbara will find almost anything she wants. If I were Barbara, as a matter of fact, I'd stop at the end of this foreword and follow the instructions at the start of the Glossary. Then I'd come back and face Chapter I high of head and heart and with my nose powdered."

Barbara worried me. I could imagine her stopping frequently to re-powder her nose. Refusing to admit that she might be brighter than I, I resolved to "translate" the book for her.

First, however, it was necessary not only to bring the text up to date but to clarify large portions for myself. I began by calling upon or writing to nearly all the men mentioned or quoted in the first edition. For their kind and patient assistance, my warmest thanks. Without their enthusiastic guidance and encouragement, this revision might have been a chore instead of the fascinating occupation it has proved to be. Their response has also represented a tribute to my father.

Early in the process, it became obvious to me that The Sophisticated Investor *is not a primer and any attempt to transform it into one would be an insult to the many professionals who assisted my father on the first edition, not to mention the readers who have supported it through ten printings.*

Therefore I have tried to remain faithful to my father's intentions and style, following wherever possible his own instructions to himself.

Where does that leave Barbara? Well, the Glossary is still there. And I have a lot more faith in her than I used to have—after all, if I can revise this book, she can jolly well read it!

Because this book has been employed by some college economics faculties, my father had decided to make the second edition more adaptable to classroom use by including a set of review questions for each chapter. The text should suggest additional class projects in testing various investment methods, as well as chart-keeping, business forecasting, etc. Some supplemental reading is listed at the beginning of Chapter I, and other recommended books are mentioned at appropriate places in later chapters.

In the pages that follow, you will find many of the ideas of professionals in the investment field or professional advisers. Wherever possible—and some of the ideas have been around so long that they have lost the laundry marks of authorship—credit has been given. The words of more than fifty authorities have been quoted or paraphrased.

In the first edition, the author offered special thanks to Harry D. Comer of Paine, Webber, Jackson & Curtis and to Ralph A. Rotnem of Harris, Upham & Co., and I should like to add my own thanks to them for their help with the revision.

Invaluable as well was the assistance received from John J. Maloney, Manager of the News Bureau, New York Stock Exchange, who went over the entire first edition with me to see where he and the News Bureau staff could supply updated material. He provided a good deal of it.

My warm gratitude to Oliver Gingold, editor of the daily stock-market column of the Wall Street Journal, for generously giving his time to reading the completed revision, and to George W. Olsen, chief of the research department at Standard & Poor's Corporation, for updating those charts which employ S. & P. indices.

I must also thank the staff of the Lippincott Library, Wharton

School of Finance and Commerce, University of Pennsylvania, where I did most of the work on this revision, not only for allowing me to use their excellent research materials but for their guidance and unfailing courtesy.

Finally, I will thank Sam Meyerson of the Simon and Schuster staff, whose suggestions gave shape to the first edition of this book and whose continuing encouragement brought about the second.

One more point: Many stocks are necessarily mentioned by name in this book. Please remember that the last one was chosen as an example in September 1963. The conditions that caused it to be mentioned have almost certainly changed between then and the time you read this. There are no tips on individual stocks in this book! *Sorry.*

SYLVIA CRANE EISENLOHR

Philadelphia
1963

BOOK ONE

Timing

CHAPTER I

How You Can Profit from
Stock-Market Timing

GOOD BOOKS on the stock market must be hard to write. I have
dipped my nose into more than a hundred and hesitate to recommend
more than three or four.* Too many of the others seem to be saying
that today will last forever.

* In the first edition of this book, I neglected to provide a list of the books
I thought worth recommending. I have since had to write several hundred
letters filling in that gap. Briefly, then, these are the books that seem to me
sound enough for recommendation:

How to Buy Stocks, by Louis Engel, Advertising Manager for Merrill Lynch,
Pierce, Fenner and Smith, Inc. (hardcover edition published by Little, Brown
& Co.; paperback, Bantam Books). It is probably the simplest book that has
ever been written about investment. It does not go into stratospheric theory;
it simply tells how the investment market works.

Security Analysis, by Benjamin Graham and D. L. Dodd (McGraw-Hill Book
Co.). This and the following book have long been considered classics in the
field.

Technical Analysis of Stock Trends, by John Magee and Robert D. Edwards
(published by Mr. Magee at 360 Worthington Street, Springfield, Mass.).

The Battle for Investment Survival, by Gerald M. Loeb, one of the principals
of E. F. Hutton & Co. (Simon and Schuster).

Financial Independence Through Common Stocks, by R. D. Merritt (Simon
and Schuster).

The trouble with this, of course, is that "today" is whenever a passage is written, or, at best, when the final proof leaves the author's desk. Printing takes time. Binding takes time. Distribution takes time. On the day when the reader sees those golden words the atmosphere of business may have changed completely. That company that looked like a terrific "growth" proposition may be eating the other side of the toadstool.

One escape for the author is to assume that the market will always make new highs because it always has. Therefore any time is a good time to buy. This is not one of my favorite arguments. I can remember that the market as a whole took twenty-seven years to climb back to its 1929 high. Although I don't prophesy it, if you pin me down I'll have to admit that any time the market dips we might be starting a round trip that could end in 1991. (The shortest round trip on record began on the day of John F. Kennedy's assassination, when stock prices dropped $11 billion, and ended on the next business day, when stock prices gained $15 billion as investors gave the U.S. economy and Lyndon Johnson a vote of confidence.)

As we learned in the third chapter of Ecclesiastes:

"To every thing there is a season, and a time to every purpose under the heaven: A time to be born, and a time to die; a time to plant, and a time to pluck up that which is planted. . . ."

There is also a time to sell General Motors, and a time to buy Consolidated Edison.

Another escape for the author of a book such as this is to assume that each kind of person needs a different kind of stock: Risk situations for the bachelor with more than enough to live on; growth situations for the young husband building an estate; chance-taking commitments for the older man whose children have left the nest, and income for the person whose earning days are over.

Mm-m-m-mm! Yes. Maybe so. But the reader should never forget that it is better to own the wrong stock at the right time than the right stock at the wrong time. In fact, we belong right back in that third chapter of Ecclesiastes:

There is a time for buying cyclical stocks. By these I mean the metals, the machine-builders and the others that run up and down madly as business prospects grow more or less bright.

There is a time for buying defensive issues. These will include bonds and preferred stocks as well as some common stocks. Among the common stocks will be electric utilities, foods, tobaccos * and food chain stores—but not all of any category. The chief qualification for buying a bond or stock is that it should seem likely to go on paying its interest or dividend no matter how bad business gets. Some call these "money-rate issues." As money rates fall, their virtually fixed returns grow more valuable.

There is a time when it is safer to be a speculator than an investor. This means that, if you are going to play the market at all, you should be willing to take profits and losses quickly and forget your obsession with long-term capital gains. (If you are in a very high income tax bracket, perhaps this is a time for you to be out of the market.)

There is a time when you—*any* you—should be out of the market completely.

To one with an old-fashioned financial upbringing, this sounds heretical. How often have we been told to keep our money at work, so that the magic of compound interest might operate in our favor? Perhaps we were even taught the little rule about dividing the interest rate into 70 or 72: Money at 6 per cent compound interest will double itself in twelve years, money at 5 per cent in fourteen years.

Sometimes this is a little hard to keep in mind. One such time was in 1957. Between the market's July high and its October low industrial stocks as a whole dropped the equivalent of 6.3 years of dividends. More recently, between the December 1961 high and the June 1962 low, industrials dropped the equivalent of 7.7 years of dividends. In both slumps, Owens-Corning Fiberglas, a "growth stock" highly favored because it paid small dividends and retained a large proportion of its profits to finance future expansion, did even worse—dropping almost thirty-seven years of 80-cent annual divi-

* Undoubtedly because of a stepped-up anti-smoking campaign in 1962–63, cigarette stocks have been greatly depressed. They dropped an average of nearly 43 per cent, from 55.3 to 32.3 (Standard & Poor's monthly average prices), in the general market decline from December 1961 to June 1962, and by October 1962 had slipped still further to 29.2. At the beginning of July 1963, they were 45 per cent below the December 1961 level. The cancer scare had much more effect on stock prices than on smoking habits: in mid-1963, cigarette companies were reporting good earnings. Because of depressed stock prices, of course, dividend yields were quite handsome. Liggett & Myers was paying better than 6½ per cent; R. J. Reynolds, 4 per cent; American Tobacco, 5.3 per cent; Lorillard, 5.4 per cent; Philip Morris, 4.6 per cent. Whether cigarettes will prove "defensive" in future recessions, however, remains to be seen.

dends in 1957 and a shade more than forty years of $1 dividends in 1962!

I believe that any person of moderate intelligence can be taught to forecast the four major periods in the stock market mentioned earlier. He may not be able to put exact dates to them. That matters little. The important thing is that he will be in the right position when the changes come. When the jammed elevator stops and the mob starts out, he won't be facing in.

The late John Maynard Keynes, one of the most consistently successful speculators of whom we have any record, once said that there are two steps in market forecasting. It isn't enough to figure what effect an economic development will have on a company. You must first decide what effect the development will have on public sentiment, then the effect of public reaction on the company's stock.

I go further than this. I believe there are three steps: (1) From the economic development to the government's reaction; (2) from the government's reaction to the public's reaction; and (3) from the public's reaction to the stock.

Put it this way: Although business seems excellent, the President's council of economic advisers and the board of governors of the Federal Reserve System note some telltale signals of a slackening ahead. Perhaps overtime hours are slipping without an increase in employment. Perhaps new orders for durable goods are declining or new contracts for building falling. Any of these (and some other indicators) can signal heavy economic weather. The Federal Reserve banks try to aid business and industry by cutting the interest rate and making money easier to borrow. This is step number 1.

How will the public react? Generally, in a confused manner. There will be some who will assume that everything is okay now that Uncle Sam has stepped in. Therefore it is all right to hold on to those wildly speculative issues. There will be others who will decide that things must have been in pretty bad shape to bring government action. Therefore the thing to do is to get out of stocks. But there will be some—and enough of them—who will quite properly realize that the lower money rate has increased the relative value of bonds and of preferred and common stocks that are pretty certain to pay their dividends come hell or high water. This is step number 2.

The third step is to adjust one's own sales and purchases to this public reaction. The market will pulse upward and downward. If you are unlucky enough to hold cyclical stocks, you will try to pick a strong day to sell those that can be most easily hurt in a slump. You will use the money to buy sure-interest or sure-dividend securities about which the word "growth" has not been breathed for years. You do *not* want an issue that has already been inflated by hopes that cannot be realized in the near future.

There was such a change-over period in 1957. The Federal Reserve banks raised their interest rates in August. In November business was sliding so badly that the rate had to be lowered. The rate reduction in November, coupled with the evidence that the more speculative types of industry were continuing to contract, was an excellent signal to get into defensive issues, not because defensive issues would save the investor from loss but *because they would rise.*

The basic idea behind this reasoning is that the government is obliged to take certain measures to control the economy. To do this, Washington's experts must read and interpret statistics. They must determine what future is likely. Because the average investor has access to the same statistics, it is not inconceivable that, from time to time, he can anticipate moves by the authorities.

Ever since history was first recorded, governments have tried to control the economy. The Egyptian pyramids may have had an additional function of serving as make-work projects to take care of the jobless. Ancient Rome experimented with controlled prices and joined with ancient Greece in reducing the precious-metal content of the as and the drachma.

Our own country had little such control (except in the supply of money and the admissibility of foreign goods) until the Federal Reserve Act went into effect in December 1914. This permitted the Federal Reserve System to raise and lower money rates and to expand and contract the supply of lendable funds. However, there was no intentional raising of money rates and no contraction of lendable funds while World War I was in progress. The System was too busy helping the Treasury sell Liberty Bonds by keeping money rates low.

Even in 1918, when the war ended, nobody in government had the courage to say honestly and brutally, "We've had enough of this foolishness. We've got to cut down the supply of money, even if it does mean that Liberty Loan prices will drop as money rates rise. Pretty soon the world is going to be back in competition with our manufactured goods and our farm products. When that happens, our prices are bound to drop. Why should we force prices higher now by providing more money and more credit than we actually need? If we do that we'll only have a bigger collapse in the end."

Instead, we had a great postwar boom based on an absurd over-supply of credit. Those were the days of HCL, the high cost of living. Finally, much too late, toward the end of 1919, the Federal Reserve System moved in and began to raise interest rates and restrict the credit available.

In the 1920s the Federal Reserve System was blamed for bringing on the business and financial crash that followed. At this late date I am not going to try to defend it. In practice, I think we may say that all business recessions of any importance are caused by governmental action. If they are severe the government may be blamed for not having checked the preceding boom before it went too far.

The government had a chance to put on the brakes in 1928. Leaders in industry and finance were summoned to Washington and asked what they thought about the mounting speculation. The joint verdict of private enterprise and government was that everything was "sound" and nobody need worry. With that pat on the back, the boom trotted happily off to make new altitude records—and the biggest crash of all. Discount rates were not raised between July 13, 1928, and August 9, 1929.

The thinking behind that verdict of "sound" was partly political. No party wants to slow down business and have a recession in the year of a Presidential election. And it is amazing how often the needs for these decisions come up in Presidential years: 1928, 1936, 1948, 1952 and 1956. The Republicans "dogged" the decision in 1928, the Democrats in 1952.

Sometimes the error is in the other direction. In 1936 the Roosevelt Administration tramped on the brake and kept exerting pressure for the better part of a year, turning a modest boom into a heartbreaking collapse. In 1948, under Truman, the matter was handled far more delicately. The dip in industry was barely noticeable.

In 1953, with activity at too great a rate because of Democratic failure to act in 1952, the first Eisenhower administration scared itself with the success of its first business-controlling measures. By the end of May Secretary of the Treasury George M. Humphrey had reversed a tight-money policy initiated in January. The government did not return to the boom-checking role until 1955. Then it had to

CHART I

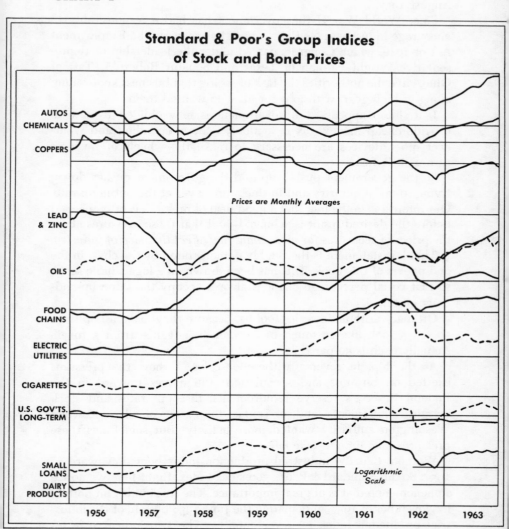

Standard & Poor's Group Indices of Stock and Bond Prices

AUTOS
CHEMICALS

COPPERS

Prices are Monthly Averages

LEAD & ZINC

OILS

FOOD CHAINS

ELECTRIC UTILITIES

CIGARETTES

U.S. GOV'TS. LONG-TERM

SMALL LOANS

DAIRY PRODUCTS

Logarithmic Scale

1956   1957   1958   1959   1960   1961   1962   1963

press harder and harder and harder. The break finally came in August 1957.

Since World War II the government has had a responsibility to encourage industry as well as to check its excesses. The Employment Act of 1946, which Congress passed under the leadership of Representative Wright Patman of Texas and Senator Robert A. Taft of Ohio, gave the authorities the task of seeing that business kept rolling along in high gear, with jobs for all who wanted them.

If a slump appears, the government is now obliged by law to provide cheap money, tax reductions, Federal spending and whatever other devices are necessary to make the wheels of business turn a little faster.

So the government pushes up and the government pushes down, trying to make industry and business turn over at the optimum rate. Our interest is in the fact that a good deal of pressure is often needed before the desired result is achieved—and that those pressures affect the prices of securities *far more than they affect the pace of industry*.

That last statement is thoroughly demonstrated by the chart in the end-papers of this book. This has been drawn on a logarithmic scale, so that equal percentage changes always occupy the same up-and-down distance.

Ordinary arithmetic scales fool us, because they make a hop from 50 to 75 look like so much more than an advance from 5 to 7½. Actually each is 50 per cent.

At the top, in reverse arithmetic scales, I show the pressures exerted on business and speculation: the moves upward in the Federal Reserve's reserve requirements, discount rates and stock margin requirements—and, of course, the easing of all three when Washington authority wanted more activity. But sometimes these pressures take time to take effect.

We note that the industrial production index bent downward in 1957. So did Standard & Poor's 500-stock index. Right here we notice a phenomenon that is of great importance. The stock index hit bottom in November of 1957, anticipating the June 1958 bottom of the industrial production index by seven months. The two indices rose together for the balance of 1958. Then there was a flattening out, and for most of 1959, stocks rose while industrial production fell. The end-paper chart shows this. In 1960, industrial production and the stock index were both falling most of the time. In 1961, they were both rising most of the time. In 1962, industrial production was rising very gently as stock prices were falling. Toward the end of the first quarter of 1963, the two indices began to rise together once again.

Standard & Poor's 500-stock index covers about 94 per cent of all the market value represented by common stocks on the New York Stock Exchange, for the price of each stock is multiplied by the number of shares outstanding. Unless I state otherwise, all index numbers, yields and other ratios for stocks used in this volume are Standard & Poor's. So it is with the groups of stocks in Chart I (see p. 21).

At the top are the curves of four industries that are exceedingly sensitive to changes in the business climate. Automobiles, of course, sell most easily when business is booming and everybody is employed and has money to spend. Chemicals, coppers and lead- and zinc-producing companies are tied tightly to the business cycle, for the companies they represent make things needed for further production. If production is easing off or gives signs of easing off, they contract fairly rapidly. They are thus among the so-called "cyclical" issues.

On Chart I notice how these four cyclical groups have tended to plow ahead despite the efforts of the Federal Reserve Board to slow them down—crumbling, however, when the Federal Reserve really got tough. All declined sharply in 1957, when the discount rate was finally raised to 3½ per cent following a series of lesser braking actions. They climbed in 1958 as the discount rate and the margin requirement were lowered, resisted another series of slow-down maneuvers in late 1958 and much of 1959, then went to pieces after the discount rate was raised to 4 per cent. Although both the margin requirement and the discount rate were lowered in mid-1960, it took a lot of coaxing to get these stocks moving again.

Electric utilities, cigarettes (see footnote, p. 17), small loan companies and dairy producers—all groups that have been fairly depression-proof—did pretty well under the pounding of government controls. Food chain stores did even better. But when the government stepped in and *cut* money rates in 1958 and again in 1960 they all shot upward.

Before we leave this subject, let me warn you: It is not anywhere so simple as I have made it seem in Chart I. To be sure, if you had been able to buy Standard & Poor's index of consumer goods stocks in May 1949, when the Federal Reserve banks began easing money to help the economy, and had held onto those stocks until September

1950, when the pressure was exerted in the opposite direction, your profit before commissions and taxes would have been 28 per cent. If you had taken the same action for the same reason in July 1953, and had held on until the government moved to check the economy in April 1955, your profit would have been 40 per cent.

There is obviously nothing wrong with the idea of buying consumer-goods stocks—the so-called "defensive" issues—at times when money rates are reduced. Our problem is that you would have made even bigger profits by buying "capital goods" stocks for those same periods, 38 per cent starting in 1949 and 60 per cent starting in 1953.

This pretty well states the problem we face for the remainder of this book: What indicators do we have that might tell us when to switch from the defensive to the more aggressive issues? What other indicators might tell us to get out of the market and wait for credit to be eased once more? Are there any market techniques that we ought to know?

Our investing method is based on taking profits now and then rather than on holding stocks indefinitely to collect dividends. Taking profits was good sense in the "good old days" before the income-tax amendment. It is even more sensible now.

Ordinary Federal income taxes on net taxable income run from 20 to 91 per cent. Short-term capital gains—that is, profits made on the sale of property held for six months or less—are taxed at the ordinary rates. Long-term capital gains—profits on property held for more than six months—are taxed at half the ordinary rates, with 25 per cent the maximum.

If an investor is in the 50 per cent income-tax bracket—which means that his next dollar of income will pay a tax of 50 cents to the Federal Government—he may keep only $3.24 out of a $6 dividend (he gets a 4 per cent credit for dividend income). If, however, he sells a stock (one he has held for more than six months) at a profit of $6 a share, he may keep $4.50 of it.

One of the favorite stories about the market has been told over and over by brokerage houses. It is the "if you only had" yarn about the man who bought something way back when, never touched it, and saw it blossom into a fortune. For example, if you had invested $9,900 in General Motors in 1913, by the end of 1958 you would have had stock worth $8,994,645 and would have received $5,373,272 in dividends and in remuneration for rights you had sold. Over the forty-five years your gain on the original investment would have been a modest 145,000 per cent.

These figures were worked out by Capital Research and Management Company of Los Angeles, which publishes such information in a booklet every five years. There was one edition for the end of 1953; the one I am quoting is for the end of 1958; and the forthcoming edition will cover the end of 1963. All are part of a larger study. At the beginning of 1913 New York Stock Exchange stocks were listed under the headings of "Rails," "Express Companies," "Coal and Mining" and "Various." Capital Research took "Various" for its historical survey and found fourteen utilities mixed in with the industrials. There were 101 issues in all. The study assumed that the investor bought at the mean between the high and low prices of 1913 and put about $10,000 into each stock. The aggregate was $1,014,855. It also assumed that nothing would be reinvested, that all rights would be sold and taken as if they were dividends. Capital Research found that market value would have mounted to $19,677,830 by the end of 1958. The investor would have received $12,670,357 in dividends and rights.

Capital Research made adjustments for changing purchasing power—the 1958 dollar was worth 34.7 per cent of the 1914 dollar—and found that purchasing power at the end of the experiment would have been about 7.2 times that at the beginning.

Now, however, we come to the question of income taxes, which started at a maximum of 2 per cent in or about 1914. In that year the investor might have retained $38,300 of his $38,842 return. In 1958 his investment income would have been $8,537,304. On the assumption that nobody pays more than 87 per cent of his income as personal income tax, this means that his investment income would have been reduced to $160,000, a gain of a little more than four times over 1914, after taxes. After adjustments for changed purchasing power, his annual income would be equivalent to $55,520 in 1914 dollars.

So it was largely futile? Not exactly. At the end of 1958 our lucky friend might have sold out, taking his profit of $10,393,000. After paying a long-term capital gains tax of 25 per cent of that amount, he would have had left $7,794,000. This he might have invested in 3 per cent tax-exempt municipal bonds, giving him an "after-tax" income of $233,820 a year.

For those who wish to buy copies of the study for themselves, the address of Capital Research Company is 900 Wilshire Boulevard, Los Angeles 17, California.

Let us nail down what I have said thus far. The critical periods for investors: what are they?

1. The time to get into defensive stocks and bonds. This starts when the government first moves to make credit easier, in order to help business. Business may not get much out of it but the "money-rate stocks" and the bonds are sure to do so.

2. The doubtful period when you can't be sure that industrial production and stock prices are going to be running in the same direction; when you have the feeling that what looks like a brighter glow on the economy may be merely a false dawn. In this period you do well to pay more than your usual attention to your investments. Perhaps you play more like a speculator, ready to take profits or cut losses quickly if there are disturbing developments.

3. The time to get into the fast-moving cyclical issues. Now you can see industrial production and stocks rising together and you can feel confidence building in the market and the economy. This is the time to go looking for stocks with the greatest leverage possibilities.

4. This doubtful period—which is almost identical with No. 2— comes when the government has moved to restrict credit, lest the boom go too far. If you still hold any defensive stocks and bonds, you get out of them in a hurry. They will go down. As for your cyclical stocks, who can tell? They will probably rise some more, but your tactics should be those described under No. 2.

5. Now and then the government has been pressing to control the business cycle. Industrial production, inventories, new orders, the length of the work week and other important indicators have been falling. (In 1961–62 stocks showed signs of reversing their upward trend. That might have been an excellent time to turn into cash all or almost all the things you held. Before long you were apt to be needing the cash to buy those bonds and money-rate stocks that were going to be helped when the government moved to keep the slump from going too far.) If you watch out, you may even be able to buy your bonds *before* the government moves.

QUESTIONS FOR REVIEW

1. What are the four major periods in the stock market?
2. What are the three steps in market forecasting?
3. What are the principal tools employed by the Federal Reserve System to control our economy?
4. What are "cyclical" issues and how have they tended to react to Federal Reserve actions?
5. What are "defensive" issues and how have they reacted?
6. What is the difference between long-term and short-term capital gains? At what rate are they taxed?

CHAPTER II

Never Mind About

Long-Term Gains

ARE THERE any *sure* ways of making money in securities? I believe there are. One way is to get a job with a brokerage house. You may not make much, but it will be money.

Another—and much more profitable—way is to buy interest-bearing securities, especially United States Treasury bonds, just before or immediately after the Federal Reserve Board starts a movement for greater monetary and credit ease. Certain sure-dividend or money-rate stocks are also good buys in this position.

You are not to be frightened away by Franz Pick's definition of a bond as "a certificate of guaranteed confiscation." I do not recommend that you stay in bonds for any considerable period. Six months is a long time. The next chapter will go into great detail about speculating on a reasonably "sure thing" at 5 per cent margin.

I believe there is one other sure-fire way, a kind of development of the above. I hinted at it toward the end of the preceding chapter.

We assume that you have bought bonds as indicated above. We further assume that you have gradually switched out of bonds and into money-rate stocks. We further assume—because this has *always* happened—that the Federal Reserve System is still pushing away, trying to get the economy back into high gear. Cyclical issues— things such as steels and machine makers and metals and other "natural resources" stocks—begin to rise more rapidly than the sure-dividend payers. In gingerly fashion, you begin to shift into these. You are watching, of course, lest there be a sudden reversal. You are protecting yourself in ways that will be described later.

Then the expected happens: the Federal Reserve Board's index of industrial production stops going down and bends upward. This, of course, is what all the shooting has been about. This is what the Federal Reserve System has being trying to accomplish.

Now, according to the record of the past, you are safe in swinging your investments almost exclusively into the fast-moving cyclical issues. The biggest profits of the past thirty-odd years have been made by playing heavily when industrial stocks and the industrial production index were both headed upward.

There were no money-rate signals to follow in 1927 or 1928, but there were beautiful uncontradictory signals and movements in 1933, 1935–36, 1942–43, 1949–51, and 1953–55.

Without stretching any probabilities, I believe I can say that— even without using margin—opportunities in each of these five periods during the past thirty years offered better than a 40 per cent profit and one of them topped 100 per cent.

Playing the market in this way, however, demands a certain amount of understanding of the principles underlying our economy. In the interests of speed and readability, I am going to postpone my discussion of these principles until the later chapters.

After all, industrial stocks and the industrial production index rise together only about 36 per cent of the time. When you pick up this book, you may just possibly have a 44-month stretch ahead of you before they do it again for more than a couple of months at a time. (This has happened.) So we're going to start out with some hints for the short-term play, hints that can be good at any time.

You will remember that I said that industrial stocks and industrial production rose simultaneously only 36 per cent of the time. Actually, this is the way market action has divided—on the long swings, between annual highs and lows—over a twenty-four-year period:

	Industrial Stocks	Industrial Production
36 per cent	Rising	Rising
24 per cent	Rising	Falling
25 per cent	Falling	Rising
15 per cent	Falling	Falling

We can see from this little table that stocks rise about 60 per cent of the time, fall about 40 per cent of the time. We can also see that stocks and business do what most people think they do—rise and fall together—only about half the time.

It ought to be fairly easy to get aboard when both stocks and industrial production are rising, but that accounts for only a little more than a third of the time. What do we do with the rest of it? How do we protect ourselves?

Play a trend and get out when it seems to be stopping. Don't wait around to be sure.

Never hold on to a loser. Sell it! And that means don't buy more of the loser in order to reduce your "average" price.

If you buy a stock because it was due to rise right away and it doesn't rise right away, get rid of it.

Don't talk about your investments until you're out of them. Then you won't be tempted to hold on to losers in order to prove you were right about them—in some far distant future.

Never "sit out a depression" with a stock. When depressions hit them, stocks take anywhere from fourteen (1953) to three hundred (1929) months to get back to their pre-depression levels.

Remember that trading in and out, especially in small amounts, costs a good deal of money. Remember the nasty little motto: "Four trades equal one year's income." This is another way of saying that commissions and taxes will add up to about 1.2 per cent on your average deal. This makes it exceedingly important for you to work hard at picking the right stocks.

The man who can pick a good stock, see it rise a bit and put in a stop-loss order that will protect some of his profit doesn't have to trade in hunger. Try to play it that way.

When listening to investment counsel, make sure that the man is talking your language. If you are looking for long-term growth and the wiseacre is thinking in terms of the next three or four weeks, for a quick turn, there are disappointments ahead. *Almost all so-called technical advice deals with the next two or three weeks.*

Never act on advice that violates good common sense, especially if the advice assumes a new era in which the old economic laws no longer govern.

Most of this advice, you will notice, would have you sell stocks. None of it tells you to "lock 'em up and forget 'em."

Frankly, I'm a person who can't forget that, between 1854 and 1933, this country had twenty-one depressions, an average of one every forty-five months. Between 1933 and 1962 we had seven depressions, an average of one every fifty months. We've been doing better since the government began cushioning the economy, but we're not yet perfect. We haven't abolished the business cycle.

Since we know stocks are going to fall as well as rise, we might as well get a little traffic out of them. A man who buys a stock at 10 and sells it at 20 makes 100 per cent. But a man who buys it at 10, sells it at 14½, buys it back at 12 and sells it at 18, buys it back at 15 and sells it at 20, makes 188 per cent—or would if there were no long-term capital-gains tax. Even if you count in the maximum tax of 25 per cent, the advantage is 130 per cent over 75 per cent.

That phrase, "the maximum tax," reminds me that there is a great deal of snobbery in Wall Street. It is good, old-fashioned, business-getting snobbery and so is not to be criticized, but we should take it into account. The average brokerage house would like to have a great many customers investing great, hulking fortunes. Naturally. An order for 1,000 shares costs the brokerage house no more to execute than one for 100. In order to attract the big-money boys, the average brokerage house pretends that it already has a great many customers in that category. It puts out literature that assumes, ever so subtly, that you, the investor, will have your next dollar of ordinary income taxed in the 76 per cent bracket—or even higher, you lucky dog, you!

This is all very flattering, but I have the greatest doubt that it applies to my average reader. The New York Stock Exchange reports that in 1962 "about two out of three [shareowners] had household income under $10,000."

I have another reason for thinking this. J. Frederic Dewhurst and his associates at the Twentieth Century Fund worked out an estimate of the number of family units in 1960 that had after-tax incomes of $10,000 and more. The figure came to 2,345,000. That happens to be less than 14 per cent of the number of shareowners in public corporations in this country. I think we may say that 75 per cent of all shareowners have after-tax incomes of $10,000 or less and before-tax incomes of $13,000 or less. I suspect that the proportion is actually considerably higher, perhaps 85 per cent. A lot of well-to-do persons own no publicly held stocks at all. Their money is in farms, stores and other businesses of their own.

Okay, okay! So what does this mean? It means that probably 85 per cent of the stockholders and probably 90-plus per cent of my readers *are in or below the 30 per cent bracket for ordinary income!*

And what does that mean? *It means that my average reader can forget about this precious distinction between short-term capital gains and long-term capital gains.* The first are those you make on stocks held for six months or less; the second on stocks held more than six months.

You want an example? Our man in the 76 per cent bracket buys a stock at $20 a share and sees it go to 28 in three months. Now he is in something of a quandary, for he knows *why* that stock went up and he figures that it has just about used up that reason. (Say the company got a rate increase and now it has had to grant a wage boost that will take away the advantage.) What does our friend do? If he sells now the short-term capital gains tax of 76 per cent will eat away all but $1.92 of his profit.

If the stock would only stay at 28 for the full six months and one day, he'd have a profit of $6 after a 25 per cent tax. The chances are he will sit watching that stock go down and down and down until both the six months and his profits are spent.

Now what about my average reader in the 30 per cent bracket? If he gets a profit he likes in one day or three weeks or three months, he can sell and have it cost him only a little bit more than the long-term capital-gains tax paid by the better-heeled investor— 30 per cent against 25 per cent. Of course, he can wait and pay 15 per cent—half his regular rate for a long-term capital gain—but he may figure that it isn't worth the risk.

So don't try to navigate your ketch with charts meant for an ocean liner. They make you feel unnecessarily cramped.

Everybody has met the man who tells him, with great sincerity and not even a trace of smugness, that he is "frozen" into a stock by the long-term capital-gains tax.

"Bought it a long time ago, when it was selling very low," he explains, "and now I just can't afford to get out of it."

Let us examine this commonly held fallacy. He bought the stock at, shall we say, $4 a share. It is now selling at $100. If he took his profit of $96 a share, his long-term capital-gains tax would be, at most, $24 a share. That would leave him with at least $76 after taxes—his original $4 plus $72 in after-tax profit. (We're not considering commissions and transfer taxes in this example.)

There are five common reasons for this kind of talk:

1. Our friend has heard other people talk this way and assumes that he is "frozen" in because he has never stopped to ask why.

2. He enjoys talking about his predicament, which casts infinite credit on his years-ago ability to pick 'em. If anything forced him to sell and stop talking about his sagacity, it would break his heart. (My suggestion here is to sell the stock but keep talking. Nobody need know he hasn't got it any more.)

3. He has no confidence in his ability to pick something anywhere near so good. And yet suppose that the stock, though selling at $100, is paying only $2 a year in dividends. This is not so rare. At the end of May 1963, four of the 200 largest New York Stock Exchange issues * were yielding less than 1 per cent in cash, 21 were yielding less than 2 per cent and 82 were yielding less than 3 per cent. International Business Machines, Xerox, Polaroid and Rohm & Haas were in the first group. Among those yielding between 1 per cent and 2 per cent were Sears, Roebuck, Chrysler, National Cash Register, Minnesota Mining & Manufacturing, Owens-Corning Fiberglas and Reynolds Metals.

Our man couldn't afford to sell? Perhaps not. But his 100 shares, worth $10,000, were yielding him $200 a year, *before* taxes. In the 50 per cent bracket, he got only $100 a year of ordinary income.

On the same date, the following issues would have yielded him better than 5 per cent: Chesapeake & Ohio, Armco Steel, Norfolk & Western, Republic Steel, Kennecott Copper, El Paso Natural Gas, Atchison Topeka and Ingersoll-Rand. Our friend might have invested the $7,600 remaining to him (after selling his original stock and paying the tax) and had a return of better than $380 before taxes or $190 after taxes.

Or he might have sunk his $7,600 into municipal bonds of the

---

* From a list compiled by Harold Clayton and staff, Hemphill, Noyes & Co.

very highest rating and received an income of $247 a year, free of all taxes.

So he "couldn't afford to sell"!

4. There is one perfectly good reason, of course: The stock that he bought so cheap may be selling at a high yield. (For example, at the end of May 1963, both General Motors and National Distillers were yielding around 5 per cent and Allied Stores was yielding 5.7 per cent.) It is pretty clear that our investor can't safely better that return with 76 per cent as much money.

5. The fifth reason is also good, but it doesn't apply to everybody. It is the reason of the stockholder who is running out of years or health. He knows that the acquisition basis of his stock will change, when he dies, to its price on the day of his death. In other words, his heirs will not have to pay a capital-gains tax on the gain in price during his lifetime.

This man's problem is a real one: If he should die tomorrow, his heirs would have stock worth $10,000 (to stay with the old example). But if he should sell the stock today and die right away, they would have other stock or cash worth only $7,600.

The job of the man frozen in by reasons 4 and 5 is to balance This against That. Is it safer to hold or to sell? Which is likely to come sooner, a 25 per cent drop in price for the stock or a 100 per cent drop in health for the stockholder?

If you are not in one of these two classes—a man with a big profit in a high-yielding stock or a man cutting the grass on the family plot—forget this monkey business about being frozen into anything. Use your head. Work out the problem sensibly, without whimsy. Before you finish this book you will find, I hope, some standards to apply to your case, so that you won't have to use more than 50 per cent of guesswork in making your decisions.

Most of the advice in this chapter is good for any time. But let us get back to the matter of timing. It is most important that an investor should have some sense of historical perspective and be able to make a pretty good guess at the stage of the investment cycle in which he finds himself. Can you? As you read this book, have you clear answers for the following questions?

Was the last credit move by the Federal Reserve System intended to inject a hypodermic needle into industry or to check a boom that was going too far?

Has it succeeded? That is, has the course of industry reversed itself as the Federal Reserve wanted?

Are industrial stocks and industrial production moving upward together or downward together?

These are things you *must* know unless you enjoy groping around in dark closets full of treacherous roller skates and venomous vacuum cleaners. You can get the information out of your daily paper if you read it carefully. But if you aren't working at it, this is the kind of thing you forget easily. You should have a handy reference.

If you are in a period when you must play the market on an in-and-out basis, your main source of information will be your newspaper. You can't afford to be a day or two days behind.

Even in such periods, however, you will need to refer to business figures to determine trends. Are inventories rising or falling? Are stocks going up so fast that the Federal Reserve System may become alarmed?

The best source for information of this kind—and for a lot of other data not obtainable anywhere else, such as price-earnings ratios for all the recognizable groups of stocks on the New York Stock Exchange—is *Current Statistics* published by Standard & Poor's Corporation, 345 Hudson Street, New York City 14. It costs $72 a year, which takes it off the shopping list of the man who goes into investing as a hobby, although it might be a wonderful Christmas present from a wife who could save that much from the butter, egg and milk money. Or the investor can check on it at his broker's.

For the family that has neither $72 for this purpose nor a nearby broker I recommend the Commerce Department's *Survey of Current Business*. Both the regular monthly edition and the weekly supplements pay some attention to common stocks and to bonds. Both may be obtained from the Superintendent of Documents, United States Government Printing Office, Washington 25, D. C., for $4 a year. From the same source you may obtain the biennial *Business Statistics*. It costs two dollars and appears in odd-numbered years. It will give you historical perspective. Also valuable are the pocket-sized stock guides published by Standard & Poor's Corporation. These cost $24 a year. Cheapest of all— but far off in the interspatial realms of economics—are the *Economic Indicators* of the President's Council of Economic Advisers. Send $2.50 to the Superintendent of Documents, Washington 25, D. C.

QUESTIONS FOR REVIEW

1. About what percentage of the time do industrial production and industrial stocks rise together?
2. In what income-tax bracket are most shareholders?
3. What are three bad reasons for hanging onto a stock that has gone up?
4. What are two good reasons for doing so?

CHAPTER III

The Almost-Sure-to-Win

Speculation

WITHOUT ANY doubt whatever the safest time for a speculative play is when a business recession is on the way. I do not mean that this is the time to go short of industrial common stocks. I mean that this is the time to *buy* bonds of the United States Treasury, municipal bonds, some corporation bonds and—if you are a rather sober, conservative type—common stocks that haven't much chance for growth but are certain to pay their dividends come hell or high water.

Here is a rather rough appraisal of the situation as you might have faced it in 1957. (Later we will see how you would have altered your approach in 1959–60 and 1962.) It assumes that you bought the bonds as a principal but paid commissions on the stock:

WHEN A DEPRESSION IS DUE

	Margin Required %	Amount Investor Could Carry for Stake of $5,000	Possible Profit on $5,000 Stake in 6 Mos. From Oct. 1957	From Nov. 1957
Long-term Treasury bonds	5	100,000	12,100	8,000
Municipal bonds	10	50,000	3,500	3,650
Highest grade Corporation bonds	15	33,300	2,376	2,409
Electric Utility stocks	70	7,100	1,306	1,454

Here we go with Casper Milquetoast, Esq., looking for the safest speculation going. After you read the not-too-fanciful paragraphs below you may decide with him that investing in stocks is too much trouble, that you can get all the action you want and all the capital gain you need by taking a wholehearted flier in the Treasury bond market each time the Federal Reserve System *begins* the process of easing credit to help the economy.

Yes, I *know* that the Treasury bond market went completely to-pieces in June of 1958 and stayed that way for a time.

Yes, I *know* that the propaganda in the stock market about stocks as a hedge against inflation caused a great many people to fall completely out of love with bonds.

Yes, I *know* that our Washington money managers made bad mistakes in handling both credit control and debt refinancing, mistakes that they have honestly admitted. But I do not believe that we have finished with bonds for good.

What is the logic of buying anything at all when an industrial depression seems to be on the way? We look back. We remember that the Federal Reserve System not so long ago was raising money rates, trying to check the boom. As money rates went up, bond prices fell. Finally, we saw that the money managers were getting their way. Industrial production began to fall.

Now the stock market begins to worry. The slump seems to be gaining momentum.

This is our signal to start buying bonds. Why? Because declining business activity itself will lower interest rates, even if the government doesn't act. But the government, in a month or two, is pretty sure to act. Off we go!

Let us note right here that the rich and the poor have to play this game by different rules. Thus, we are not even going to consider the man who embarks on a speculation in Treasury bonds with $50,000 and takes 1,000 bonds—a commitment of $1,000,000—but we note that he can do a little better at interest, and so forth, than the less well-heeled gentleman whose situation is described below.

In *The New York Times* or any other sober-minded newspaper you will find Treasury bonds quoted in this fashion:

$$3\tfrac{1}{4}s \text{ '85 May} \quad 99.8 \quad 99.16 \quad -.4$$
$$3\tfrac{1}{2}s \text{ '90 Feb.} \quad 102.12 \quad 102.20 \quad -.4$$
$$3s \text{ '95 Feb.} \quad 95.0 \quad 95.8$$

The first line means that, at 3:30 P.M. on the preceding day, somebody was willing to pay 99 and $\frac{8}{32}$ dollars plus accrued interest (that is, interest that has piled up since the most recent payment date) for $100 face value of United States Treasury 3¼ per cent bonds due in May 1985, and that somebody else was willing to sell such bonds for 99 and $\frac{16}{32}$ dollars. The bid price had dropped $\frac{4}{32}$ from the previous day. The bonds of which we are talking are, of course, in $1,000 denominations. For simplicity, we are not going to deal in actual bonds but in Standard & Poor's averages, by months. In other words, we are not going to assume that our man gets the best price in any month, merely the monthly average.

Let us talk first of a man who is going to risk at least $5,000 in a speculation in Treasuries—a "hundred-bond customer." His ordinary way of doing business would be, I suppose, to go to his broker, a member of the New York Stock Exchange, and tell him to buy 100 of such-and-such bonds. The broker buys the bonds at the best price he can and charges a commission. This commission is not an established rate. It is agreed upon by common consent. A not unusual rate for a deal of this size is 62½ cents for each $1,000 bond— $\frac{1}{16}$ or $\frac{2}{32}$.

Our friend's next question concerns interest. The brokers as well as the banks use a little slow motion when the lowering of interest charges is concerned. The banks move slowly and, for stocks, the brokers charge ½ per cent more than they pay the banks. For bonds, they are allowed to reduce the mark-up to ¼ of a percentage point.

Let our friend make sure that he is getting this lower mark-up. Let him also make sure that he will get the advantage of interest rate reductions. After all, there's something a little grasshopperish about borrowing money at 4½ per cent to carry bonds that are yielding only 3½ per cent.

Our friend does not have to do this business through a New York Stock Exchange firm although he will find almost any firm willing to co-operate if he shows that he knows what he wants, and the greater convenience will naturally bend him that way. He may also trade for the bonds without benefit of commission and arrange to have the dealer get payment from the bank or other agency that is financing him. This is not apt to be a home-town bank. Home-town banks keep their home-town rates as high as they can for their regular customers and send their idle money to other cities. In New York a man who wanted to buy 1,000 bonds or so would probably go to an agency of one of the Canadian banks or the Bank of Tokyo or perhaps of the Cleveland Trust Company. These lend in New York at rates considerably better than they get on Treasury bills but considerably less than they charge their home-town customers.

The man with a smaller amount to borrow, however, would probably get the money on the first bounce through a money broker such as D. H. Blair & Co. or Garvin, Bantel & Co. Both are Stock Exchange members.

To get the lowest available rates, our friend would borrow on 90-day notes. He would then be able to renew halfway through the deal and take advantage of any further reduction in interest rates. In this manner, according to Charles Miller of D. H. Blair & Co., our friend could possibly make a few pennies on interest. In the 1957–58 market a 1,000-bond customer could probably have made ⅛ per cent in interest.

I am assuming, however, no more than that our friend gets what is called a "free carry." Bond yield equals interest on borrowed money. To make the figuring easier, I am assuming that our friend trades for his bonds—that is, he does not pay commission. Note, however, that the one-way commission on 100 bonds need only be $62.50.

We are starting off our man with $10,000 in 1949. He decides to buy long-term Treasury bonds on 5 per cent margin each time the Federal Reserve System *starts* to ease credit—at the beginning of each business slump. He also resolves to sell immediately (1) if

there is a threat of war, (2) if the Federal Reserve moves to contract credit, or (3) if the price of Treasuries starts to fall because
people are switching out of them to invest in a booming stock
market. He also makes up his mind to keep an eagle eye on the
story about the condition of the Federal Reserve banks that appears
in his Friday morning newspaper and to read all the articles about
impending Federal financing. He also remembers, if he is in a low
income-tax bracket, that he doesn't have to be a snob about long-
term capital gains. In the 30 per cent bracket, he can take a 100
per cent profit at any time and do almost as well as the mogul
who has to wait six months to come in under the long-term capital-
gain 25 per cent minimum!

Our little man has settled everything with his bank and in May
1949—the Fed's move was on May 5—buys 185 bonds ($185,000 in
face value) at $1,080 a bond for his $10,000. The average price of
long-term Treasuries runs up to 110.9 in December of that year and
slips to 110.6 in the following January (the figures after the deci-
mals here are not 32nds). Our friend thus makes a gross profit of
$26 on each of his 185 bonds, or about $4,800.

We shall assume that our man is in the 30 per cent bracket for
ordinary income, so his long-term Federal capital-gains tax on this
will be 15 per cent or $720. Let us call his whole tax bill $800 and
assume that he now has $14,000. He puts this money into a couple
of savings banks and bides his time.

Before we go on to brighter things—that is, to the next nation-
wide slump—let us make two observations: First, our friend would
have wanted to arrange to refinance his loan, because interest rates
would have been slipping steadily throughout the period. Therefore,
if he had any interest loss at the start, it should have been more than
made good at the end. Second, this was not an especially good time
for his trade in bonds, because the Federal Reserve banks in 1949
were still supporting government bonds all the time, and they were
at high levels. As you can see in the chart on the end-papers of this
book, the main instrument for easing credit was the lowering of
reserve requirements.

Sitting there in the savings banks, our friend's nest egg has turned
into about $15,400 by the time he has his next chance, which comes
in 1953.

Every Friday morning *The New York Times* carries the report on
the condition of the Federal Reserve banks for the previous Wednes-

day night. It is easy to see whether they have raised or lowered
their holdings of Treasury bonds, notes and bills* by "open market
operations." If they have bought more of them, they have increased
the reserves of the member banks and made them better able to
lend money. In other words, they have tried to boost the economy.

The reader will probably remember that Secretary of the Treasury George M. Humphrey, even before he took office in January
1953, was talking about bringing about a return to "honest money."
He set about tightening the money market, persuading the Federal
Reserve to raise the discount rate in January. Down went bonds.
In fact, between November 1952, when Mr. Humphrey began talking, and June 1953, Standard & Poor's index of long-term Treasuries
fell from 103.7 to 98.8. Figure that one on a 5-point margin!

But back to our friend with his $15,400 in May 1953. Even with-
out any knowledge of what was going on in banking circles, a person who read the weekly reports of the Federal Reserve banks in
his daily paper could see that the Humphrey "honest money" policy
was being washed down the drain. Money was being pumped back
into the economy as the Fed bought Treasury bills (the Fed
customarily buys the shortest maturities available, but the effect
is quickly transmitted to the longer ones).

Let us say that our cautious friend invests about half his money
at the June average price of 98.8. He buys 154 bonds for $152,152
and puts down a little more than $7,600.

On July 1 the Fed lowers its reserve requirements. Our friend
buys 154 more bonds at the July average of 100.2, or $154,308.

In November the booming stock market begins to take a little
money away from the bond market. In December, scanning Standard & Poor's *Current Statistics*, he makes due note that the average
for long-term Treasuries was 102.3 in November against 102.6 in
October. Is this a signal to get out of them? Perhaps, but my guess
is that even our timid friend will wait a little. When the six-month
long-term-capital-gains holding period has passed he sells the first
batch of 154 bonds and gets an average of 103.1, or $158,774.

He still has 154 bonds bought in July. He decides to hold on a
little longer for three reasons: first, bonds are rising again; second,
he wants to get a long-term capital gain; third, he'd rather take his

---

* The name differs with the maturity. "Bills" mature in as little as 91 days,
"certificates" in a year, "notes" in periods up to five years and "bonds" in more
than five years.

profit in the next year. For a person whose ordinary tax rate is less than 50 per cent, the long-term capital gains tax rate keeps rising as gains advance. Try not to take all profits in one year.

Our friend waits until January, finds that bonds are still rising and decides to let them ride a while longer. By April, perhaps, he is getting a little nervous, so he sells his remaining 154 bonds at 107 or $164,780. Assuming again that the interest charges on the loan were equaled or more by the interest yield of the bonds, we find our man had a gross profit of $17,094. Suppose we figure his after-tax profit at $13,500, giving him $28,900 to parcel out among savings banks as he waits for the next slump. He waits from April 1954 to October of 1957. Savings-bank dividends have raised his nest egg to about $32,000.

Once more? He buys 350 bonds at 92 in October and 330 bonds at 95 in November.

A little softness develops in February. Does he sell? No. The Federal Reserve is still anxiously injecting energy into the economy. He comforts himself with the thought that, since World War II, the *first* move to check the economy has always come at least eleven months after the *last* move to boost the economy. Even back in 1931, when the Hoover Administration was trying to end a recession by raising money rates, there was still a five-month free-wheeling period between the last push up and the first push down.

Mr. Milquetoast is in for a surprise. After pushing up steadily for five months, the Federal Reserve will wait only a little more than three months before pushing down.

But our boy is out of the market. He waits the full six months in each case, selling 350 bonds at 102.6 and 330 bonds at 102.1. No, let's assume the worst and trim about $\frac{8}{32}$ or 0.3 point off each of those prices. Even with that bow to understatement, I think you will find that Mr. Milquetoast, after all taxes, has turned his original $10,000 into about $75,000—all in nine years. That is 25 per cent a year at compound interest.

There have been two recessions since the first edition of this book was published in 1959 but only the earlier one, that of 1960, offered much opportunity for a speculative play in bonds.

Even then, our friend had to act well ahead of the Fed if he wanted to make any money. The interest rate was cut to 3½ per cent in June and again to 3 per cent in August. Had he bought long-term Treasuries at the June average price of 89.6, his profit

at the end of six months would have been .7 per cent. Had he
bought in August, he would have had a small loss—about .8 per
cent.

Let us say he felt encouraged to buy his bonds in early 1960,
when a lot of other investors were becoming attracted to Treasuries
because of their high yields (5 per cent and better). There were
other tempting signs. Industrial stocks were beginning to slide.
Industrial production, after a slight rally in December and January,
was falling too.

Hindsight shows us that the best time for his move would have
been January 1960 when, after a long series of downward pushes
on credit, the price of long-term Treasuries hit a low of 84.1. Selling six months later at around 91.1, he would have made upwards
of 8 per cent. Let us say, however (because we know him pretty
well by this time), that he climbed aboard in February, when
the average price had risen to 86.1, and climbed off again in
August, when it hit 91.9. He still would have made better than
6½ per cent.

How would Mr. Milquetoast have behaved in 1962? Stock
prices over the first six months were declining at a monthly rate
of 5.2 per cent (as against 7.5 per cent in the three-month slide of
1957) but as far as anyone could see, they were falling under their
own weight—not as a result of "tight money." The Fed had not
changed the discount rate since August of 1960. After a brief dip
early in the year, industrial production was rising.

During that brief dip, might he have decided to try again with
part (certainly not all) of his money? Say he went in at the
February average of 87.70. Getting out six months later at 89.16, he
would have made 1.7 per cent. Had he hung on until the following January, in order to take his profits in another year, he might
have done a shade better—2.4 per cent. If he had waited until
June, right after the market "break" of late May, he might have
come out a little better than even.

But the 1962 market was really no place for the likes of Mr.
Milquetoast. There were too many straws in the wind, too many
contradictory speculations about the direction of the economy. My
guess is that he would have kept his money in savings accounts—
conceivably in a string of savings and loan associations paying 4¾
per cent—and that he is, at this writing, biding his time.

So much for government bonds. For the time being we shall also pass over corporation bonds and debentures, convertible and otherwise. There will be times when they interest us. This is not one of them.

In the opening chapter we recognized that there were times when coppers and steels and machine-makers might be falling but when money-rate stocks—sure-dividend payers—would be rising, *provided* nobody had ever mentioned them in the same sentence as "growth." When growth seems to have stopped and unlikely to start again for some months or years, growth stocks lose ground, or fail to gain as much as they might. But you might have bought General Foods at 124½ on June 13, 1960, the business day following the Federal Reserve Bank's first move in the most recent campaign to relax credit. That stock had been on a kind of plateau for nine months. Six months and a day later, you might have sold it for 151¼ (pre-split price: the stock split two for one on August 24, 1960).

Where are you now? At the start of a business depression you have bought Treasuries on small margins and have taken a good profit as soon as you could. You may have bought other bonds or sure-dividend stocks.

As the stock market begins to recover you will notice that the cyclical stocks, as a group, will begin to do better than your sure-dividend payers. Some investors are getting rid of the money-rate stocks in order to get into issues that may be moving more rapidly.

It is easy to look back at the chart of a market and say, "But of course that was when you switched into Inspiration Copper (or Merck, or Chrysler or U. S. Smelting)!" Hindsight, however, is denied us at the time of any investment decision. We know this is an upturn, of course. We can see it. But is it going to be a false alarm? How do you play this kind of market?

You may find some usable suggestions in the following chapter.

QUESTIONS FOR REVIEW

1. What business signals tell us that a recession is on the way?
2. What is a "money-rate" stock? Why buy it?
3. What is the total amount (face value) of long-term Treasury bonds an investor could carry for a stake of $7,500?

4. What are three good reasons to get out of bonds?
5. Why do the Federal Reserve banks buy Treasury bonds, notes and bills?

CHAPTER IV

Cut Your Losses:

Let Your Profits Run

FOR REASONS that are not always clear at first glance, there are always some stocks that out-perform the rest of the market by a country mile.

In the first half of 1963, for example, when Standard & Poor's composite index of 500 stocks was up 7 per cent, six New York Stock Exchange issues rose more than 80 per cent. These were American Agricultural Chemicals (96 per cent), Soo Line Railroad (94 per cent), Pan American World Airways (91 per cent), Trans World Airlines (88 per cent), MetroMedia (85 per cent), Chrysler (83 per cent).

During 1962, when the market was down 9 per cent and Big Board stocks had shown a dollar loss of $50 billion, Chrysler was up 51 per cent, Hayes Industries 65 per cent, Delta Airlines 67 per cent, and National Airlines 77 per cent.

In 1961, the market went up 20 per cent, Korvette 287 per cent.

In 1960, the market was down 4½ per cent, but Brunswick was up 135 per cent.

Why such bursts of virtuosity?

(1) Brunswick, maker of bowling equipment and a leasing manufacturer of automatic pinsetters, heavily promoted bowling as a respectable family activity and scored as the craze spread throughout the U.S. and beyond.

(2) Korvette was expanding its chain of discount houses as

sales boomed, and in the process was acquiring a stock interest in Alexander's Department Stores. (In 1963, the proposed takeover was still in litigation.)

(3) Under the firm management of President Lynn A. Townsend, Chrysler underwent a rigid cost-cutting campaign which, with a new styling approach and a greatly strengthened dealer network, helped the company to a generous slice of record 1963 automobile sales.

(4) Hayes Industries, manufacturer and supplier of auto parts and equipment for General Motors, Ford and Chrysler, naturally went along for the ride and hiked per share earnings from $1.20 in 1961 to $3.18 in 1962.

(5) A boost in air travel in 1962–63 helped domestic as well as international airlines.

(6) News that Continental Oil Co. proposed to acquire it doubtless accounted for the jump in the stock of American Agricultural Chemical Co. Merger talk (with Chicago Great Western Railway Co.) may also have increased the attractions of the Soo Line Railroad. Keeping pace with the times, the line has also expanded its trucking business via the piggyback method.

(7) MetroMedia, which derives 60 per cent of its earnings from broadcasting and 40 per cent from the outdoor advertising business, had a strong plug from an investment advisory service as a result of its 1963 expansion plans.

These are not the only reasons for such gains. Here are a few

: for control. Each battle in the struggle for Alleghany
as caused the stock to rise sharply: from 3½ to 11 in
) 15 between 1957 and 1959 (year ends) and from
ı5 in 1961–62.

process. Early in 1957, when General Plywood was
American Stock Exchange for about $8 a share, word
at it had developed a heat-treating process that
need for expensive sanding and polishing of ply-
k sold above 23 in 1958.

arkets can be created by new products. On the
Exchange, the shares of Syntex Corporation, mak-
ngredient for oral contraceptive pills, went from a
igh of 260 in 1963 before they were split three for
ear.

Yes, there seem to be plenty of investment or speculative opportunities for those who have the techniques to seek them out.

There is a recognizable amateur technique in investing. You buy a stock. It goes down. You grit your teeth and hang on. Of course you aren't going to sell it! That would mean a loss and a loss would prove that you are not infallible. Finally, perhaps years later, the stock gets back to the price you paid. You sell and puff out your chest. You are a financial genius. You didn't take a loss.

This is about the silliest imaginable way of behaving. All that money tied up all that time, and all you get out of it is an even break—*if* you're lucky. And who ever said that you were infallible? Nobody has been declared infallible since 1870.

The sensible philosophy, it seems to me, is to consider that the unit is the whole investment account, not any individual stock in it. *It might help you not to talk about any of your investments until you have closed them out. Then you will find it easy to remember only the brilliantly successful ones.*

How does one adopt a more logical, more professional approach? Quite simply.

You buy a stock for any one of a number of reasons: (1) Because you have made a careful study of the company's prospects; (2) because there are rumors of a split or a merger or a big defense contract; (3) because somebody told you that a lot of "wise" money was going into it; or (4) because somebody had said that somebody had told him that "They" were going to put it up to 90 by the year's end. In essence, you buy the stock because you feel that it might go up.

Now the stock doesn't go up, so you sell it. It is as simple as that. Even though you may be taking a loss, you sell it. Obviously this was not the right stock to buy. The next one may be.

We are assuming here, of course, that the reasons you had for buying the stock were immediate reasons—reasons that were going to set the stock moving right away. When the stock didn't move right away, the reasons were proved wrong. This is entirely different from deciding that coppers or papers or steels ought to be in good demand three or four months hence and moving in now to pick up a few bargains.

The first edition of this book, which appeared in April 1959, explained the technique of the stop-loss order. This is an order that your broker will leave with the specialist in the stock. It is an order to sell (or buy) if the price should drop to a given level. For example, suppose you bought a hundred shares of BOQ at 20. You might then put in a stop-loss order at 19. Now, suppose the stock drops to 19 or even "sells through" to some lower price. That changes your stop-loss order to a market order. The specialist will now try to sell your stock at the best price he can get. You have no guarantee, of course, that you will get 19 a share or even 8 for it.

One difficulty with this kind of order is that the market may be breaking badly at the moment it goes through your stop-loss price. Your order will merely exaggerate the tendency. Your stop-loss order thus puts you into the position of selling on a breaking market, which is seldom wise. You do much better, for the most part, when you sell on the rallies.

One year after the publication of *The Sophisticated Investor,* a book appeared by Nicolas Darvas, an adagio dancer. It was called *How I Made $2,000,000 in the Stock Market.* Mr. Darvas ascribed almost all his success to the use of the stop-loss order, or rather to the "trailing" stop-loss order. A trailing stop-loss order means that as the price rises, the stop below it rises as well. For example, you buy at 20 and set a stop at 18. The stock goes to 24, so you set a stop at 21½, and so on. In other words, you preserve part of your paper profit each time there is a gain. All this emphasis on a single technique, one of several hundreds in use in the market, naturally attracted a great deal of attention among unworldly-wise investors. Before long, the so-called "Darvas Effect" was being noticed in the market. It was definitely a factor as early as July 1960. A break in the market shortly became a rout. Unlike short selling, which exaggerates upward movements, this exaggerated the slumps. Stock Exchange suspensions of the right to use stop-loss orders became more frequent.

Another method is to use the stop-limit order. This establishes a definite price. The specialist may sell at that price and no other. Or you may combine both methods.

Whichever you chose, you would raise your "stops" as the price went up. At 22, you might have your "stop" at 20½; at 24 a "stop" at 22, and so on.

This mechanical way of playing the market falls down now and then, most notably when too many speculators are trying to use it. Then stop piles on stop and, in the language of the Street, "the amateurs get their brains kicked out." At such a time I suggest the

"John Magee stop." Mr. Magee would have you set your stops in your head. Then, when your stock *closes* below the mark you have set, you courageously sell out the next morning *at the market*. No fooling around. But may I suggest that you dodge the opening crush of excited orders by selling after 11:00 A.M.?

You realize, of course, that if you can cut your losses and let your profits ride you don't even need to be right half the time. Since most of us are right less than half the time this is an important consideration.

How do we pick out the stocks that are going to do spectacularly better than the average? The easiest thing in the world is to pick out a good, sound, solid, respectable stock, one that wears woolen underwear and brushes its teeth after every meal. Such a stock will earn its dividend year after year. It will never go up with the other flighty stocks—at least, that's the way it seems—but it will go down just as enthusiastically as everything else.

We, however, must be on the lookout for stocks that wear tight sweaters and no girdles. We want stocks that have attracted attention and have followings or are just growing up to that nubile state. The most profitable—and, for a time, the safest—stocks to own are those that investors are talking about.

In the first edition of this book, I made a pretty detailed examination of two methods of picking stocks that seem to be on the way up. One was the method of selecting issues from among those that are making new highs for the year. Some experts say, buy such stocks the first time they make new highs. This is pleasant, I suppose, but an unnecessary refinement. Every stock has to make a new high at least once a year. That is why the Associated Press does not give the 1964 high until some time in March. Up to then it reports the 1963–64 high.

The important thing, it seems to me, is that the stock has enough following to be making a *string* of new highs.

The other method examined was that developed by Harold Clayton of Hemphill, Noyes & Co. Mr. Clayton held—at that time —that the one great test was the market itself. If volume rises substantially, then somebody knows something. If the price rises at the same time, you have a "buy signal." If it falls, you have a "sell signal."

In Mr. Clayton's view, the actual nature of the "something"

matters little. Perhaps there is to be a split or a merger or an extra dividend. Perhaps a juicy new contract has been or is about to be signed. Perhaps operating results have been surprisingly good. Then, says Mr. Clayton, somebody will know. Insiders and the brothers of insiders and the kissing cousins of insiders and (possibly) the brokers of insiders will all be on the bandwagon, buying stock. Weekly volume will jump to two or three times its normal pace.

Before we go on, file this in your memory: There is no magic about "buy signals." They are only devices by which we call our attention to stocks that have already begun to attract the attention of others.

In 1958 I made a comparison of the "new-high method" and the Clayton "change in volume" method, covering the period from February through June. Here are the ground rules:

For the "new-high method" I chose alphabetically the first five stocks that made new highs in each month on weekly volume of 15,000 shares or more. There seemed little point in moving on a new high that had come on negligible volume.

When I asked Mr. Clayton's assistance in making the comparison, he pointed out to me that he made daily reports to the Hemphill, Noyes & Co. offices about the country, naming the stocks that had moved upward and downward on unusual volume. He invited me to go through the card index file in which he made his daily notations. For my test of his method, I decided to pick out alphabetically the first five stocks mentioned three times in a month, naturally starting from the beginning of each month.

For both methods, I decided to put in stop-loss orders 10 per cent under the purchase prices. As the stocks rose, these stop-loss orders would follow the prices upward. This, I thought, would provide a good test. However, in making my test, I considered *only weekly closing prices* as peaks. In other words, a stock might close one week at 43, rise as high as 47 in the course of the next week and then close at 46. The figure of 46 would be marked down as a peak and the stop would be set on the round number nearest to 10 per cent below it, in this case 41.

The reader will understand that I was not actually buying any of these stocks. I was working considerably after the dates when purchases should have been made. What I did was check the

Clayton lists against the microfilm files of *The New York Times,* grinding over them week after week to mark new highs and to make sure that stops had not been touched off.

Mr. Clayton doesn't like to sell except when sold out, but I felt I had to wind up the comparison somewhere. I brought purchases to an end in June 1958 and then left enough time so that the fortunate choices could be turned into long-term capital gains. Only three commitments were ended by this fiat of mine:

THE CLAYTON "CHANGE IN VOLUME" METHOD

							Net Gain or Loss*	
Stock	Date Bought	Price Bought	Peak Price	Reason Sold	Date Sold	Price Sold	Long-Term	Short-Term
Minerals & Chemicals	2–5	20⅜	20⅜	Stop	3–8	18		$(294)
Continental Motors	2–14	8⅛	9¾	Stop	6–6	9		42
Philip Morris	2–17	51⅛	61	End	12–9	61		106
Carter Products	2–19	25½	29½	Stop	4–4	27	$891	
Campbell Red Lake	2–19	7¾	9⅛	Stop	6–6	8		(11)
February Totals							891	(157)
Basic Products	3–10	22	23⅜	Stop	3–29	21		(154)
Polaroid	3–10	61	68¼	Stop	5–23	61		(97)
Food Giant	3–11	25⅛	25⅛	Stop	4–4	22		(379)
Bell & Howell	3–11	54	64½	Stop	6–4	58		305
Siegler	3–12	14	31⅛	End	12–9	29⅝	1,500	
March Totals							1,500	(325)
Ritter	4–9	30¼	34⅛	Stop	4–18	31		(19)
Eastern Corp.	4–9	27⅝	43	Abs.†	11–26	43	1,459	
White Dental	4–10	40⅜	48	Stop	8–22	43		178
Artloom	4–10	7	22½	Stop	9–7	20		1,252
Boeing Airplane	4–11	39⅞	54⅝	Stop	11–28	49	833	
April Totals							2,292	1,411
Haveg Industries	5–5	28⅞	32½	Stop	5–29	29		(60)
Hilton Hotels	5–6	22½	32½	Stop	11–21	30	680	
Rexall	5–7	16	16	Stop	6–13	14		(250)
Sperry Rand	5–7	19⅛	24⅛	Stop	11–28	22	236	
American Motors	5–8	12¼	13½	Stop	6–27	12		(69)
May Totals							916	(379)
Argo Oil	6–6	32⅝	39¾	End	12–9	38½	509	
Shahmoon Ind.	6–10	13½	15⅝	Stop	11–28	14		3
Chance Vought	6–6	45⅝	54⅛	Stop	11–28	49		242
Filtrol	6–6	47⅜	48	Stop	10–31	43		(139)
Allied Kid	6–10	29½	32	Stop	11–28	29		(123)
June Totals							509	(17)
Grand Totals							$6,108	$533

* This is net gain or loss on each transaction after deduction of Stock Exchange commissions, New York State and Federal stock transfer taxes and the Securities and Exchange Commission fee. Because readers will want to see how such a system will work in the future, I have used the commissions and Federal tax rates in effect at the beginning of 1959. Both were changed in 1958. † Eastern Corporation was absorbed by Standard Packaging. I assume here that it was sold just before the merger took effect. Numbers enclosed in parentheses, thus ( ), indicate losses.

Let us suppose that our investor is in the 30 per cent income-tax bracket. His maximum commitment has been $31,500—without any use of margin—so his net capital gain on that amount, *after taxes*, has been close to 18 per cent; adding $1,521 of dividends, more than 22 per cent.

Here are the results of the new-high method:

THE NEW-HIGH METHOD

Stock	Date Bought	Price Bought	Peak Price	Reason Sold	Date Sold	Price Sold	Net Gain or Loss* Long-Term	Short-Term
Disney Productions	2–3	17	20⅜	Stop	4–4	19		$144
Florida P. & L.	2–3	60	90¾	End	12–9	89½	$2,849	
Hertz	2–2	44	44	Stop	3–27	40		(488)
J. Kayser	2–3	14⅜	14⅜	Stop	2–12†	13		(175)
Phila. & Reading	2–4	29¼	71¼	Stop	11–28	64	3,389	
February Totals							6,238	(519)
ACF-Wrigley Stores	3–3	17	20⅜	Stop	7–18	18		45
Food Giant Markets	3–3	23½	25	Stop	4–4	23		(116)
Parke, Davis & Co.	3–4	68⅜	109	Stop	10–24	98	2,859	
Rexall	3–5	12½	15⅝	Stop	6–13	14		104
Bell & Howell	3–10	53½	64½	Stop	6–6	58		354
March Totals							2,859	387
Campbell Red Lake	4–1	8¼	9⅛	Stop	6–6	8		(60)
United Fruit	4–1	45¼	50⅜	Stop	11–21	45		(114)
Raytheon	4–4	24¾	59⅜	End	12–9	58⅞	3,330	
Texas Instruments	4–2	31½	49½	Stop	8–29	44		1,168
Transamerica	4–2	39	27⅝	Stop	7–18	24		(462)
Firstamerica	‡	‡	22¾	End	12–9	21½	994	
April Totals							4,324	532
Amer. Water Works	5–1	13	15¼	Stop	8–8	14		53
J. I. Case	5–1	17¼	22½	Stop	11–28	20		218
Colgate-Palmolive	5–1	62	86½	End	12–9	84½	2,150	
Deere	5–1	33½	53½	Stop	11–28	48	1,365	
Ex-Cell-O	5–1	38¼	44	Stop	10–17	40		92
May Totals							3,515	363
Air Reduction	6–2	59½	82⅜	End	12–9	78⅝	1,814	
Alleghany Corp.	6–2	5⅜	8¾	Stop	10–3	8		233
American Airlines	6–2	19⅜	25⅜	End	12–9	24¼	410	
American Can	6–2	48½	52	End	12–9	49⅞	44	
American Metal Climax	6–2	22½	29	Stop	11–28	26	283	
June Totals							2,551	233
Grand Totals							$19,487	$996

* This is net gain or loss after deduction of commissions and transfer taxes at the 1959 rates. † This commission is at 1½ times the ordinary rate plus $5, then allowed for a round trip within fourteen days, but abolished March 30, 1959. ‡ Transamerica distributed the stock of Firstamerica as a dividend.

The maximum amount committed here was $63,500, so that the return was 27.2 per cent *after capital-gains taxes*. With dividends

included, the *after tax* return for the period of about eleven months
was 30.5 per cent.

The reader will notice one big difference between this method
and the Clayton method: It called for the involvement of about
twice as much money over the same period. This may have been
partly accidental but at the same time we must remember that
high-priced stocks are less likely to be chosen by a method that
demands that volume double or treble. In other words, the Clayton method leans toward stocks that are more moderately priced.
It would show to better advantage if equal amounts of money
were invested each time.

Under my method of presentation, the Clayton method bought
100 shares each of Bell & Howell and Siegler for an aggregate of
$6,800 and made a combined profit of $1,805, or about 25.3 per
cent. If an equal amount had been invested in each stock, the account would have held 60 shares of Bell & Howell for a profit of
about $180 and 250 shares of Siegler for a profit of $2,675. The
combined profit would have been $2,855, or 42 per cent.

Mr. Clayton protests the use of arbitrary 10 per cent stop-loss
orders, quite rightly reminding us that while 10 per cent of a $50
stock may be $5, 10 per cent of a $10 stock is only $1. The alpha-
betical method we used for both systems was also a little confining.
I have an idea that either would have done better had an intelligent
man used discrimination among the many candidates for investment, and if the stop-loss orders had been set a little more realis-
tically.

After the publication of the earlier edition of this book, Mr. Clayton decided to employ a combination of the two methods in making
his daily reports, which now list new highs and new lows as well
as up and down moves on unusual volume. In addition, Hemphill,
Noyes put out a weekly *Sentinel Service* sheet, rating every Big
Board stock on the basis of its performance. Each issue leads off:
"The obvious way to be successful in the stock market is to buy
or hold stocks making new highs or exhibiting unusual upside
volume, and to sell or avoid issues having unusual downside volume
and those making new lows. Since it is impossible for the average
investor to follow on his own more than a handful of stocks,
Sentinel Service has been developed to enable him to evaluate

weekly the technical price-volume relationship of more than 1100 listed securities."

Stocks "experiencing buying pressure" are marked "F" for Favorable, those experiencing selling pressure are marked "U" for Unfavorable and those doing little either way are marked "N" for Neutral. Those in each category are totaled weekly so that the investor can get an over-all picture of the market. Early in 1962, for example, he might have noted with alarm (and perhaps acted upon) the almost steady decline in the number of "F" ratings from 229 (February 9) to 5 (May 25) and the concurrent rise in "U" ratings from 264 to 920.

Chrysler, says Harold Clayton, was the outstanding example in 1962–63 of a stock whose rise was well signaled by the combined methods. "Back in October 1962," he recalls, "when people would ask me what I thought of Chrysler, I'd say, 'Well, I don't like Chrysler, but the market does. Therefore I *must* like Chrysler.' " Mr. Clayton's *Sentinel Service* had rated the stock "N" or "U" for six weeks before it started, in late October, on a nearly perfect string of "favorables" (broken by one "neutral" the week ending March 25, 1963) ending June 21. It had gained 146 per cent before it got its first "U."

Any investor who paid good attention to his daily newspaper could have had an eye on Chrysler from late September 1962, when it began to be included with some regularity in the daily lists of the most active stocks, moving down as well as up. By careful study (we will discuss some methods in Chapters XI and XIII), he might have timed his purchase to coincide with one of the early series of dips in price as Chrysler seesawed upward. Between November 2 and November 16, while remaining for the most part on the "most active" list, it made six new highs and was off and running.

QUESTIONS FOR REVIEW

1. Name five good reasons why stocks go up.
2. What is a stop-loss order and how does it work? Why is it sometimes banned on the Stock Exchange?
3. Put together your own portfolio over any period of time, selecting theoretical purchases by the "new-high" or "change in volume" methods or by a combination of the two.

CHAPTER V

Buy on the Rumor:
Sell on the News

YOU MAKE more money in the market on rumors than you do on news. You also lose more, unless you bring a little common sense to the business.

Don't be too eager to get in on the ground floor. Sacrifice a little of the profit to make sure that somebody else believes what you've been told. In other words, let volume and price go up a bit before you buy.

Rumors about big companies are more likely to be true but less likely to be profitable than rumors about small companies. The "fast movers" who start rumors for their own advantage know that widely held companies don't move fast or far enough on tips to give adequate profits.

If you are willing to go in and out, like a trader, you may assume that any rumor that moves a stock has some truth behind it. It may not be the truth you've been told, but somebody knows something.

Increased price and volume are the only confirmations that matter. If you wait for official confirmation, you will lose money. Buy at once if you're going to buy at all.

Our study of the stock market divides fairly neatly into market analysis and security analysis. Market analysis, in which we are now engaged, splits easily into the short-term and the long-term. We are tackling the short-term first, because most investors are almost completely ignorant of it. They do not realize that their relatively low income-tax brackets let them take short-term profits that the big earner must avoid.

In the preceding chapter we took up two mechanical methods of playing the market, the new-high method and the Clayton method. As we went through them we asked no questions whatever about the value of a security. We bought because a stock had made a new high on good volume or because it had increased volume at a rising price. In many cases we were buying the wrong stock at the right time but both methods proved profitable, and a combination of the two proved even more so.

In the next chapter we shall talk about the techniques of the floor traders on the New York Stock Exchange and the men who run the trading desks for its firms. Often they too buy a stock merely because it is moving well, not because they know anything about it. There is even one trader who calls me up now and again to say, "I've just bought some So-and-So because it looks good on the tape. Do you know anything about it?"

I don't know about you, but I always feel uncomfortable when I risk actual money with no rationale other than a tape movement. This chapter, therefore, is an attempt to quiet the abdominal butter-flies by discussing the various ways of handling news and rumors.

Generally speaking, you buy on the rumor and sell on the con-firmation—but make sure you're not the only one buying.

You take some risk when you're doing this, of course. Now and again insiders (or somebody) will see bad news coming up and cir-culate good rumors. For example, a sugar company was driven up to a new high in August 1958 just before it announced a dividend slash. This kind of thing, however, is not quite so common as in the past, thanks to the vigilance of the Securities and Exchange Com-mission and the stock exchanges themselves.

Mergers and splits always seem to send stocks higher, although neither necessarily does the company any good.

Regardless of this, investors seem to think a merger is going to be invariably helpful. Stocks go up—at least, the stock of one of the merger partners is pretty sure to go up. The reason for this, I be-lieve, is a kind of race memory. Without thinking things through, we somehow expect the surviving company to gain monopolistic ad-vantages or, perhaps, some of the sheer bullying advantages of big-ness. Whatever these gains may be, it has been demonstrated that they are not always big enough to offset the handicaps.

How about stock splits and 100 per cent stock dividends? Here the chances for the investor are a little better. The company will remain unchanged instead of deteriorating, as it might in a merger. Here we have a company with 100 shares outstanding, selling at $100 a share and earning $10 a share. It declares a 100 per cent stock dividend. Now there are 200 shares, each earning $5. Why should it sell for more than $50 a share? Or it splits 4 for 1. Why should it sell for more than $25? But it does. There is always the chance that the company may increase the dividend. But in that case, of course, the important news is the decision to increase the dividend, not the decision to split.

There may be good business reasons for splitting some stocks. A man who owns Chrysler and only Chrysler among the motor stocks is far more likely to buy a Dodge than an Oldsmobile—or so the marketing experts tell us. But I am quite sure that Mrs. Crane doesn't stop to consider whether she owns B. T. Babbitt, Colgate-Palmolive or Procter & Gamble before buying Bab-O, Ajax or Tide. And I doubt that most other stockholders do either. (Our daughter, however, insists that when she and her husband owned Scott Paper, she suffered excruciating guilt feelings every time she bought a box of Kleenex.)

For some years I had noticed—or thought I had noticed—that stocks about to merge or split went up ahead of any announcement of such an intention and then did little. In March 1957 I decided to test out the accuracy of this observation. I dug into all the New York Stock Exchange issues that had had splits since the end of the previous June. This was an excellent period for the test, because stock prices, on the whole, were about the same at either end of this period.

In all, there were forty-three splits or 100 per cent stock dividends, but fifteen were not complete by March 20, when I made the study. I examined the other twenty-eight stocks.

How was I to know when the rumor first got around in each of these stocks? There was no way. I couldn't consult my column in the *Times*. Many stock-split rumors go unprinted for days, sometimes because they seem unlikely, sometimes because I don't hear the story in at least two trustworthy places, most often because the stock makes no one-day move big enough to match the rumor.

The best way seemed to be to assume that the rumor got under way in the three months that preceded its announcement. Directors' meetings are commonly three months apart. I took prices on these dates:

1. The day before the directors' meeting that announced the split or 100 per cent stock dividend (there were six of the latter). *Directors*, in table that follows.

2. A date three months before Item 1. *Rumor*.

3. The day before the shareholders' meeting that approved the suggestion of the directors. (Not necessary for the 100 per cent stock dividends, so that identical prices for these were noted under *Directors* and *Shareholders*.)

4. The *Distribution* of the new stock.

5. A *Recent* date. This was three months after the shareholders' meeting for twenty stocks. At the close on March 20, 1957, not quite three months had elapsed for the other eight, so the March 20 closing price was used.

The following table shows how the twenty-eight stocks behaved:

	Rose	Fell	No change
Rumor to *Directors*	23	4	1
Directors to *Shareholders*	9	12	7*
Shareholders to *Distribution*	10	18	0
Rumor to *Shareholders*	20	7	1

* Including six stock dividends.

It was clearly profitable to buy stocks when they started moving on split rumors, but how profitable? How much of that upsurge between *Rumor* and *Directors*, for example, might have been caused by the strength of the general market? Here are the figures, compared with *The New York Times* industrial average:

ACTION ON SPLIT RUMORS

	28 Stocks	N.Y. Times Industrial Average
	(In percentages)	
Rumor to *Directors*	+10.85	+0.53
Directors to *Shareholders*	+ 4.20	—0.54
Shareholders to *Distribution*	— 1.82	—0.90
Distribution to *Recent*	— 1.15	—2.09
Rumor to *Shareholders*	+15.51	—0.01
Rumor to *Recent*	+12.09	—2.99
Directors to *Recent*	+ 1.12	—3.50

The first four entries above make clear that the only profits worth trying for are those made preceding the directors' meeting. In fact, the day before that meeting might be an awfully good time to sell. If the split is not voted, the stock will fall as disappointed holders sell. If it *is* voted, Wall Street professionals will be taking their profits. The old rule is to "buy on the rumor and sell on the news." You can see for yourself in the first table that you'd have a better chance to lose money than to make money if you hung on.

Your problem now is the fact that you would be taking a short-term capital gain. In every case you would have to add more than three months to the holding period in order to turn it into a long-term gain. There are things you can do. Two or three of them will be discussed in Chapter XIX, which deals with taxes. But I am afraid that the real decision rests with you and your own view of the future.

In all honesty, however, I don't feel that anybody whose tax bracket is higher than 40 or (at most) 50 per cent belongs in this kind of speculation. The rumor, if such a man follows it, should promise something of more intrinsic value than a merger or a split.

The average gains are possibly a little better than I have indicated above. For example, El Paso Natural Gas, Louisville Gas and Electric and Panhandle Eastern Pipe Line declined in the whole Rumor-to-Directors period. Rhodesian Selection Trust also declined, due to a crumbling in world copper prices. Royal Dutch Petroleum held even, affected by trouble over Suez. Since these stocks did not rise on the split rumors, you would not have bought them and their losses would not have diminished your profits.

Some of the profits were pretty good. Here is a table of the issues that had the more violent movements:

	Rumor	Directors	Recent*
Boeing Airplane	77¾	89½	108¼
Crescent Corp.	65	79	74⅜
Gardner-Denver	58⅜	70¾	71½
Georgia-Pacific	54⅝	80⅜	59
Greenfield Tap & Die	34¾	44⅜	37½
Jaeger Machine	36½	57	49¼
National Supply	77¼	93	93¾

* Prices "unsplit" to provide comparison.

There is one thing, of course, that is missing in all this calculation: I have said nothing about the number of splits and mergers that are rumored but don't come off. There are plenty of those, believe me! One day in late 1957 I listed the names of six companies that had been mentioned *that day only* as possible merger partners for Gulf Oil. Five years later all were still waiting at the church.

A. Wilfred May, executive editor of *The Commercial and Financial Chronicle,* has done a great deal of research on these lines. Early in 1957 he examined the eighty stocks that split 2 for 1 or more in 1956. Between the admission of the new shares to trading and the end of 1956 only forty-three of the eighty out-performed the remaining companies in their respective industry groups.

Mr. May then took the sixty-six stocks that split in the first eleven months of 1955. Of these, only twenty-one out-performed the Dow-Jones industrial average up to the end of 1955 and only twenty-four did so up to the end of 1956.

In another examination of the eighty issues that split in 1956, he found that seventy-two out-performed the market in the one-month period before the directors met and only thirty-six issues did so from then until the new shares were admitted to trading.

All these data bear out my conclusions, although I prefer the dates I have chosen to those used by Mr. May.

In going over the first edition of this book to see where he might provide updated material for the present revision, a representative of the New York Stock Exchange pointed to the title of this chapter and said, "You'll find we don't have this trouble with rumors so much nowadays." He then produced a letter from Stock Exchange President Keith Funston to the presidents of all listed companies sternly reminding them that prompt disclosure of any corporate news that might affect the price of securities is a requisite of their listing agreement. "When unusual market activity in a security accompanied by a substantial price change occurs shortly before the announcement of an important corporate action or development," wrote Mr. Funston, "it is extremely embarrassing and may work a disservice to shareowner and to the public."

In fairness to the Exchange, without whose assistance this revision would have been enormously more difficult, it must be said that Mr. Funston's letter was aimed chiefly at public-relations officers who had been sending out corporate news on a "Hold for Release" basis to newspapers, brokerage offices and the like, giving all sorts of people plenty of time to get into or out of a security before the publication date.

Has it affected the sort of rumor we have been discussing? The following table shows the action in a number of issues which were split in the first six months of 1963:

	Rumor	*Directors*	*Share-holders*	*Distribu-tion*	*Recent*
Beatrice Foods	52	56	61¼	62	62¾
Chrysler	63⅝	82⅞	109⅜	107	128½
Cleveland Electric Illuminating	61	67¼	65	65	67
Inspiration Consolidated Copper	53½	62¼	63½	69¾	70¼
Long Island Lighting	47⅜	56⅜	58⅞	62¾	63¾
Magma Copper	63	75	77½	80	76½
Singer Manufacturing	107	111⅛	136½	136	151½
Sterling Drug	65¼	77	84⅛	79	81
Sunshine Biscuits	97¾	103	110	110¾	106
Union Electric	46¼	51¾	53⅜	55½	54½
Virginia Electric & Power	57⅝	62⅞	64⅝	65¼	63½

The above stocks were chosen at random. While Chrysler and Singer do not precisely prove our point, there still does not seem to be much of a case for dropping this chapter from the book.

What interests you most, I take it, is whether you ought to speculate on the rumors that a company is about to merge or split its stock. For a little while, anyhow, the stock will be higher. Why not apply these three simple tests?

1. Is the market action right? Has the stock moved in the right direction on appropriate volume? If it has, perhaps you don't need to worry too much about the truth of this rumor. *Something* is happening.

2. Is the rumor reasonable or is it something to the effect that American Home Products has discovered a cure for Rumpelmeyer's Disease? (Since there are only twenty known victims of Rumpelmeyer's disease in the world and thirteen of these are on county poor farms, this is hardly likely to mean an increased dividend, is

it?) Or had you heard that Owens-Corning Fiberglas is making both the glamshishes for the TGBM—trans-galactic ballistic missile —that is to make the trip to Alpha Centauri and back? (Alpha Centauri is four light-years away and, even at ultimate speed, at least nine years must pass before we know whether these glamshishes are any good. Maybe Haveg Industries will get the 1970 contract, after all.)

This razzberry attitude may cost you a good speculation now and then but it will save you more bad ones. After all, why—within limits—should you care how many you miss? There are always plenty more.

3. As I said, there are lots of rumors about lots of stocks. Why not, then, take special interest in stocks that seem likely to do pretty well even if the rumor should not be true? Then, if the rumor happens to be true and you have a pleasant profit at the end of three months, you can hold on for another three months with less quivering behind the belt buckle.

Shall we talk about lies? The earlier pages of this chapter have given the impression that Wall Street rumors are true if enough people believe them. This is not correct, as you may have guessed, but from the point of view of the speculator it may be correct enough. Perhaps he can take his profit and leave before the rest of the customers start looking for the escape hatch.

There are some brokers who would like to "buy stock at 8 times earnings and drive it up to 50." There are others who—perhaps from too much anxiety to please—have an annoying habit of promoting possibilities into rumors. I have found still others who seemed a trifle overanxious to persuade me that such-and-such a stock was a gorgeous buy. Their customers had probably bought on their recommendations and they wanted to make those recommendations stand up.

Perhaps these practices are not quite up to the best Sunday School standards but I do not criticize them. When a broker is accepting a commission to sell an already listed stock—and could make just as big a commission by selling almost any other stock— you can put this kind of thing down to boyish enthusiasm. It is "just his way." If he doesn't tout the stock and drive it up beyond the limits of safety, somebody else will.

I do object, however, when the same man is acting as a salesman. Your broker should represent *you* all the time. If he is hawk-ing a new issue or a secondary distribution of an already listed stock he is using your broker-customer relationship in a way that can be easily misunderstood. He certainly is not representing you. He is representing the issuing corporation or the owners of second-ary-distribution stock who are trying to get out from under by paying more than the regular commission.

How would you like your doctor to take kickbacks from the drug manufacturers? The broker is obliged to recite a little formula when he suddenly turns into a salesman. Perhaps he is "acting as a prin-cipal" or there is "no commission to be paid by you." But what he says is apt to be so perfunctory that it is ignored or not understood.

Most of the liars who affect us in Wall Street are, I am afraid, corporation officials, not brokers. Time after time I have had com-pany presidents deny that their concern was considering a merger with Watsis, Inc., "or with any other company," only to have the same solid citizen announce a merger with another company a week or so later.

According to Revelation 21:8, all liars "shall have their part in the lake which burneth with fire and brimstone: which is the second death."

If I could only be sure of that!

QUESTIONS FOR REVIEW

1. From the viewpoint of the investor, what are the best confirmations of a rumor about a company?
2. Why are stock splits more likely than mergers to improve a company's position?
3. In general, when is the best time to sell a stock you have bought on a split rumor? Why?
4. Should an investor in the 50 per cent income-tax bracket speculate on split rumors? Why?
5. What three tests should the investor apply before acting on a split or merger rumor?

CHAPTER VI

Tips from the Big Traders

BECAUSE LIFE moves in rhythms, the studious are continually trying to find special repetitive patterns in the universe, signals to guide them through their lives. They examine the proportions of the Great Pyramid, the fifty-eight "sevens" in the Revelation of St. John the Divine—and the stock market.

There was once a man who ran a fairly successful investment advisory service based on his "readings" of the comic strips in *The New York Sun*. His trouble lay in adding astrology to comicology. When the authorities found Leo the Lion, Cancer the Crab, Wally the Walrus and other animals of the zodiac creeping into his stock-market forecasts, they decided he must be nuts.

I have been assured in utter seriousness that the dots between prices on the ticker tape are a code used by the Big Boys to signal each other for market coups. I have even been shown what purported to be a decoding of the dots. (The dots, in fact, are used in slow markets to move the last price out from under the typewheel so that it can be read.)

The tape, however, does have signals for those who can read them. Wall Street mentions the names of the "good tape-readers" with respect. Some are floor traders such as Edwin H. Stern of E. H. Stern & Co. and Albert E. Fagan; some are specialists such as Robert L. Stott of Wagner, Stott & Co., John A. Coleman of Adler, Coleman & Co., William M. Meehan of M. J. Meehan & Co., and James Crane Kellogg III of Spear, Leeds & Kellogg; some "office partners" such as Milton Leeds of Pershing & Co. or Roy Neuberger of Neuberger & Berman.

All these men "trade off the tape." They do not come to conclusions merely for doctoral theses or books such as this or market letters. They risk their own money on their conclusions. I decided to stage a kind of piecemeal interview of traders on the New York

Stock Exchange to see if I could extract (1) a few tips on tape-reading and (2) some trading precepts for the beginner. I believe that I have succeeded.

Floor traders, all members of the New York Stock Exchange, naturally have some advantages over the general public. They pay no commissions if they trade for themselves. In other words, they can get out quickly at small cost if they find that something is wrong. (But they still have to pay the State and Federal transfer taxes.) They know which brokers are apt to be representing which institutional investors. They stand there in the "crowd" surrounding a specialist. They hear broker after broker ask "the market"—the price bid and the price asked—and "the size"—the number of shares to buy or to sell. They can get the "feel" of the market that is denied to any outsider.

Their days are probably numbered, however. In July 1963, the Securities and Exchange Commission's Special Study Group for Reorganizing Securities Markets published the second segment of a three-part study dealing, among other matters, with the practice of floor trading. Stating that floor traders apparently served no useful purpose and that their activities seemed to worsen market fluctuations, the study group recommended that all floor trading on the New York Stock Exchange and American Stock Exchange be abolished by January 2, 1965.

The S.E.C. itself endorsed most of the study, and could end floor trading under its present rule-making power. However, Chairman William L. Cary promised not to do so without talking it over thoroughly with those who would be affected.

Whether or not they are permitted to stay on the floor, their past experiences can certainly teach us a few things.

Tom Frank, a floor trader not mentioned above, once asked me rather cynically if my interviews with his colleagues had given me the idea that anybody was making any big money. I replied that my over-all impression had been of a great yearning for a six-*hour* holding period for the long-term capital-gains tax. He nodded approval. Mr. Fagan says, "Something always seems to go wrong in the last three weeks of my six months."

I think we may say that a man who has a good deal of capital and a good deal of nerve can make a pretty good living trading *if* he has the flair. He will also have a good deal of fun. The floor traders I have talked to are among the most completely *alive* men I have met in Wall Street.

There is almost no magic in reading the tape. James Crane Kellogg III, a former chairman of the board of the New York Stock Exchange, says that when he trades in stocks other than those in which he specializes, he is using the tape as a signal.

"I usually try to trade in the kind of stocks that others avoid," he says. "Other people pick stocks that can be moved by their own trading. I'm more interested in finding stocks that have values, stocks that should have gone up but didn't. *However, I don't want to buy them if nobody else is interested in them, so I wait until the tape tells me that volume is developing and the price is rising. Then I buy.*"

Roy Neuberger says that tape-reading is merely the timing device for him. He doubts that it counts for more than 10 to 20 per cent in the making of his speculative decisions. Before he moves he has appraised the market, the industry and the stock. He has decided whether he wants to be long or short of it. But he has gone through the same process for half a hundred issues. Which he chooses to buy or sell will depend upon the action of the tape.

What kind of action can the tape have? What can it say? Here are a few examples:

In the market as a whole, expanding volume must confirm rising prices for the movement to be bullish; expanding volume must confirm falling prices for the movement to be bearish.

If prices rise on falling volume the move is neither *bullish* nor *bearish*; if prices fall on falling volume the move is neither *bearish* nor *bullish*.

These indications are important from hour to hour as well as from day to day. Sometimes a market starts out with a rush in one direction or the other and then dries up.

When the market goes one way and an individual stock goes in the other, a trader sometimes can draw useful conclusions. Suppose, for example, that the market is falling on larger volume but that SOS has risen steadily. Somebody is in there accumulating stock for his own reasons.

Sometimes there are things to be learned from the size of orders. "All ones and twos"—orders of 100 and 200 shares—commonly mean a large involvement by the general public. Institutional investors and big professionals do not trade that way.

Sometimes the time of the day or the week or the year is important. Now and again the market will run along for weeks at a time with sessions in which all the important action takes place before 1 P.M. Again, especially in rising markets, the final forty-five minutes of trading will see a burst of activity and higher prices, day after day. Traders do not like to carry large positions over weekends. A market without fundamental strength is apt to reveal itself on Friday afternoons. And, of course, there is always "tax selling" at the end of each year.

Such influences as these are seldom important by themselves. They must be measured against the news and other knowledge in the mind of the trader.

What kind of knowledge? Well, certain company managements are known to be notably "stock conscious." This need not mean that the officers are trying to drive up the price of the stock so as to make personal profits. It may mean that they are trying to improve the investment rating of the stock so that new financing will be easier.

I remember wondering out loud why a certain eager electronics company's stock should have risen in a certain market. "It jumps every time the company sends its officers East to talk to market analysts," a broker told me. "I hadn't heard that they'd started, but the market action seems to put them about Cleveland."

The best time to buy or the best time to sell is not invariably the time that you suddenly awake to the fact that the market has started to move. Try to pick your moments for getting in and out of the market. The techniques of the traders may not apply all the time—*but they apply at least 90 per cent of the time!*

Be like a trader. Watch out for patterns in the market.

Here is one of the commonest market patterns: Overnight there has been news of the kind that usually moves a market in marked fashion. Let us say it is bad news.

The traders—and they are not all professionals, but include a good many who sit around boardrooms or have their customers' men call them after the opening—watch the way the market begins. The pressure of overnight selling orders is not so great as might have been expected. There are fairly general losses of ⅛ or ¼ but nothing much worse than that. Here and there a stock is higher on some trifling development or the half-hearted recommendation of a wire house. In other words, the market does not want to go down. It acts as if it were waiting around for an excuse to rise.

At this point a few important purchases of easily moved stocks may set the market on its way. A thousand shares here, 2,000 there, and public support may come in. As the brokers say, this kind of market moves upward more easily than downward.

There will almost always be some support attracted in a case such as this. If it is healthy and vigorous, the professionals will help it along. If it is doubtful, the professionals will sell and wait for a better time to push the market ahead.

Unless you are a member of the Exchange, you cannot trade in and out on this kind of signal. Getting a 1-point profit in a $40 stock doesn't leave you with anything worth having after commissions and transfer taxes. But you may save yourself money by watching the market with this in view when you are about to sell or buy. Bad news and you're selling? Why not wait and see if there isn't a rally sometime after eleven o'clock? That would be a better time to sell, at least two-thirds of the time.

Mr. Fagan insists that the floor trader is a follower, not a leader. "Nobody," he says, "is big enough to stem the tide when a stock is ready to go or to start it when it doesn't want to go."

This does not mean, of course, that nobody has ever "started" a stock. There are numberless examples to prove that this has been done and is being done. It means that Mr. Fagan feels that the floor trader, for the best success, should hitch onto trains already in motion, not try to set them going.

And let us note here that the registered stock exchanges have sternly enforced rules to prevent traders from "congregating" on their floors (presumably to plan joint action) or from "dominating the crowd" in any stock.

Is there one piece of advice on which all the top traders agree? Yes: *Take your losses in a hurry. Don't hang around, pretending that you haven't already made up your mind. Move!*

"Nothing is worth more than it is selling for," says Mr. Fagan. "If you bought it at 40 and it goes to 39, a good, smart trade would be to sell it at 39. The first loss is always the best loss."

"Never forget you're a trader. Never argue with the tape. If the stock doesn't do what you thought it would, get out," says Milton Leeds, who would have you execute all decisions promptly and not quibble over small price fluctuations. "If a stock is a purchase or a sale," he insists, "action should be taken at once. The market does not consider your trade in its fluctuations. I have seen many people miss a sizable move because they would not pay ⅛ of a point up or sell ⅛ lower. If you make up your mind to act, put your order in at the market."

"The man who plays the market as a trader," says Mr. Stern, "must be relaxed. If a friend of mine wanted to come down here, there would be two important factors I would check on: First, that he had enough capital so that two or three bad years wouldn't hurt him enough to make him tighten up. When a man starts to get hooked in the market his whole judgment can become warped.

"He can buy a stock, see it go down and decide he's got to have a little more faith in it, hold on. *That little more faith almost always means a much bigger loss.*

"The second thing he'd have to guarantee is that he'd sell when a stock went against him. Any man who will do that will be all right.

"Some people say," he goes on, "that a trader who cuts his losses and lets his profits run doesn't have to be right even half of the time. Maybe that's true. I don't know how often I'm right. But if I had to pay non-members' commissions I think I'd prefer being right at least 60 per cent of the time."

Most maxims of the traders are merely more reminders that stocks going the wrong way are the wrong stocks to be in.

"Never," says Albert Fagan, "average a losing position." You buy 100 shares at 40. The stock drops to 30. You buy 100 shares more, so that your average price is 35 and your loss, *mirabile dictu*, has become $5 a share instead of $10 a share.

This is what is called "averaging." Whole investment systems, including the installment sales of the mutual funds, have been built upon it. But the traders sneer at it.

Milton Leeds contributes a maxim that does not say "cut your losses." It is: "Bulls and bears make money; hogs never."

Mr. Stern disagrees with this. "Now and again," he confides, "hogs make money, too—nice hogs, that is." Then he goes on: "*The main thing is to play a trend, but don't overstay your market. When it reverses itself, run like a thief. You can't win by bucking a trend.*

"*Never be bigger than the size of the market you trade in.* If the market for a stock will let you get in and out with no more than 5,000 shares, why louse yourself up by playing with 10,000?

"Don't press. If you've got to make the money to buy baby new shoes, you don't belong in the market at all. The man who sticks out his jaw and talks of 'making a real play of it this time,' is asking for punishment.

"When everybody is bearish, everybody is apt to be wrong. When everybody is bullish, everybody may be right now and then."

The principal technique of the traders, the tape-readers, is to follow a trend as long as it continues and get out of the commitment as quickly as possible as soon as that trend shows signs of ending. Here we are discussing year-long, month-long, week-long, day-long and hour-long trends. The trader makes little distinction among them. He knows, however, that it is easier for a stock to go the way it has been going than it is to change direction.

Sometimes the trader is attracted to a stock by the fact that it does not go down when other stocks in its group are weak. It has support, even though the trader may not have the faintest idea of the reason for it.

Says Mr. Stern, "If today should be the top of the market, I'm going to lose money. When stocks dip, I'll buy them again. In fact, I'll buy them on each dip until I can see that the dips are part of a receding tide and that the market has changed. I don't want to sell the market short until I see real evidence that something is wrong with it."

Mr. Leeds has a little something to add here: *"When a bull swing turns into a bear swing, sell the stocks that have been going up most and the stocks that have been going up least."* Those that have been rising rapidly may be out on a limb through overconfidence, overspeculation and overpricing. Those that have not been rising in spite of everything may be in trouble because they have no sponsors, no friends.

"The late Eddie Bruns, a great floor trader and the man who gave me my first lessons in this business," says Mr. Fagan, "used to say that a stock at 100 was a buy and a stock at 10 was a sell. This had nothing to do with the prices. It meant that a stock that was in the public eye and was going up would probably go up farther. A stock that had sold off and been neglected would probably go down more. *In other words, he didn't have much sympathy for the idea*

*of picking out stocks that were 'behind the market' unless a lot of
other people had decided they were behind the market and were
engaged in driving them up."*

All the traders speak respectfully of the effect of a big block of
stock at a rising price—not at the opening but in the course of the
day. Each trader must learn for himself, of course, what constitutes
a big block of stock in each issue. For example, 5,000 shares is a
lot bigger block in National Lead than it is in Bethlehem Steel.

Stories are told of one old tape-reader who used to shake his head
whenever he saw 900 shares cross the tape. "That's a signal of something," he would say, "but I don't know whether it is up or down."

Mr. Neuberger feels that a large block almost always brings on a
rise. Big blocks, he says, are bought only after somebody has made
a pretty exhaustive study. The buyer is apt to be an institution or a
big trader or investor. There are enough market tape watchers willing to bet that such a buyer is right 70 or 80 per cent of the time
to give such a stock a following. The result is that an investment-
type issue might go up 5 per cent, merely on the buying generated
by the printing of the big block on the tape. A speculative issue
might rise 10 to 20 per cent.

This is something for anybody to watch.

The remarks above refer chiefly to a big block that trades on an
uptick—that is, at an advance in price over the previous sale. Mr.
Leeds is sure that "the big block generally is bullish for the short
term," even though the price may have fallen a little. "The market
knows," he says, "that the overhanging barrier has been removed."

Mr. Leeds points out that some stocks will rise or fall on the basis
of regularly published reports of "insiders'" stockholdings showing
major purchases or sales of securities by officers, directors and large
stockholders of listed firms. "If an officer has disclosed that he purchased a large block, this is interpreted as being bullish, and
conversely on the sell side," says Mr. Leeds.

Scanning a list made public on Wednesday, July 10, 1963, we
find that G. M. Sadler, vice president of American Airlines, Inc.,
bought 3,500 shares, increasing his holdings to 3,600 shares. The
stock closed at 26⅛ that day, up a quarter. On Thursday it closed
at 26½, a new 1963 high; on Friday it made another new high of
26¾, but eased off to close at 26⅝. The more spectacular example is
on the "sell side." Following a report that S. C. Allyn, chairman of
the executive committee of National Cash Register Co., had sold

10,000 shares, the Wednesday, Thursday and Friday closings were, respectively, 70 (off ¾), 69 and 68½.

"When a stock stays for a long time in a very tight area—that is, when all its movements stay in a rather small range—and then comes out of it on the up-side, you can assume that the stock has been under accumulation," says William M. Meehan of M. J. Meehan & Co., a leading specialist. The natural assumption in such a case would be that the floating supply has been reduced and that new buyers may have to bid a little more in order to get it.

"If a man is picking up 100,000 shares of XYZ," explains Mr. Meehan, "he isn't going to reach. He will try to let the stock come to him. He isn't going to get it at a reasonable price if he moves too fast. He buys some. He takes everything that is offered at his price, perhaps. Then, if traders start to pick up the stock in the expectation that he will raise his bid, he may pull away for a while. He can afford to have more patience than they can. But the effect on the chart is that the stock has not been allowed to drop and has drawn a mildly wavering line from left to right. The longer that line has been, the wider the movement of the stock is apt to be.

"But if you lean too heavily on devices such as this," says Mr. Meehan, "Heaven help you!

"There's an old maxim that says, 'Never sell a dull tape.' Maybe a thing like that works nine times, but the one time in ten that it works in reverse is apt to be a violent surprise.

"I once had a friend who used to work by rules such as that. He wasn't hurt much in 1929 or 1937 but the averages caught up with him in 1938 and 1939. Why? Because in 30-odd years in the market he had never seen stocks go down with volume declining every day. To him, this was a bullish signal. So he bought something at 25 and kept buying as it fell. They picked up the pieces of his fortune when it hit 11.

"Generally speaking, however, watch for a stock that goes up on increasing volume—and especially, watch for a stock that rises on bad news."

Earlier I mentioned Mr. Neuberger's reasons why a big block crossing the tape is usually followed by a rise in price. The same reasoning supports the so-called "sympathetic" buying of apparently similar stocks. If Reynolds Metal gets going with a large parcel and moves up a bit, there will be traders who figure that whatever goes for Reynolds may apply equally to Alcoa and Kaiser Aluminum.

This kind of thing is especially noticeable when the "sympathetic" stock is priced at 10 or less.

Sometimes Wall Street gets a laugh when the well-meaning seekers after "sympathetic" stocks jump to buy before they know what they're buying. More than once Seaboard Air Line Railroad has risen on good news for the airlines.

And sometimes the traders figure coldly on the chances that sympathetic magic will work. "The news that Alaska was becoming a state arrived over a weekend," Milton Leeds recalls, "and I went to the office Monday determined to buy Alaska Juneau. If there had been a market for Baked Alaska, I'd have bought that, too." Alaska Juneau, no longer a gold mine but a rather unexciting utility, came through with some nice profits for traders in those first few days.

More recently (1963), however, Mr. Leeds advised against this type of play. "Don't buy the sympathy stock," he said. "Don't buy Southern Pacific because Union Pacific has gone up. Buy the stock that is going up. Buying the sympathy stock is a great fallacy."

Traders also have to watch carefully for tips from investment services, outfits such as Standard & Poor's *Outlook*, Moody's, Fitch's, United Business Service, Value Line, Capital Gains Research, John Magee, Garfield A. Drew and others. Many of them, like the bigger brokerage houses, have substantial followings. Their definite recommendations bring quick action.

"For example," says Milton Leeds, "a stock may close at 29, get a boost such as that and open at 31 to 33, with apparently nobody selling but the specialist. There is a possibility that the stock will close higher than it opened but the greater likelihood is that higher prices will bring out stock for sale and there will be a slight decline. If not that day, then the next day."

"When a Walter Winchell tip comes along," says Mr. Fagan, "I always take the opposite side. As a matter of fact, I'm apt to do the same thing when one of the big investment services comes out with a strong recommendation. If this results in a bunching of orders to buy or to sell, I do the opposite and make money more often than I lose. This, of course, is almost always a one-day or two-day operation."

We have barely noted Wall Street's tendency to underplay any development that has previously been rumored. Stocks, we have been told, never discount any development twice. Therefore traders tend to assume that something that has been known to a section of the community has been adequately discounted. Often it has not.

Mr. Fagan notes how often the publication of actual news brings about a kind of reverse psychology. The insiders—and here we are including the traders who took a chance and bought or sold on the rumors—are taking their profits. Thus the news sometimes results in the opposite of what an ivory-tower student of economics would expect.

Among his fellows Mr. Fagan has a reputation as a "great player on the up-side." He is particularly effective when he finds a stock with what he calls "mystery." "Mystery," he says, "makes stocks go higher than they ever should.

"There is a saying," continues Mr. Fagan, "that a stock generally moves toward the largest order in it. Put this in another way: When there is a large offering in a stock, it is usually going up. When there are large bids in it, it is going down.

"Does this seem like another paradox? Then consider this: All the time that Lorillard was going up"—and here he was referring to the period between September 1957 and July 1958—"there was never a bid on the specialist's book; nothing but offers to sell it. But in the last couple of weeks of July 1958, the specialist had nothing but bids and the stock broke.

"This is a little hard to explain, so suppose we try an example: Let us say that there is an offer to sell 40,000 shares at 43 on the specialist's book. Now let us say that I sell short 10,000 shares at 42⅞. In ninety-nine times out of a hundred I'll have to cover that stock at 43 or higher. Why? Because if I could sell 10,000 at 42⅞, the support was there to send the stock even higher."

Professionals, those who operate on the floor for themselves or behind the trading desks of New York Stock Exchange firms, do not like to be heavily involved over weekends. They have a tendency to even up.

When times are normal and the professionals are playing the long side of the market, this usually means that they try to sell out on Friday or on the day before a three-day weekend. That ordinarily brings about a heaviness. When it does not, when prices seem to lift against pressure, the market may well end the day with a burst of strength.

Milton Leeds confesses that he likes his trading accounts to be fairly well cleaned out before a weekend. "But if I'm long of something that I feel I should hold, I try to match it with a short line.

Naturally, I try to keep the things that are solid and be short of those that are not.

"If bad news breaks—and in recent years a lot of our bad news has broken over the weekends—I find that I can usually make more on my shorts than I lose on my longs."

QUESTIONS FOR REVIEW

1. What major advantage does the floor trader have over the general public (non-members of the Stock Exchange)?
2. In the market as a whole, if prices rise on falling volume, is the movement bullish?
3. If a particular issue rises steadily in a falling market, what conclusion can be drawn?
4. What would a tape-reader conclude if most orders on the tape were "ones and twos"—orders of 100 and 200 shares?
5. What is meant by "averaging"? What are its advantages or disadvantages?
6. What can we conclude when a "big block" crosses the tape?
7. What is "sympathetic" buying?

CHAPTER VII

What You Should Know

to Go Short

TUCKED AWAY at the bottom of the agreement you make with your broker when you open a margin account are these words: "I hereby authorize you to lend either to yourselves or to others any securities held for me on margin." This commitment, readily made and seldom revoked—it can be revoked by notice in writing—makes it easy for stocks to be sold "short."

Stocks can almost always be borrowed readily. Brokers are happy to lend their customers' stocks because this is the only way in which they can borrow 100 per cent of the value. Banks give no such terms. Does that sound like a paradox? Let us see how it works:

You decide to sell General Motors short at 70. To do this, you put up the normal margin. Let us say that it is 50 per cent. This does not necessarily mean that you provide extra cash. Your equity in "long" stocks in your account may be enough to cover the operation.

Now your broker borrows the stock you want, either from another customer or from another broker. To do this, he has to put up the value of the borrowed stock, dollar for dollar. This is easy for him, of course, because he has already sold the stock and has collected the sales price. But whenever asked he must "mark to the market," keeping the cash deposit equal to the value of the stock.

Ordinarily, stock is lent "flat," which means that neither side pays the other anything. Very rarely one reads that a stock is lending at a premium. The premium we most often hear about is $1 per 100 shares per day, but premiums may also be quoted at $2, $3, $6, $10, $15 and in multiples of $10. Back in 1927, according to J. E. Meeker's *Short Selling* (Harper's, 1932), Wheeling and Lake Erie Railroad set the historic high by lending at $7 a day *per share:* $700 the way premiums are now quoted!

Nowadays, sometimes a year goes by without a stock being lent at a premium.

If dividends are paid, the borrower of the stock has to make them good. In this case we have General Motors, paying at the rate of $2 a year. A quarterly dividend can theoretically cost you $50 on the 100 shares, but GM would probably drop that much on the ex-dividend date, and if you covered in the next three or four weeks the dividend might not cost you anything in actuality. But let us set up an imaginary short sale (see page 76).

You will notice that on a short sale the margin is calculated against the net proceeds, not against the gross amount received for the stock sold short. This is the *initial* margin.

The New York Stock Exchange also has a "maintenance margin rule." Other exchanges in this country have rules that are replicas of it or exceedingly close copies. For any stock selling under $5 a share, the short sale margin is $2.50 a share or 100 per cent of the market value, whichever is *greater*. For any stock selling at $5 or more a share, the maintenance margin is $5 a share or 25 per cent of the market value, whichever is *greater*. (However, many brokers have set even higher minimum maintenance requirements for their customers—averaging 33⅓ per cent.)

GOING SHORT OF GENERAL MOTORS

Short sale of General Motors at 70		$7,000.00
Costs:		
Commission	$46.00	
Federal transfer tax at 4¢ per 100	2.80	
New York State transfer tax	4.00	
Securities and Exchange Commission fee	.14	52.94
Net proceeds		6,947.06
Margin: 50% of net proceeds		3,473.53
Credited to account		10,420.59
Short covering of 100 shares at 65	6,500.00	
Commission	45.50	6,545.50
New credit balance		3,875.09
Less margin deposited		3,473.53
Net profit on short sale		$ 401.56

In other words, you have to *keep* more than 100 per cent margin if a stock is selling under $2.50. In fact, the rule means that your margin on a short sale must be *kept* at more than 25 per cent unless the stock sells at $20 or more.

There are a couple of handy formulas for figuring maintenance margins on stocks selling at $20 or more. For the first one, add the net proceeds and the initial margin—the sum called "credited to account" in the table above—and divide that figure by the present market value. From this fraction subtract 1.00. That will give you the percentage by which your short account is margined.

Take the accounting above and suppose that, after you have gone short at 70, General Motors rises to 75. Then your margin will be figured this way:

$$\text{Margin} = \frac{\$6{,}947.06 + \$3{,}473.53}{\$7{,}500} - 1.00 = 1.39 - 1.00 = 39\%$$

The second formula lets the short seller figure where his margin call will come—if it comes. This is a kind of rule of thumb, so we shall not figure it exactly. Suppose that he sells 100 shares short at 50 and that the *initial* margin requirement at the time is 90 per cent. He puts up as margin $4,500—actually, as we have seen, a little less.

Now 25 per cent of $5,000—the amount he received on the short sale—is $1,250, so our man at the start has an excess of *maintenance* margin amounting to $3,250.

Each time the stock rises a point our friend has lost $100 but he also needs $25 more of maintenance margin. You therefore divide $125 into the excess maintenance margin of $3,250 and discover an answer of about 26. Add that to 50, the original short-sale price, and you know that more maintenance margin will be required when or before the stock hits 76.

A short sale—that is, any sale of borrowed stock—cannot be made unless the *last different price* was lower. This is the so-called "up-tick rule." Suppose a stock sells at 60⅜, then at 60¼, then at 60⅛, then at 60, then at 60⅛, then at 60⅛ again. Stock may be sold short at the first up 60⅛ trade and on the second and third and all successive 60⅛ trades. If the stock rises to 60¼, the speculator may continue to "put out his short line." If it should then drop back to 60⅛, he could not sell short unless he did so on a subsequent advance.

Much of our short selling takes place in connection with the conversion of preferred stocks and debentures into common shares. For example, a $1,000 debenture may be convertible into 50 shares of stock. A floor trader, let us say, is able to buy two debentures for $2,000 and at the same time sell short for $2,200 the 100 shares of stock he will get for the debentures. That kind of short sale is exempted from the application of the "up-tick rule" just recited.

Another point: Sometimes people sell short shares that they actually own. This is called "selling against the box." This is done by persons who expect the market to fall—or want to be hedged in case it does fall—and for various reasons do not care to sell.

Shall we set up an exaggerated example? You are a young man still in a low-income bracket but you have been left 1,000 shares of stock in Grandpa's company. They are now selling at 20. The immediate future looks pretty bad but you expect everything to be all right for the long pull. Instead of selling out your stock, you sell 1,000 shares "against the box"—that is, you borrow 1,000 shares more (with your own 1,000 shares as collateral) and sell them short. If you do this, you are giving up your dividends, for you have to deliver those you receive to the person from whom you borrow the 1,000 shares.

If the stock drops to 10 you have a paper loss of $10,000 on the stock you own but, as you close out your short sale, an actual profit of about $9,533 on the operation "against the box." After paying your income tax on the short-sale profit—which is, unfortunately, a short-term capital gain and taxed at your ordinary income rates— you may have enough left over to buy another 600 or 700 shares in Grandpa's company. Then, if you are right about the good prospects for the long pull, you'll be a lot better off.

For you, this has been an apparent loss. Your 1,600 or 1,700 shares do not carry the market value that your 1,000 shares had at the start. If you had merely held on, however, you would have had only the 1,000 shares, now worth half as much.

Doing as you did, you were fairly safe right along. You paid no interest on borrowed money and you lost only your dividends. If a "squeeze" had developed and frightened shorts had rushed to cover, driving up the price of the stock, you could have joined them, making a good profit on every share you managed to buy and knowing that you could always deliver your own stock in time of need.

A "squeeze" in a stock? Yes, something new has been added to this stock market. For years, about 75 per cent of all short sales were made by members of the New York Stock Exchange and 50 per cent of all short sales were made by specialists on the floor of the Exchange. The specialists had to make them in the normal way of business in order to supply stock when people wanted to buy it. Only about 3½ or 4 per cent of all sales were short sales.

But then came 1957 and 1958, the former with what was probably the most publicized recession in the history of the New York Stock Exchange. Everybody knew it was coming. So brokers began to talk about "more amateur short selling than we've ever seen," short sales jumped to 6½ or 7 per cent of all sales and the non-member public began doing as much as 42 per cent of all the short selling. The short interest on the New York Stock Exchange expanded in this pattern:

Year and Month	Shares	Year and Month	Shares
1953: Jan. 15	1,785,725	1956: Jan. 13	2,289,880
July 15	1,812,352	July 13	2,289,136
1954: Jan. 15	2,564,467	1957: Jan. 15	2,238,573
July 15	3,026,205	July 15	2,737,779
1955: Jan. 14	2,831,191	1958: Jan. 15	2,832,740
July 15	2,739,976	July 15	6,087,260

Not until 1962, with its severe May-July slump, was there another really sharp run-up in short interest. Then the November figure of 6,858,168 toppled the July 15, 1958 record. Here are monthly figures, beginning with December 1961, the market's high:

Date	Shares Sold Short
December 15, 1961	3,406,805
January 15, 1962	3,024,541
February 15, 1962	3,164,292
March 15, 1962	3,119,209
April 13, 1962	3,205,840
May 15, 1962	3,266,873
June 15, 1962	4,611,961
July 13, 1962	5,168,349
August 15, 1962	5,400,104
September 14, 1962	5,354,450
October 15, 1962	6,101,531
November 15, 1962	6,858,168
December 14, 1962	6,436,215

The level remained high through 1963.

When the average man buys 100 shares of United States Steel at 48 and sees it drop to 44 he isn't especially concerned. After all, that's what usually happens to his investments. Besides, he can always comfort himself with the thought that he can't lose much more than 100 per cent: $6,000 plus commissions and taxes.

When the average man goes short of 100 shares of United States Steel at 48 and sees it rise to 52, we have a different animal entirely. He isn't used to being short of stocks. And—if he is the kind who hears noises downstairs at night and goes to investigate—he remembers that there isn't any real limit to the amount he can lose. Why, when you come to think of it, a man who put up $9,000 to sell E. L. Bruce short at 18 might have had to cover at 192, a loss of more than $180,000—*and he hasn't got that kind of money!* (Change that from 1,000 shares to 100 and it still looks scary.)

No wonder amateur shorts are nervous people, always afraid of trolley cars.

You can understand, therefore, that the professional finds it a fairly easy job to "run in a few shorts." He sees that the short interest in a stock is about three times as large as a normal week's volume in it. He buys 1,000 shares. Perhaps that "cleans up the book," takes all the shares offered for sale at, let us say, 48. He then buys another 1,000 shares "at the market," that is, for whatever he has to pay. The price goes to 49, perhaps to 49½. Three or four nervous shorts, who have been promising themselves that they'd get out "in just a little while more," finally decide that the little while has come and gone. They cover and the price rises. Interested professionals see on the tape that something is happening. They buy, too. Pretty soon the professionals and the non-member boardroom traders who followed them in are selling the stock they bought to the shorts rushing to cover.

The above has happened again and again. Throughout the 1957–58 period, moreover, brokers talked constantly of "new shorts selling to old shorts." In other words, those who had grown tired (or scared) of waiting for stocks to go down were covering their commitments by buying from those who figured that stocks simply couldn't go any higher on lower earnings and lower dividends. So these new shorts were borrowing stock and keeping the ball rolling. We saw the whole thing over again in 1962–63.

When a general movement to cover begins, prices rush up even more rapidly. The following brief table gives an idea of what has happened in 1963. In each case the short interest is for the middle of the month preceding the price (see table on p. 81).

Even a small dip in the short interest, you will notice, brought a run-up in the price of most stocks. And why not? The short interests in Ampex, Bell & Howell and Xerox were all greater than a week's normal volume. If anybody really got scared about the business prospects of, say, Xerox or IBM quite a few even more scared shorts were waiting to buy any stock he felt he wanted to unload. In other words, a big scare was going to be necessary before such stocks could return to where they should be.

Milton Leeds recalls Crucible Steel on July 23, 1958. In one week, due to a slightly insane wave of enthusiasm for the second-grade steels, Crucible had risen from 19½ and on that day had made a high of 24⅞. When it declined a bit, Mr. Leeds sold it short at 23¾, saw it close at 23⅛ and locked up his desk well satisfied with himself.

"Then came the second-quarter report," he recalls. "Just six cents a share, making eleven cents for the first half, against $1.80 a share in 1957. If you annualize those earnings—multiplying the eleven cents of the first half by 2—you discover that Crucible, at the close,

SHORT INTERESTS & PRICES
(Prices rounded and short-interest 000's omitted)

	Dec. 28 1962	March 30 1963	June 28 1963
AMERICAN CYANAMID: Price	50	54	58
Shorts	31	28	9
AMPEX CORP.: Price	17	16	20
Shorts	66	45	43
BELL & HOWELL: Price	22	21	26
Shorts	47	44	40
CHRYSLER: Price *	37	46	63
Shorts *	372	330	265
CBS: Price	45	52	58
Shorts	5	9	5
GENERAL MOTORS: Price	58	65	70
Shorts	38	43	49
IBM: Price	395	420	436
Shorts	40	29	14
MERCK: Price	78	83	90
Shorts	30	24	16
PAN AMERICAN AIRWAYS: Price	21	30	36
Shorts	6	15	52
REYNOLDS METAL: Price	24	25	34
Shorts	23	15	54
TEXAS GULF PRODUCING: Price	43	54	58
Shorts	7	22	14

* Both prices and shorts at levels before the two-for-one split May 13, 1963.

was selling at 105 *times* annualized 1958 earnings, against an unusually high 10 *times* at the end of 1957.

"Just on logic, the stock, after all the wonderful extra enthusiasm that had sent it up 5½ points in a week, should have opened the following day at about 21. Did it? It opened at 22⅞, rose to 24½ that day and closed the week at 24¼."

Whenever such a thing as this happens—that is, when a market begins to operate as if all the old laws had been repealed—there are three or four things to remember:

Don't try to fight such a trend. You may be right in the long run but, as John Maynard Keynes once reminded us, "in the long run we're all dead."

If you have the nerve, play the market *as it is,* rather than as you would like it to be—but go to bed with your clothes on. In other words, be ready to jump and run when the trend shows signs of wearing itself out. Use stop orders to cut your losses.

Remember that the upward course of prices is due to the trading of comparatively few persons. After all, only 12 to 15 per cent of the shares listed on the New York Stock Exchange turn over in any one year. A great many shares are being held by investors who are wondering just when they ought to get out. On May 15, 1963, the short interest in Polaroid was 110,543 shares and that was larger than the volume of a normal week. At the same time it was only 2.8 per cent of the 3,900,000 Polaroid shares outstanding.

Any general feeling by the public that—in the light of Washington's credit and fiscal policies and the rate of business revival—present prices of the leading stocks are about as much as can be expected can bring a sharp change.

Remember also that this kind of thing *can* go on much longer than anyone would expect. It might go on until war or some other development brought a great boom in business and rescued everybody—except the shorts.

By and large, my advice is to stay away from the short side of the market, unless or until you can feel a ground swell of public sentiment working your way. In other words, the advice is the same as that for the long side: "Wait until somebody else has started it. Pioneers don't get rich."

Thus far we have been talking about market analysis. Now we are going on to security analysis. I think you'll have fun with it.

QUESTIONS FOR REVIEW

1. What is the initial margin on a short sale? How is it calculated?
2. What is maintenance margin?
3. Explain the "up-tick" rule.
4. What is selling "against the box"? What is the advantage of such a procedure?
5. About what percentage of the shares listed on the New York Stock Exchange turn over in any one year?

BOOK TWO

Quality

CHAPTER VIII

Why You Should Not Lock
Away and Forget Your
Investments

To THIS point we have being talking almost entirely about buying the wrong stock at the right time. There was one exception. In Chapter III we discussed buying the right bond for an exceedingly brief right time. Otherwise we were concentrating on the methods to use when nobody can be sure.

We now move into a field that somehow seems a little more respectable. It is that of security analysis, which is probably the art of choosing the right stock for the wrong time.

There are some New York Stock Exchange firms that don't even bother with market analysis. They figure that if a man gets enough of the right stocks, he can carry them through fire, flood, war and panic and come out all right in the end.

Maybe they are right. They can talk about General Motors (especially if it was bought back in 1914, when it had only 258 stockholders; or, at any rate, well before 1940). They may hint at International Business Machines, which has done about six times better than the market since 1940. They will cough lightly when you mention air transport companies, to remind you that they had them on their lists way back when. Natural gas producers? Of course! Xerox? Chrysler? Columbia Broadcasting? How can you possibly imagine that a concern concentrating on security analysis would not have spotted them all shortly before Guy Fawkes's Gunpowder Plot?

Let me put it this way: Every now and again there are stocks so geared into the future that they will rise no matter what. Lorillard was like that in September 1957. Between 1940 and the end of 1961 IBM multiplied itself forty times, with setbacks as large as 10 per cent only in 1946, 1950, 1955, 1956, 1957 and 1959. Then came the big slump of 1962, when it dropped about 50 per cent. At mid-1963, though it was still more than 25 per cent below its 1961 high, you could still say it had multiplied itself nearly 35 times since 1940. (The man who failed to sell his 1932 legacy of $4,000 worth of IBM stock because he didn't know how and was too lazy to find out is today, of course, an expert on almost every subject and is constantly consulted by Presidents and their advisers.)

This kind of thing always bothers me. I look at a chart of IBM and my lips move. They are saying, "Suppose you had put $5,000 into IBM back in 1943, buying it on margin. Suppose every time the stock rose a point, you bought as much more stock as the broker would let you. Do you realize that you never would have had a margin call and that by 1958 your $5,000 would have changed into something like $3,150,000, not counting cash dividends?" (This "leverage" pyramiding technique is discussed a little later in Chapter XII.)

The trouble is that no really sane person ever acts that way, not for fifteen continuous years. Even though I might have started out that way, the first couple of hundred thousand dollars would have cured me. Or you. We'd have become conservative, switched most of the cash out of IBM and begun playing the market "rationally." While the stock was multiplying itself by 5 between the ends of 1953 and 1957 we'd probably have been in some "dynamic growth stock" in artificial fertilizers or civilian electronics, both of which were falling smack on their faces in relation to the rest of the market.

Theoretically I agree; it is possible to pick out stocks that you can lock away and forget. Practically, I feel it is impossible.

Up to now neither you nor I have been too particular about quality. We have agreed that we'd get along all right if the stocks we picked were in the public eye, if they were moving and if we cut our losses promptly and let our profits run. If our almost mechanical methods of picking stocks should happen to turn up a stock worth holding, that was so much gravy. For the most part, we were content to trade in cats and dogs, provided that they were freshly turpentined cats and dogs.

When discussing the new-high method and the Clayton method I did let fall the thought that, other things being equal, the sound company might be the better. If for no other reason, it *did* give you a better chance of holding out for a long-term capital gain.

But how does one pick a sound company? Can the method be taught? In other words, can I teach you?

Yes, I believe you could be taught, but, unless you intend to go into the securities business, I'm not sure that learning would be worth your while.

You see, it isn't enough to know how. To make security analysis mean anything you must have not only the technique but the entrée. There are hundreds of good security analysts on Wall Street. They know how to break down a balance sheet or an earnings statement. They can assay the potentialities of new products and new markets. They are experts at weighing the effects of taxes or the removal of taxes. They can balance one company's chances of growth against those of another company. And, because they work for an investment service or an investment house, they can and do call up the officers of corporations and ask, How come?

You may learn all the other techniques and, clever as you are, still be unable to get anybody at the other end of the line when you want to ask, How come?

Another thing: Brokerage houses that pride themselves on security analysis seldom come up with more than a handful of worthwhile studies a year. (I am not talking about hasty rewrites of somebody else's research, but of studies that probe deeply and end by planting an actual idea in the reader's mind.) Even if you had the time *and* the entrée your painstaking singlehanded analysis could hardly turn up enough good investment opportunities to be worth your while.

All I am going to try to do, therefore, in the chapters that follow is show you how to read the reports that analysts turn out. If you feel you need more all I can do is recommend the standard book on the subject: *Security Analysis* by Benjamin Graham and D. L. Dodd. McGraw-Hill Book Company, Inc., published a fourth edition in 1962.

Most of the questions that security analysts try to answer about a stock boil down to: How safe is it? What can it yield? How good are the chances for growth? Should I buy, hold or sell it? Here are a few of them, enough to give a sampling:

Is the dividend being earned by a comfortable margin? Since most companies, in good times, pay out about 60 to 65 per cent of net earnings as dividends, the answer, in a slump, is almost invariably No.

Then the question becomes:

Does the company have enough loose cash to continue the present dividend even if it is not completely earned? Does its pride in being an "investment-quality stock"—which can be an asset when it is raising new capital—make you think it will do that if it can?

As a guide to this company's ability to meet competition, how does its net profit ratio compare with that of the rest of the industry? For example, a certain company in a given quarter is carrying about 8.6 cents of each sales dollar down to net profit. The average for its industry is 5.5 cents.

For how many successive years has the company been paying dividends? Note, please, that this figure is often most deceiving. Some companies have managed to stay on the list for more than 100 years by paying single pittances in bad years. This is not the same as paying at a steady rate or an increasing rate, quarter after quarter. But it does show that the company is anxious to retain its investment rating.

How do the company's ratios compare with those of its competitors? Dun & Bradstreet publish these each year in a small brochure. They will tell you, for example, how often the company should turn over its working capital and the average ratio of cash and quick assets to current liabilities.

Can your company operate profitably on 60 per cent of capacity? On 50 per cent?

How rapidly have net profits risen in the past? Are there yard-sticks to let you measure possible future growth? We have a chapter on this a little later.

Your company is earning at the rate of, say, $2 a share a year and selling at $30 a share. That means that its ratio of price to earnings —its price-earnings ratio—is 15 *times.* How does this compare with the ratios of competing companies? Is its ratio apt to go down or up to meet theirs?

What percentage of sales are civilian, what military? What does that mean for the immediate future? If times look good, a large proportion of civilian orders is grand, because these pay more than government orders; but when a slump is in prospect, heavy government orders can almost exempt a company from the business cycle.

If sales rise 10 per cent, will net profits rise 20 per cent or 5 per cent?

Are there any special reasons why this company should benefit in the immediate future? Are there any reasons for thinking that this may be what William Swartz of Goodbody & Co. calls a "thesis stock"—a stock with a special reason for rising?

Adding together the findings of market analysis and of security analysis, should you buy, sell or hold?

If the results are very doubtful, should the speculator play along on the edges of the market or should he get out until he can generate more confidence?

My answer is this: If the investor has the time to pay adequate attention to the market, let him stay in through this doubtful season. If he's apt to forget about it for a couple of weeks hand-running, he'd better get out. There are professionals who *work* at the market. Amateurs should not expect to beat them blindfold with one arm tied behind the back.

There are hundreds of well-equipped, curious-minded security analysts in Wall Street. Some work for big statistical outfits, some for investment advisory services, some for great wire houses with as many as a hundred branches, more for smaller member houses of the New York Stock Exchange. They are constantly flooding their customers with studies of companies arranged by industries, companies arranged by yields, companies arranged by sensitivity to (Heaven forbid!) excess-profits taxes, companies that may be going to split their stocks, companies that have shown terrific growth ratios, companies that have convertible debentures and preferred stocks and companies that have more cash behind each share than the entire market price.

Some of these brokerage houses are big firms that try to cover everything; some are little fellows known for specializing in narrow segments of the market. (One I can think of has three outstanding experts in oil stocks.) There are others that concentrate on market analysis rather than security analysis. Here and there are the eager-beaver firms that gnaw away to uncover the reasons that make this stock or that stock rise or fall more rapidly than the rest of its group. They are quick to jump on signs of unusual market activity.

I have a suggestion to make: If you have enough money, open two brokerage accounts, one with a great big brokerage house that will shoal you under with literature, the other with a small energetic "on-the-ball" kind of house.

Before we leave this subject, however, I want to add a couple of thoughts. There is a built-in risk in playing the market. Don't add unnecessarily to that risk by dealing through a brokerage house of no reputation. Your best bet is always a member of a registered stock exchange in this country. Such firms are policed by the Securities and Exchange Commission as well as their own exchanges, and they are proudly jealous of their records for fair play.

Never never never never buy stock that anybody seems unduly anxious to sell you. High-pressure tactics—"If you don't buy today you'll miss the opportunity of a lifetime"—are the surest warning signal. If you are a doctor or a dentist be especially careful. Doctors and dentists are the world's worst suckers.

QUESTIONS FOR REVIEW

1. What is the difference between market analysis and security analysis?
2. Why do some New York Stock Exchange firms claim they do not even bother with market analysis?
3. What is a company's net profit ratio?
4. How do you calculate the price-earnings ratio of a stock?

CHAPTER IX

What Are Earnings Worth?

MOST OF us over the age of forty, unless we are completely without market knowledge, subconsciously think of yields of 6 per cent and price-earnings ratios of 10 as about right.

For those who came in late, the yield is obtained by dividing the price today *into* the dividends paid in the four preceding quarters.

The price-earnings ratio we get by dividing today's price *by* the per share earnings of the four preceding quarters, or by the earnings of the last quarter multiplied by 4, or by the estimated earnings of the current year, or by the estimated earnings of the year to come. The commonest method is the first, but in 1958, for example, analysts rather generally agreed that 1958 earnings were "unrepresentative" and took to dividing 1958 prices by *1957* earnings.

From this you will gather that a price-earnings ratio, like a machine gun, is not a tool to be used indiscriminately. Judgment is necessary.

Those race memories of ours about 6 per cent yields and price-earnings ratios of 10 times: just how good are they? Pretty good. From 1935 to 1962 the mean average yield of Standard & Poor's industrials was 4.65 per cent, for the utilities, 5.20 per cent.

Over the same period, the mean average price-earnings ratio for the industrials was 13.28 times, for the utilities 13.58 times.

We look over the 112 quarters ended in 1962 and we find that the yield on Standard & Poor's industrials—figured at the ends of quarters, with dividends for the four preceding quarters—has been as low as 2.75 per cent and as high as 7.76 per cent.

Over the same period, Standard & Poor's industrials have had price-earnings ratios veering between 23.32 and 5.64 times. That last figure was as recent as 1950, in case you were wondering.

Our trouble is that both yields and price-earnings ratios each contain two variables. Yield can be changed either by the size of the dividend or by the price of the stock. The price-earnings ratio moves with a shift in either price or earnings. Thus it can rise in either a boom or a slump. It is like a compass needle with both ends marked the same. Pretty bad in a fog.

Consider what happened to Chrysler in 1962. In 1961 it earned $1.24 a share. At the end of January 1962, it was selling for about $54. That gave it a price-earnings ratio of 43.5 times. Suppose the price had dropped 50 per cent to $27. Then the price-earnings ratio would have been halved as well, going to 21.8.

That didn't happen, although Chrysler took a pratfall along with the rest of the market. Instead, Chrysler earned $1.31 a share in the first half of 1962, an annual rate of $2.62—a little better than double its 1961 earnings. So in the middle of August 1962, when the stock was again quoted at 54, the price-earnings ratio was calculated at 20.4 times.

No, the price-earnings ratio isn't much of a measurement when you go up and down the calendar, and yet every now and again it comes in handy as a check.

Sometimes I find myself toying with the idea that the price-earnings ratio is merely a tool for selling stocks to the general public. (I don't really believe this but I don't think I'd do so badly if I picked that side in a debate.)

A broker can use it to make a stock look cheap. "Do you realize," he will ask, "that Boggles Cordage is selling at twelve times earnings? Every other stock in its group is at twenty or better."

If prices have risen so that price-earnings ratios are much too high, the broker can pat your head and make you feel like a six-year-old: "Things have changed, my boy. People are sophisticated now. They are getting trained to expect lower yields. With all these built-in supports and cushions we've given the economy, they're being schooled to considerably higher price-earnings ratios.

"You've got to realize, sonny, that if you're going to get worthwhile long-term capital appreciation, you've got to look forward to those great ages of future growth. You're *never* going to be able to buy anything at eight times earnings again—not anything *good*." This is the line we are being given in the 1960s.

If earnings have fallen faster than prices, we are told that the price-earnings ratios are unrepresentative. That will be in the first breath. The next will use the ratios to suggest that Such-and-Such is undervalued in its group.

Or, when things have gone amiss, we are reminded that Such-and-Such "normally" sells at some higher price-earnings ratio.

But what would you have? It is a broker's job to find (relative) bargains for his customers and any stock is a bargain as long as it is going up.

Eventually—and this has always happened and always will happen—prices are persuaded to levels beyond the power of earnings to support. Or earnings shrink. Then prices come down, sometimes slowly, more often rapidly. Actually, stocks seem to spend about half again as much time rising as falling.

Are there any ways in which we can use yields and price-earnings ratios to guide our investment programs? Yes, I believe there are, but only in the most general way.

You might, I suppose, work out a system that would have you buy stock only when the price-earnings ratio of Standard & Poor's industrials was below nine times and sell when it topped 13 times. *Under such an arrangement, you would have bought twice and sold twice since 1935!* The first round-turn would have made you a profit of 32 per cent, the second one of 241 per cent, if we ignore commissions and taxes. This sounds wonderful, I know, but it only works out— over the 28 years—at 6.2 per cent on your money, compounded semi-annually. You ought to be able to do better than that.

No market is cheap because the price-earnings ratio is low and no market is dear because the ratio is high. In June 1962, at the market's bottom, the price-earnings ratio for Standard & Poor's industrials was 15.5. Many of us think that figure is high. Yet the trend since the mid-1950s has been to price-earnings ratios above 15. In 1958, when the first edition of this book was written, it was possible to look back and observe that good rallies hardly ever seemed to start when the ratio for industrial stocks was above ten times. There had been only two occasions since 1935. The first was the nine-month advance that started in April 1939, when armaments orders were pouring into our economy. This situation raised industrial stocks 25 per cent. This was followed almost immediately by a 30 per cent decline in five months. The second rally, which came in 1957 (from a base of 12.91 times earnings), had equaled the 1939–40 gain by September 13, 1958. The 1957 rally apparently set a new trend. In 1960–61, industrial stocks rose 33 per cent between the October 1960 low (price-earnings ratio: 18.92) and the December 1961 peak. Between June 1962 and June 1963, the gain was 27½ per cent. But the following table makes it all much clearer.

PRICE-EARNINGS RATIOS AT PEAKS AND TROUGHS
(S. & P. Industrial Indexes)

	At Peaks				At Troughs		
	Index	Month	P/E*		Index	Month	P/E*
1937	18.10	3	17.08				
1938					8.39	3	9.21
1938	13.66	11	23.25				
1939					9.92	4	15.46
1940	12.42	1	15.15		8.70	6	9.85
1941	10.62	1	9.48		8.47	12	7.92
1945	17.06	12	19.74				
1946	18.53	5	23.26		13.64	11	13.90
1947					13.40	5	9.81
1948	16.93	6	8.63				
1949					13.23	6	5.69
1949	16.52	12	6.76				
1950	20.60	11	7.51				
1951	24.33	10	9.62				
1952	26.92	12	10.22				
1953					22.70	9	8.55
1954	37.24	12	12.17				
1955	49.54	11	12.65				
1956	53.28	8	13.53				
1957					41.52	10	12.91
1958	57.09	12	20.40				
1959	64.23	7	19.06				
1960					56.90	10	18.92
1961	75.81	12	19.57				
1962					58.32	6	15.50
1963	73.61	6	19.07				

* The price-earnings ratios are for the ends of the quarters in which the peaks or bottoms were hit and therefore are not completely accurate. Earnings are cumulated for the four quarters before the date of calculation.

Look at that ladder of rising prices between 1949 and 1956, with only one rung missing. It may help you to keep things in focus to remember that in that period per-share earnings rose from $2.40 to

$3.58, an advance of 49 per cent. The price index, however, rose 194 per cent. As you will discover by dividing 149 into 294, much of that advance was due to the virtual doubling of the price-earnings ratio. Little by little, bemused by the hopes of future profits, investors let themselves be hypnotized into capitalizing earnings more and more generously.

You might notice also that at the 1962 bottom, when prices had fallen 23 per cent from the 1961 high, they were still 253 per cent above the 1949 high. Earnings were up 129 per cent.

What is the story on yields? Can we use them as infallible guides into and out of the market? Perhaps we can. You will remember that the mean average yield of Standard & Poor's industrials from 1935 onward was about 5 per cent. If you had bought every time the yield topped 7 per cent and sold every time it dropped below 4 per cent (using the figures at the ends of quarters) you would have bought in 1937, 1941 and 1949 and sold in 1938, 1945 and 1955, with profits of 27, 90 and 208 per cent. Your aggregate profit would have been 633 per cent or about 8½ per cent a year for the 24 years, compounded semiannually.

Should we sell, then, whenever the yields on industrials average less than 4 per cent, as they did in thirty-six of the 112 quarters from the end of 1934 to the end of 1962? If we did so we'd be losing some of our more profitable movements. In 1935 and 1936, for example, the market was anticipating prosperity faster than companies could raise their dividends, so yields were below 4 per cent for six successive quarters. Selling on the first drop below 4 per cent would have cost an impending profit of more than 50 per cent.

In 1955, 1956, and 1957, yields were below 4 per cent in five out of seven quarters before the market break came. From the first under-4 to the last under-4 the industrial index rose from 42.98 to 51.21. As of August 1963, we can say that yields have been under 4 per cent since the second quarter of 1958.

The above reminds me of a bit of advice we often hear quoted: When stock yields drop below those for high-grade bonds, sell the stock and buy the bonds. Later, you are told, you'll be able to pick up the stock at half its present price.

This is one of those sayings that sounds wise and hardbitten but is actually composed completely of horsefeathers.

Between March 1933 and November 1936, the yield of industrial stocks was constantly below the yield of Moody's triple-A bonds. Why? Investors were anticipating the full recovery of business. Stock prices were rising faster than dividends.

In that 44-month period industrial stocks rose 239 per cent. High-grade corporation bonds gained 26 per cent, long-term Treasuries 14 per cent.

This is a complicated subject and I'll have to discuss it later, under "Fundamentals." All I care to say here is this: There should be a close relationship between the yield of bonds and the yield of stocks. Such a relationship is destroyed when people begin to lose faith in the solidity of the currency. When the value of the yen was dropping from 6.66 cents to 0.278 cents in four years of MacArthur's occupation of Japan, investors shied away from 9 per cent bonds but rushed eagerly to buy common stocks that were paying no dividends.

A man who bought long-term Treasuries at the end of 1952, when they were yielding 2.74 per cent, would have seen more than half his interest return nullified by the 7¾ per cent drop in the purchasing power of the dollar between then and mid-1958. Wall Street's shouts that common stocks were "a hedge against the inevitable inflation" could hardly be called helpful.

For our economy to function, our government must be able to sell its bonds. If the Washington money managers should undertake to rectify their mistakes and bring people back to bonds by issuing them with coupons of 5 per cent, 6 per cent or 7 per cent—and I'm not recommending this, simply pointing it out as a sad possibility—that would not mean that stocks should *necessarily* be thrown overboard. Japan's experience might be repeated. In other words, these are relative things and each situation deserves study rather than mere labeling.

Ralph A. Rotnem, economist-partner of Harris, Upham & Co. and a former president of the New York Society of Security Analysts, recognizes the price-earnings ratio as a measure of hope, hope that earnings will rise to justify the price. To make this a little clearer, he subtracts book values from Standard & Poor's index of 50 industrial stocks.

S. & P. calculates the book values annually, adding up all of each corporation's assets and then subtracting all liabilities. If there are preferred stocks, their liquidating values (the amounts holders are supposed to get if the corporation is wound up) are also subtracted. The figure that is left is net asset value. That is divided by the number of common shares to get book value.

"Some puzzling trends," says Mr. Rotnem, "are evident when we use the ordinary method of figuring price-earnings ratios on the general market averages. The ratios averaged higher in 1930, 1931 and 1932 than they did in 1929 despite a market decline of 86 per cent from the 1929 peak to the 1932 low.

"Earning power," he continues, "also cost more in 1938 than it did in 1937 despite a decline of 53 per cent in stock prices."

Mr. Rotnem defends his decision to subtract the book value figures: "There are plenty of good arguments that book-value figures are rather fictitious. But aren't earnings and stock market averages themselves fictitious and dirty? No one knows what real earnings are today. Are they too high because depreciation rates are too low? And in certain cases are they too low because of the influence of accelerated amortization?"

He points out several other places where the statistics are "dirty." For example, Dow-Jones includes the value of stock dividends when figuring yields; S. & P. and Moody count only cash dividends. Thus, in July 1963, Dow-Jones gave the industrial yield as 3.34 per cent, the others figured the average at 3.13 per cent.

Mr. Rotnem figures his use of the (only available) "dirty" statistics is "a little like the scientist who takes some dirty coal and produces a piece of white nylon." It works like this: In a certain quarter the range of Standard & Poor's industrials was between a high of 52.25 and a low of 45.71. Their book value at the end of the preceding year was 23.08. Subtracting the book value, the high and the low become 29.17 and 22.63. Dividing those by the average earnings, which we shall call $3.85 a share, we get a price-less-book value times earnings ratio ranging from a high of 7.68 to a low of 6.39.

There have been times—in 1929, 1930, 1931, 1937, 1938, 1946 and 1959 through 1962—when the high of this ratio was near ten or above it. And there have been times—1931, 1932, 1933, 1934, 1935, 1942 and 1949—when the stock market averages were for a time, at least, below the book values, so that there was nothing left to divide. Strangely enough, the high for 1931 was almost ten points after it had been divided by earnings but the low was under water. The whole year of 1932 was under water.

My feeling about this amended price-earnings series is that it makes a little clearer that we are working with two variables, but that the fundamental trouble remains. Those high ratios in declining years still bother me. I like the north end of my compass needle to be marked so that I can recognize it.

In April 1958 J. Walter Leason of Gregory & Sons made an ingenious study of the depression-resistant qualities of 104 electric utility companies. He has not revised the study. "However," he wrote in August 1963, "the findings are still current. An earlier interest in 1954 produced almost identical results. The reason is that the basic characteristics of the territories served change very slowly and rates are based upon cost and profit factors which also remain reasonably constant." I have chosen thirteen of his companies and applied prices for May 16, 1958. They are arranged in order of price-earnings ratios—the old-fashioned, not the Rotnem, kind:

COMPARISON OF ELECTRIC UTILITIES

Company	*Price 5–16–58*	*1957 Earnings*	*Dividend indicated*	*P/E Ratio*	*Yield %*
Florida Power	63½	$2.96	$2.00	21.5	3.15
Virginia E. & P.	30⅝	1.53	1.00	20.0	3.26
Texas Utilities	50⅝	2.56	1.60	19.6	3.16
Southern Co.	29⅝	1.65	1.20	17.9	4.05
Long Island Ltg.	24¾	1.44	1.20	17.2	4.85
Boston Edison	52⅜	3.12	2.80	16.8	5.35
Commonwealth Edison*	46⅝	2.85	2.00	16.7	4.28
Public Service E. & G.	35⅜	2.22	1.80	15.8	5.09
Consolidated Edison	54⅜	3.44	2.80	15.7	5.15
Detroit Edison	39⅜	2.62	2.00	15.0	5.09
Empire District El.	21⅝	1.49	1.20	14.5	5.53
Minnesota P. & L.	33⅝	2.49	1.60	13.5	4.76
Kansas P. & L.	27½	2.05	1.30	13.4	4.73

* Commonwealth Edison's year is to 9–30–57.

At a time like the middle of May 1958, why should there have been such great variations in the yields? We know that a good many investors had been looking for defensive issues, for cyclone cellars in which to hide until the cold economic winds stopped blowing. Was there all that difference in safety between, say,

Florida Power and Consolidated Edison? Let us examine that question.

Mr. Leason, one of our more imaginative security analysts, had asked himself what would happen were the electric power companies to lose 10 per cent, 20 per cent or 30 per cent of their industrial business. Would their dividends be in danger? Would these defensive issues be defenseless? This is a useful question, because, using full-year totals, we find that aggregate power use dropped only 14 per cent from its temporary peak in 1929 to its temporary trough in 1932.

Industrial users of electricity buy at wholesale. According to Mr. Leason, in 1957 they consumed 50.8 per cent of all the kilowatt hours used but (with an average rate of 0.91 cent to the kwh.) provided only 27.9 per cent of the revenues of the electric utilities. Residential customers used 26.2 per cent of the power and provided 40.5 per cent of the revenues. Commercial and other users took and paid for the rest of the power.

Between 1929 and 1932, says Mr. Leason, *industrial* kilowatt sales fell 28 per cent and revenues from them dropped 20 per cent. But residential sales actually rose—for who is going to turn off an electric refrigerator to save 83 cents a month? A television set costs 66 cents a month, to bring the matter up to 1959.

Therefore the question is: How dependent is any electric utility on its industrial business? How much would its earnings fall if it lost 10 per cent, 20 per cent or 30 per cent of its industrial load? If the company lost 30 per cent of its industrial sales, what would be the margin remaining over its present dividend?

Boston Edison, at the time Mr. Leason wrote his report, showed 1957 earnings of $3.12 a share and was paying a dividend at the annual rate of $2.80. That left a margin of only 32 cents. If the company lost 10 per cent of its industrial power sales, Mr. Leason figured, it would exceed its $2.80 dividend by only four cents. If it lost 20 per cent of its industrial sales, it would fail to earn its present dividend by 24 cents a year. A 30 per cent loss in industrial sales would find its dividend 52 cents a share under water, or 19 per cent.

On the other end of the line, Texas Utilities would be covering its dividend by 145 per cent, even if it lost 30 per cent of its industrial power sales. Here is a comparison of the dozen companies, arranged by coverage in the event of such a loss in industrial sales:

COVERAGE OF PRESENT DIVIDENDS

Company	Over coverage of present div. if ind. sales fell 30% %	Ratio of 5–16–58 price to 1957 earnings	Yield %
Texas Utilities	45	19.6	3.16
Virginia E. & P.	44	20.0	3.26
Kansas P. & L.	42	13.4	4.73
Florida Power	38	21.5	3.15
Commonwealth Edison	19	16.7	4.28
Southern Co.	15	17.9	4.05
Consolidated Edison	14	15.7	5.15
Minnesota P. & L.	12	13.5	4.76
Long Island Ltg.	8	17.2	4.85
Detroit Edison	8	15.0	5.09
Public Service E. & G.	—	15.8	5.09
Empire District El.	(−12)	14.5	5.53
Boston Edison	(−19)	16.8	5.35

You may do your own browsing among those long-past bargains. Obviously Consolidated Edison was a better defensive buy than any of the stocks mentioned below it in this table. Imagine losing 30 per cent of industrial power sales and still covering the present dividend by a seventh!

Only if one were expecting a more complete disaster than that of 1929–32 could any of the stocks listed above Consolidated Edison look better on a yield and safety basis. One might hope for an increased dividend, perhaps, but suppose that Texas Utilities were paying $2 a share instead of $1.60 or Florida Power $2.50 instead of $2. At the mid-May prices of 1958 they'd both still be yielding less than 4 per cent. Not even if they were paying as dividends every penny they earned would their yields at those prices be as high as that of Consolidated Edison. No. Those prices and those low yields were obviously predicated on the hope of further "growth." Texas Utilities, Virginia Electric and Power and Florida Power were what some analysts were then calling growth utilities.

The concept of "cash flow," now increasingly popular among brokerage houses, is another way of looking at company income.

"Cash flow," says Samuel C. Greenfield, economist for Hardy & Co., "is that portion of the year's sales that remains with the company. You add net profits (profits after taxes) to the amount set aside for depreciation and depletion. If you then divide by the number of shares of common stock outstanding you can get cash flow per share. Part is paid as dividends. Part is used to reduce debt. Part is reinvested in new equipment. Thus cash flow is the main source of company expansion. It really is not too significant whether a cash flow of $5 a share is composed of $1 profits and $4 depreciation and depletion or the other way around. That is why the cash flow figure is so important. Then again, in oils, metals and other extractive industries, the tax laws permit huge deductions of depreciation and depletion. In these industries the cash-flow figure is particularly important."

Mr. Greenfield gives the following examples of cash flows in 1962, to which he has added comparative figures for mid-August 1963.

A FEW EXAMPLES OF CASH FLOW

Company	1962 Earns.	D.&D.	Cash Flow	Price End of 1962	Price-C.F. Ratio Jan. 1, 1963	Price Aug. 14, '63	Price-C.F. Ratio Aug. 14, '63
Atlantic Refining	$4.89	$5.30	$10.19	48⅞	4.7	54⅝	5.3
First Nat'l Stores	4.75	7.53	12.28	50	4.1	56	4.6
U. S. Steel	2.56	5.15	7.71	43⅝	5.6	49½	6.4
Allied Chemical	2.19	2.83	5.02	44¼	8.8	49¾	9.9
RCA	2.79	2.35	5.14	57½	11.1	71⅜	13.9

An analyst for the now defunct Ira Haupt & Co. put cash-flow figures to an interesting use early in 1958, comparing Chrysler with General Motors and Ford. He found these figures:

	GM	Ford	Chrysler
Profit per unit produced*			
1954–1957 average	$517	$332	$135
Profit per unit for first			
1958 quarter	500	180	90

* After amortization of tools and dies but before depreciation.

The reader must understand that the figures used here are not the correct ones—although reasonably close—because the Ira Haupt analyst was estimating on the basis of the first eleven weeks of 1958. He estimated per-share earnings for the quarter at 65 cents for General Motors and 35 cents for Ford and then "annualized" them, multiplying by 4. His next move was to add a tax saving of 50 per cent of the amount deducted for depreciation. Like this:

PER-SHARE FIGURES ON THE MOTOR MAKERS

	GM	Ford	Chrysler
Annualized 1st Q. net profit	$2.60	$1.40	($1.20)
50% tax saved on depreciation	.78	1.84	4.80
Profit plus tax saving (A)	3.38	3.24	3.60
Cash-flow basis (B)	4.16	5.08	8.40
Price divided by (A)	10.8	12.5	14.6
Price divided by (B)	8.5	8.0	6.1

The small number of shares outstanding for Chrysler was, of course, the main reason that this company could be made to look like such a good gamble for the future. "If it ever returned to supplying its old 21 per cent of the market! . . ." I mused in 1958. In 1963 its common shares were split two for one and its share of the market was up to 15 per cent (from 10.3 per cent in 1962).

QUESTIONS FOR REVIEW

1. What happens to the price-earnings ratio of a stock when a) price goes up? b) earnings go up? c) price goes down? d) earnings go down?
2. What happens to a stock's yield when the price falls?
3. How do we calculate the "book value" of a stock?
4. What is cash flow? Why is this figure particularly important in such extractive industries as oils and metals?

CHAPTER X

If They Say "Growth,"
Make 'Em Prove It!

MY FAVORITE definition of a growth stock is "a stock that somebody is trying to sell you."

Many a stock remains a growth stock only as long as somebody is actively interested in selling it. When it becomes a little hard to move, when the salesmen switch to another line of goods, it stops being a growth stock, no matter how rapidly its earnings may be rising.

The "growth" label can be (and probably has been) applied to any stock that made more this year than last. In its worst form it is merely a selling tool; in its *usual* form, let me say, it is merely a selling tool. Too few investors are equipped to distinguish between the increase in price and earnings that reflects a mere upturn in the business cycle and the increase that has more fundamental causes. Another pitfall is that hundreds of stocks retain their "growth" labels long after changes in fundamental conditions should have washed them off. Chemicals and airlines and frozen foods and distillers and papers were high on the list of growth stocks in the early 1950s, but between 1955 and 1958 their growth was barely discernible to the naked eye. Some of them got started again in 1959 and later but their record was a reminder that they could stall again.

Yes, I think we may say that most so-called "growth companies" today are those that have already had their growth and no longer deserve the label. You don't need a map of that old petrified forest. What you need is a crystal ball and the intuition to pick out the new growth stock, the one you can still buy "almost for free."

Do you wait around for a new industry to get cracking, something like television or transistors or hi-fi or canasta or residential heating by thermofusion or air conditioning? If you do, you are almost certain to be disappointed. In the first place, you never know how much growth you can count on. (Production of television sets rose 445 per cent between 1947 and 1948 and 207 per cent between 1948 and 1949. Between 1953 and 1954 it made the impressive gain of 2 per cent! How are you going to figure that in a growth-stock investment program?)

In the second place, when a new industry is concerned, you never know which entrant in the race is going to win. It is apt to be the biggest company, but success in a new line by a big company would mean relatively little in extra profits. Investors who try to follow this new-industry method almost always figure that "you can't win enough by betting on the favorite." They pick hundred-to-one shots, the kind that come in once in a thousand times.

No, the best way to pick a growth stock is to go after it for "company reasons" rather than "industrial reasons." Such as these:

Has the company got a virtual monopoly or an impregnable position in an industry that seems absolutely certain to expand for the next few years at a rate of 13 per cent or more? In a public utility, 9 per cent will do.

Has the company embarked on new financial tactics that cannot help but improve its earnings over the years? For example, if it were in an industry that could turn over its capital profitably several times a year, it might get rid of its real estate and adopt a build-sell-and-lease-back policy. This might multiply by two or three times the profits available from the money already invested.

Is it a company designed for growth?

Has it got the kind of sponsorship that can take it places?

The concept of a company "designed for growth" is possibly a new one to you. Let me back into it with an illustration:

Here is an electronics company that earns $2 a year on each of its 2,000,000 shares. The market gives it a price-earnings ratio of 16 times. This makes each share worth $32 and the common stock as a whole worth $64,000,000. This is Company A.

The description of Company B is identical except that its stock is given a price-earnings ratio of 8 times. That makes each share worth $16 and the company as a whole worth $32,000,000.

Now suppose Company A offers one share of its stock for each two shares of Company B stock and suppose that the deal is accepted. The combined earnings are now $8,000,000 or $2.66⅔ for each of the 3,000,000 shares. But there is a very good chance that Company A's price-earnings ratio of 16 will adhere to the merged company. Each old shareholder of Company A would have shares worth $42.60 each instead of $32. Each half-share of Company A stock given an old Company B man would be worth $21.30, instead of the $16 he started with.

Or take another example: Our merged Company A-B decides not to pay any dividend out of its annual earnings of $8,000,000. Instead, it buys outright, for $8,000,000 in cash, a company that is making $1,200,000 a year. This means 40 cents a share for the 3,000,000 shares of Company A-B. Those 40 cents are multiplied by 16 and the stock (potentially, at least) rises $6.40.

Instead of a dividend of perhaps $1 a share—on which he'd have had to pay taxes at his ordinary income-tax bracket rates—the shareholder gets a potential capital gain of at least $4.80 *after maximum taxes*.

Naturally, that kind of thing gets to be exceedingly popular with top-bracket taxpayers. They go after companies for which this has come to be a recognized pattern of behavior. Soon that price-earnings ratio of 16 times will rise and rise! Then the company gets even more leverage when it buys for stock or cash.

Does this sound far-fetched, a little on the imaginative side? I assure you that it isn't. It is common and would be a lot more in your consciousness if almost every company didn't want to end up as top dog! There would be many more such mergers if junior partners weren't so hard to find. Following is a list of companies that we may judge to have adopted acquisition policies:

COMPANIES WITH ACQUISITION POLICIES

(Figures in parentheses show number of
acquisitions between 1952 and 1963)

Allied Supermarkets (13)
(formerly ACF-Wrigley)
Amerace (3)
Babbitt (6)
Crescent Petroleum (6)
Federal Pacific (9)
Food Giant Markets (9)

Haveg Industries (8)
Howe Sound (25)
(formerly Haile Mines)
Litton Industries (30)
Nautec (9)
(formerly Motor Products)
Philadelphia and Reading (10)

COMPANIES WITH ACQUISITION POLICIES (*Cont.*)

Plough (13)	Textron (34)
Rexall Drug (16)	U. S. Industries (10)
Studebaker-Packard* (11)	Vulcan Materials (22)

* When this company was selected in 1958, it had not yet made any acquisitions.

These companies have all shown signs of being acquisition-minded. When I first selected them in October 1958, most were in the popular 10–25 price range. Checking them over in October 1961, I calculated that an equal number of shares in each company would have shown an aggregate gain of 81 per cent since October 1958. Five years later, in August 1963, only two were selling for more than $40. I have not meant to slight bigger and more seasoned acquisition companies such as Air Reduction, American Home Products, Otis Elevator, Minnesota Mining and Manufacturing and International Business Machines. Most of these seemed to me so big that even a favorable acquisition could hardly mean enough in added price or earnings.

Obviously, the relatively small company has the better chance of improving both earnings and price-earnings ratios by these methods. You may wish to note in this connection that all the stocks named above are on the New York Stock Exchange. They come out of a list of 86 Big Board stocks selected by Daniel Cowin of Burnham & Co. and myself as being fairly representative of their breed. There are a great many more of the same kind on the American Stock Exchange and in the over-the-counter market, but they are a little harder to identify. When you are searching for them, take along an interested and savvy broker.

What else makes a company appear "designed for growth"? It may have a large tax-loss carry-forward. If such a company were to merge with a highly profitable concern, the profits of the latter for a time would be tax free. In mid-1963 General Dynamics, Studebaker, New York Central Railroad and Underwood Corp. were all attractive merger partners because of their past losses, if for no other reasons.

We come to our last question: "Has the stock got the kind of sponsorship that can take it places?"

Here I come to swampy ground. What exactly *is* a sponsor? Is he the kind of fellow who once told me, "The way to make money in this game is to grab a stock at eight times earnings and drive it up to fifty times"? Perhaps, because we have seen that, with the proper suggestions and the right acquisition plan, this can be done honestly. It can even be done without any actual growth in the original property—although growth helps.

Yes, the ground is *really* swampy. The sponsor of a stock may be (1) merely a house seeking a good buy for its customers but with so many customer's brokers of its own that their activity alone is enough to move a stock; (2) a "pool" or "group" creating activity in the stock in order to suck in the public; or (3) a firm engaging in creative finance.

Creative finance? Suppose an investment house spots a bag and carton company that is barely breaking even or possibly losing money. Sales cost it too much. Setting up the jigs and patterns for short runs costs it too much. Maintaining a fleet of its own trucks— idle most of the time—costs it too much. Suppose that this invest-ment house determined that a certain large manufacturer nearby would be willing to contract to pick up the entire output of the little bag and carton company if it could get it at such-and-such per cent off the market. And suppose that that would enable the little company to bring fifteen cents of each sales dollar down to net profit—instead of one cent.

Would you say that the investment house might justifiably buy a few shares for itself and have its customers buy a few shares more, so that present management could not prevent the deal? (This story, which happened, did not happen because of a brokerage house— but it might have.)

Or suppose that your investment banker realizes that a movie company (Loew's) might become highly profitable if it stopped making movies. Or a publishing company (Crowell-Collier) would do much better if it stopped publishing its famous magazine and concentrated on books. And then there are dozens of acquisitions such as the Sylvania-General Telephone deal, and a few that re-mind one of the manner in which Roger L. Stevens bought the Empire State Building. In rough summary: He sold the ground out from under it (leasing it back, of course) and got enough for the land to pay for the equity (the amount over the mortgage) on the building itself.

I am not going to name any of Wall Street's "good sponsors" for you. "Good" in this connotation is too indefinite a word. If you play around in the market you will soon find out their names.

Their stocks? These are constantly cropping up in the most-active lists. They are almost always low-priced. If you combined the new-high method or the Clayton method with the most-active list of your favorite Stock Exchange you'd almost certainly be aboard four or five of them in three months.

If you are, watch out! You can never know when the "sponsors" are going to pull the plug. Go easy on buying this kind of stock on margin. And take some of your profits fairly promptly, to protect yourself. When a real drive is on with one of these stocks, the sponsors always seem to try to push the profit far beyond 100 per cent. Suppose the movement started when the stock was at 3, you got aboard for 300 shares at 4 and it is now at 6. If you sell 200 shares now for $1,200 you have the remaining 100 for the commissions and taxes.

Don't get the impression, from the paragraph above, that I invariably distrust such fast-moving stocks. But what I said earlier about a stock being a growth stock only as long as somebody is actively pushing it goes double in these cases. The sponsors almost always carry positions of their own. These they sell when they see more profitable uses for their money. You should, too.

There are very few New York Stock Exchange houses that engage in the kind of dynamic "sponsorship" described above. Yet, if we talk of the better-grade issues—more thoroughly seasoned and higher-priced—the effect is almost exactly the same. Incidentally or accidentally, you get the same growth-stock talk from all the brokers. They are geared for selling stocks, not for getting their customers out of the market. In my years covering Wall Street I have seen many a day when the main influences were the buying suggestions of brokers and investment services.

In the first edition of this book, I showed how the five largest American chemical companies, which had virtually quadrupled in price between the low of 1949 and the high of 1955, had obviously "grown out of growth" by 1956. The point I was making was that, although they all declined between 1955 and 1958, they retained their high price-earnings ratios. Here is the table showing their growth rates for that period, along with their price-earnings ratios in August, 1958 (1958 price divided by 1957 earnings):

YEAR-TO-YEAR GROWTH RATES

Earnings per Share
Rate of Increase

Stock	1958 Over 1957	1957 Over 1956	1956 Over 1955	Price-Earnings Ratio (8/58)
Du Pont*	(26)	3	(12)	23.2
Union Carbide	(16)	(11)	(1)	24.5
Allied Chemical	(26)	(6)	(10)	20.2
Dow Chemical	—	(16)	(13)	29.8
Monsanto	(35)	(5)	(8)	20.2

( ) indicates percentage decline.   * Accelerated amortization and tax normalized.

Here is the record of the same stocks from 1959 to estimated 1963 (earnings estimated at end of first half, 1963):

	P/E Ratio 1963	1963 Over 1962	1962 Over 1961	1961 Over 1960	1960 Over 1959	1959 Over 1958
Du Pont	25.5	(2.5)	8.1	9.8	(9.3)	23.2
Union Carbide	20	(1.4)	8	(10)	(8)	37.3
Allied Chem.	22.1	17	(7)	(9)	2	46
Dow Chem.	25.5	2.4	12.3	(24.2)	28.4	33
Monsanto	18.9	2.2	12.5	—	(4.8)	75.5

I think they all took that big leap in 1959 just to embarrass me. However, my point about the high price-earnings ratios still holds. Look at Du Pont, Union Carbide, Dow and Monsanto in 1963.

Quite obviously there is a good deal of guesswork about price-earnings ratios. What is the value of probable future growth? How do you put a price tag on it? How do you compare one growth stock with another?

In the first edition of this book I examined the work done in this field by the late Samuel Lee Stedman of Carl M. Loeb, Rhoades & Co. Unfortunately, according to his firm, the type of study made by Mr. Stedman and his staff has not been continued since his death in 1961, but the concept he developed can certainly continue to serve us as a guide.

Here it is in essence: Say you are looking at a stock that has doubled its annual net profit over the past four years. That means that its compounded rate of growth has been 19 per cent a year (see the compound interest table on page 112). It is a bona fide "growth stock," so far. What are the chances that it will continue to grow at the same rate for the next four years?

You decide that they are pretty good, so you multiply present annual earnings of $15 a share by 2. If they double again, they will be $30 four years hence. You remember that price-earnings ratios, once established, tend to stay up there. Up to now, ratios that aren't deserved have fallen far less often than they should. You therefore use the present ratio of 25 times earnings (the price of your stock being $375 a share). You multiply those possible future earnings of $30 a share by 25 and get $750 as the possible price of your stock in four years.

Now you have a problem: What is the *present* value of that future price? In other words, how much should your money earn a year? Armand Erpf of Loeb, Rhoades once told me it should earn you at least 12 per cent or you ought to put it to some other use, put it into some business other than investing in the stock market.

All right. Let's see what a "discount factor" of 12 per cent will mean at the end of four years. Using a logarithmic table (see page 113) we find that a 1962 dollar has a present value of 63.5 cents. So we multiply our $750 by 0.635 and come up with $476.

If we figure 20 times earnings instead, we'll have a present value of about $381. Even that isn't bad.

Let us make sure here that we know exactly what we are doing. We are not determining any actual values for anything. All Mr. Stedman's method gives us is a framework on which to hang our best guesses regarding possible future rates of growth, possible future price-earnings ratios and the present value of our future dollars.

One thing the formula—or the research preceding the use of the formula—will let you do is weed out cyclical issues from among the growth stocks. Steels and coppers and aluminums don't really belong in the "growth" classification, as you undoubtedly have discovered by now.

Your best use for the formula lies in comparing one alleged growth stock *today* with another alleged growth stock. You may decide that its rate of future growth will be bigger than the figure I used and that it is likely to sell at 35 times earnings in four years ($30 \times 35 \times .635 = 666\%$).

In the first edition of this book, which appeared in 1959, we used Mr. Stedman's formula to make some guesses as to the 1962 values of a few of the many growth stocks he had studied. We are now in a position to see how we came out. Because of the 1962 market slump, I am including December 1961 prices as well as those for the end of 1962.

FAMOUS GROWTH STOCKS ANALYZED 1958–1962

	Merck	Polaroid	CBS*	American Photocopy Equipment*	Rohm & Haas*	Corning Glass Works
A. Avg. annual growth 1953–57 (%)	22	25	25	37	12	0
B. Est. avg. annual growth 1958–62 (%)	18	20	25	23	5	0
B'. Actual growth rate 1958–62 (%)	1½	8	5	18	12.9	13
C. Multiplier for est. 1958 earnings	1.939	2.074	2.441	2.289	1.216	1.000
D. Est. 1958 earnings per share (as of 8/58)	$2.60	$1.95	$3.15	$2.85	$12.00	$2.05
E. C. × D. (est. '62 earns.)	$5.04	$4.04	$7.70	$6.52	$14.60	$2.05
F. Price-earnings ratio on 9/5/58	25.0	34.6	10.9	17.2	28.2	37.9
G. E. × F. (est. 1962 price)	$125½	$140	$89	$112	$412	$54
H. G. × 12% discount factor of 0.635 (adjusted 1962 price)	$80	$89	$56½	$71	$262	$33
I. Est. 1962 earnings × 20 × 0.635	$63½	$51½			$185½	$26
J. Est. 1962 earnings × 15 × 0.635	$47½	$39		$62	$144	$19½
K. Prices of 9/5/58	$65	$67½	$34½	$49	$405	$92
L. Prices of 12/61 (close)	$89	$220	$43	$270	$550½	$192
M. Prices of 12/62 (close)	$77½	$143	$50½	$103½	$454	$162

* Prices of 1961 and 1962 "unsplit" to provide comparison.

Although I realized that stocks to which the "growth" label has once been applied sometimes retain high price-earnings ratios long after they have stopped deserving them (see the tables on the chemicals, p. 109), I did not like to bet that this would be true in any individual case for as long as four years. For this reason, I worked out 1962 prices on the table immediately preceding at twenty times and at fifteen times projected earnings for stocks selling above those ratios on September 5, 1958.

There is another point you might note: When the accumulation factor is bigger than the discount factor you are using, the farther you look into the future the better picture you get. Take Merck, which I guessed might increase earnings at the rate of 18 per cent a year. We looked in the table and found that, in four years, each 1958 dollar of Merck earnings could be multiplied by 1.93877. That gave us $5.04. If we multiplied that by a price-earnings ratio of 20 and then multiplied by the 12 per cent discount factor of 0.635 (also for four years), we got an answer of $63.75 against a 1958 price of $65. Not much of a bargain.

If, however, we had said we were looking ten years into the future, we would have found that each dollar of Merck 1958 earnings could be multiplied by 5.23382. True, over ten years our discount-factor multiplier would drop to 0.3219 but we would come out with a pleasant 1968 estimated value of $87.64. That can make any growth stock look a lot better.

I wish to warn you, however, that a ten-year guess is more than two and a half times riskier than a four-year guess. But here are the figures you need. They come to me from Borden Helmer of Union Carbide Corporation on a kind of bounce and dribble through Samuel Lee Stedman and Robert Barbanell of Carl M. Loeb, Rhoades & Co.

GROWTH OF $1 AT COMPOUND INTEREST IN FOUR YEARS

%		%		%		%		%	
1	1.041	11	1.518	21	2.144	31	2.945	41	3.953
2	1.082	12	1.574	22	2.215	32	3.036	42	4.066
3	1.126	13	1.630	23	2.289	33	3.129	43	4.182
4	1.170	14	1.689	24	2.364	34	3.224	44	4.300
5	1.216	15	1.749	25	2.441	35	3.322	45	4.421
6	1.262	16	1.811	26	2.520	36	3.421	46	4.544
7	1.311	17	1.874	27	2.601	37	3.523	47	4.669
8	1.360	18	1.939	28	2.684	38	3.627	48	4.798
9	1.412	19	2.005	29	2.769	39	3.733	49	4.929
10	1.464	20	2.074	30	2.856	40	3.842	50	5.063

DISCOUNT FACTORS FOR FOUR YEARS

%		%		%		%		%	
4	0.8548	5	0.8223	6	0.7924	7	0.7628	8	0.7353
9	0.7082	10	0.6831	11	0.6587	12	0.6353	13	0.6135

Once more? Here's a company that earned $1.24 a share in 1958 and $2.55 in 1962. You divide the first into the second and come out with 2.06. You look in the growth table above and find that that works out at about 20 per cent a year.

Will the company add to its earnings at that rate for the next four years? You're not sure. Maybe 15 per cent would be a safer rate. Opposite 15 per cent in the growth table above you find 1.749. You use this to multiply the 1962 earnings per share and come up with $4.35 a share for 1966. What price-earnings ratio do you want? Perhaps 15 times? OK. That makes $65.40. Now you apply one of your discount factors to compensate for the use of your money for four years. Shall it be 9 per cent? Right. That leaves you with a present value for your stock of $45.30.

How can you be guided in your selection of growth stocks? A number of investment advisory services now concentrate upon them, and most insist that their choices meet certain growth standards. Standard & Poor's Corporation publishes *The S. & P. 200 Rapid Growth Stocks* as a monthly supplement to its weekly *Outlook* (subscription price, $18 quarterly, $65 annually). The list, according to S. & P., is "the end product of the screening of nearly 6,000 issues by electronic data processing methods. As such it represents a purely mechanical process and is not to be regarded as a 'buy list.' . . . The major criteria employed are:

"(1) If growth in share earnings over the past five years has been steady, it must have amounted to at least 7 per cent per annum, compounded;

"(2) If growth has been interrupted in only one year and the decline has been less than 5 per cent, annual growth must have been at least 10 per cent;

"(3) If growth has been interrupted in more than one year, or in one year has declined more than 5 per cent, annual growth rate must have been at least 12 per cent.

"Selections have been limited generally to issues with more than

500,000 shares outstanding, and to those with earnings of at least $0.25 a share in the last full year."

S. & P. calculates a "growth premium" for each of its listed growth stocks. This is described as "the extent to which the price of a given issue is in excess of the general level of stock valuation, as measured by the price-earnings ratio of the S. & P. index of 425 industrials based on estimated current year earnings." To get the growth premium, you divide the price-earnings ratio of the stock by the price-earnings ratio of S. & P. industrials and multiply the result by 100 to get a percentage. "The difference between this percentage and 100 per cent is the indicated premium (if a plus figure) or discount (if a minus figure)." Undervalued stocks will show a minus figure and could be good buys. S. & P. selects a few stocks from the list each month for recommendation.

Here are a few examples taken from S. & P.'s lists of January 21, 1963 and June 24, 1963:

	American Distilling	Bobbie Brooks	Crown Cork & Seal	Fram Corp.	S. & P. 425 Industrials
January 1963					
Price	41	24	32	32	
Price-Earnings Ratio	14.5	21.9	17.8	11.9	18.36
Growth Premium	−21	+20	−3	−35	
June 1963					
Price	38	25	37	36	
Price-Earnings Ratio	13.1	22.7	17.6	13.3	19.07
Growth Premium	−27	+19	−2	−26	

A relatively new service (inaugurated in 1958) which has gained recognition among Wall Street analysts is the monthly *America's Fastest Growing Companies*, published by John S. Herold, Inc., at 25 Greenwich Avenue, Greenwich, Connecticut. Mr. Herold lists some 150 companies each month, insisting that they show an uninterrupted compound growth rate of 10 per cent annually over the most recent three years. Like Mr. Stedman, Mr. Herold tries to forecast future values of the listed stocks, basing his prognostications on past performance, and takes the following precautions to reduce "the downside margin of error": 1) earnings are projected on the basis of either a five-year historical growth rate or the most recent growth rate, *whichever is lower*; 2) projections into the future are limited to three years; 3) growth projections are revised and checked every time earnings are reported.

An accompanying manual, *Growth Stock Investing*, gives you the mathematical tools for calculating growth, including a compound growth table which lets you figure the value of $1 at rates from 10 per cent through 200 per cent for periods up to seven years. It also provides tables and formulas for arriving at "prudent" values and "prudent capitalization rates" for growth stocks, as well as "payouts." Borrowed from "the corporate manager's concept of 'payout' as it applies to capital investment in plant and equipment . . . the term as used [by Herold] is the time required for per share earnings, compounding at a given growth rate, to accumulate to current market price."

As one might have expected, Mr. Herold is just as unhappy about traditional price-earnings ratios as any other student of growth stocks, and he has his own formula for adjusting them. This is done by dividing the traditional P/E ratio by $1.00 of current profit compounding over a period of three years, as follows:

Stock	Price	Net Income	P/E Ratio	Growth Rate	$1.00 of Current Net Income at end of 3 years*	Adjusted P/E Ratio†
A	$10	$1.00	10	0%	1.00	10.0
B	10	1.00	10	10%	1.33	7.5
C	10	1.00	10	30%	2.20	4.5
D	10	1.00	10	50%	3.38	3.8

* Taken from compound growth table in·manual.

† Represents P/E ratio divided by figures in preceding column.

"From the adjusted P/E ratios in the above table," observes Mr. Herold, "it will be seen that Stock B is 25 per cent cheaper than A, and D is 70 per cent cheaper, disregarding other considerations. Through the adjusted P/E ratios the relative attraction of growth stocks, based on their earning power and growth rate, is brought into proper focus."

As I said in the previous chapter, yield is the base on which the market rests. Aunt Millie with her legacy, the college trustees with their inadequate endowments, the little worshipers of the magic of

compound interest that have been lured hesitantly away from bonds
—all these want a return in the form of income.

When such investors get into a growth stock, I feel some element
of luck is involved. Perhaps the stock is tagged with the "growth"
label after they have bought it. I'm sure they don't go shopping for
Bobbie Brooks with its cash-dividend yield of 1.5 per cent, Bristol-
Myers at 1.6 per cent or Magnavox at 1.7 per cent. Even Xerox at .5
per cent—these are all yields from the end of May 1963—is not
precisely what they are looking for. Such investors seldom know
how to evaluate the chances of growth. Nevertheless, these are the
people who make most of the values in the market, in the long run.

Jacques Coe, now senior partner of Jacques Coe & Co., tells a story
of his early days with Bache & Co., a house that then, as now, had
a great many small and middle-sized accounts. Those early days, of
course, were before the formation of the Securities and Exchange
Commission, before the imposition of any effective controls on market activities.

"Whenever I'd hear," says Mr. Coe, "that the smart boys of Wall
Street were going to 'do a job' on such-and-such a stock, I'd go into
our back office and ask questions. If I discovered that Bache customers were loaded with it, I knew that that was a stock that
couldn't be pushed around very much by clever shenanigans. It
was solid."

The reverse, of course, is true, now as then. There are certain
stocks that seem designed for long-term capital-gain play. Xerox
pays a niggardly dividend, hoes earnings back into growth. There
are Canadian investment trusts designed the same way: They
pay no dividends but in due course the investor can sell, profiting
only through capital gain.

Early in this chapter I remarked that "growth stocks" have some
qualities of safety, because the old stardust refuses to rub off and
you can sell them for good prices long after they should have gone
down. From 1955 to estimated 1958 Minneapolis-Honeywell, Owens-
Corning Fiberglas, Corning Glass and Rohm & Haas had profit
declines in every year and yet each held up at 28 times earnings
or more. Minnesota Mining and Manufacturing, with no appreciable
gain since 1956 and a decline in 1958, was selling on September 5,
1958, at 39.6 times 1957 profits, 46.1 times those estimated for 1958!

The yields on those five issues, only one of which paid a stock dividend, ranged from 0.49 to 1.76 per cent. The run-of-the-mill investor isn't in them except by accident or luck. A special breed of well-heeled investor holds them and probably will continue to hold them. He can see no reason at all for selling, save to take a profit. In spite of their miserable showings, two of them actually rose in 1957 and all five gained an average of almost 50 per cent in 1958.

QUESTIONS FOR REVIEW

1. What was Samuel Stedman's formula for measuring growth?
2. How does Standard & Poor's calculate its "growth premium" for growth stocks?
3. Why all the dissatisfaction with traditional price-earnings ratios among those who specialize in the study of growth stocks?
4. What is the advantage to the high-bracket taxpayer of a growth stock paying small dividends?

CHAPTER XI

Using Charts for Profit

THE MAIN reason charts work is that investors have a nasty habit of remembering what they paid. This I have on the authority of Harry D. Comer, economist-partner of Paine, Webber, Jackson & Curtis.

In fact—and I may as well make a full confession right now—most of what I am about to write about charts I got from Mr. Comer, from Alan C. Poole of New York Securities Co., from Edmund and Anthony Tabell of Walston & Co., from Morris Goldstein of F. I. du Pont & Co. and from others whose names will be dropped ostentatiously here and there in this chapter. I am not a constant chart-user. I draw charts now and again to illustrate an article or a book, but I have never kept the movement of any stock posted from day to day, from week to week or from month to

CHART II

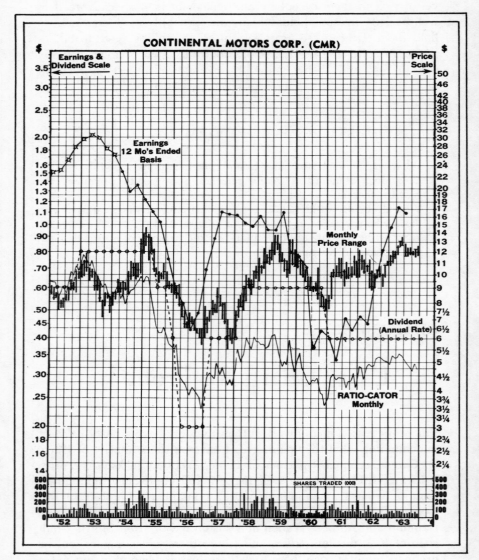

Courtesy of Securities Research Corporation, Boston

CHART III

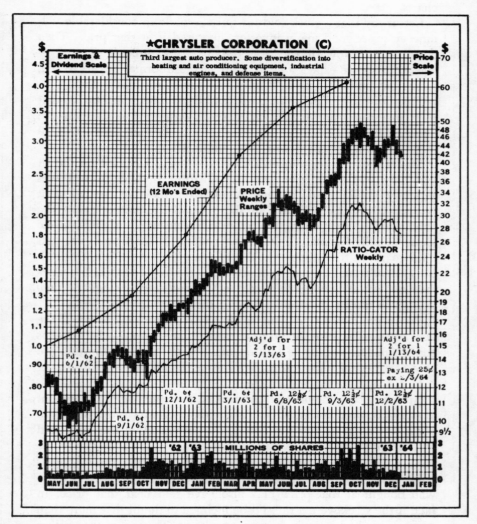

Courtesy of Securities Research Corporation, Boston

month. And you probably must do this to get the most out of charts.

Let us say that a stock sold for quite a while in considerable volume at 40. A good many investors acquired it at that price. Then it fell away. Now, if the price climbs back through 35 and 37 and 39 to 40, we expect a good many of those former buyers to sell, for 40 has now become a "supply area" or a "resistance zone."

Much of the technique of chart reading is based on the fact that most investors use the amateur methods described in Chapter IV: They buy a stock, see it fall, grit their teeth and hang on until it gets back to where it was. Then they sell it.

The rest of the technique of chart reading is founded on the "if you only had" idea mentioned in Chapter I. The investor was seriously thinking of buying Whiffenpoof Oils at 10 when it jumped to 15. As he hears all those wonderful stories about the values in Whiffenpoof Oils—the stories that explain the rise—he kicks himself. He really missed the boat! If Whiffenpoof ever gets back to 10 or thereabouts, he'll buy some for sure! This, theoretically, should make 10 a "support area" for Whiffenpoof. *Investors may not actually think this way but market analysts believe they do, which makes the results exactly the same.*

We return to the stock that has finally climbed back to 40: If the new advance in price should have enough momentum—which means enough people willing to buy enough shares—to carry through the area of expected selling at 40, Wall Street technicians would expect it to continue to rise for a time.

Naturally the amount of resistance at 40 depends on the amount of stock acquired at that price in the earlier period. On this point you can never be sure. You can determine, perhaps, that the stock sold within a point of 40 for twenty weeks, during which average volume was 10,000 shares a week. That does not mean that the market is going to be hit with 200,000 shares of stock. A good many of those who bought at that price may also have sold near that price. In fact, if the stock were a rail, I'd be inclined to doubt that more than 5,000 shares had actually found a new home. The rest of the trading would have been the hopping in and out of professional traders.

Some chart services approximate the value of accumulation at a given level by multiplying price by volume, and this can help. How much it helps depends partly on your knowledge of the kind of buying in the stock and partly on guesswork.

Yes, quite a bit of chart reading is guesswork. The experts tell me that if you stay at it long enough you develop either a tremendous flair or a tremendous frustration.

It is not necessary to draw charts in order to read charts, and this is good, because most of them don't mean much most of the time. Now and again, however, something will pop up on a chart that indicates that such-and-such a stock may be worth studying. Perhaps a trend is about to end. Perhaps a "sleeper" is about to be kissed by Prince Charming.

All (I believe) of the big investment services use charts in advising their customers. Then there are a number of chart services, some of which let you draw your own conclusions. Here are a few: John Magee, 360 Worthington Street, Springfield 3, Mass.; R. W. Mansfield Company, 26 Journal Square, Jersey City, New Jersey; M. C. Horsey & Co., 37 Wall Street, New York City 5; F. W. Stephens, 87 Nassau Street, New York City 38; Securities Research Corporation, 211 Congress Street, Boston 10, Mass.; Trendline Corporation, 82 Beaver Street, New York City 4.

Underlying all chart-reading, says Mr. Comer, is an idea from the original Dow theory: Markets are like the sea, with ripples, waves and tides. You come to the seashore, look at the wet sand and wonder whether the tide is coming in or going out. You set a stake in the sand where the last long wave creamed. You wait. There are small waves for a time, then another big one. Perhaps it goes beyond your stake. Perhaps it falls short. In either event, you know which way the tide is setting at the time.

Mr. Comer identifies major swings, which run in the same direction for a year or more and move stocks by 20 per cent or more; intermediate or secondary movements, which normally last from one month to six or more months and retrace one-third to two-thirds of the ground covered in the preceding rise or fall; and minor trends, which generally last a week or less and are meaningless in themselves. They do, however, make up the intermediate and major swings, when added together.

My chapter on the techniques of the traders emphasized the importance of following a trend but of being constantly on the lookout for a reversal. Chart-reading, say the technicians, is one of the best ways of spotting reversals.

To Mr. Poole, the "greatest danger in the use of charts" would be for the investor to rely entirely upon them. It is equally bad to rely entirely on a single group of indicators of a different kind.

"One of the best examples of the value of charts," he writes, "was the sharp rise of stock prices in the summer of 1958. Based on the fundamentals, no such rise in stock prices appeared justified and yet a study of the chart formations of the market averages indicated strongly that such a rise would occur.

"At the present time," he wrote in late August 1958, "the market continues to advance in the face of high price-earnings ratios, low yields and a very unfavorable relationship between bond and stock yields. The advance has been sparked by inflation fears, the flight from senior securities into equities and by large sums of money awaiting investment. How long it will continue is difficult to predict but if the fundamentals prevail, as they always have in the past, stock prices will eventually adjust themselves to more realistic values. The timing of that adjustment may well be best interpreted by the reader of charts."

What good can chart-reading do *you?* Can you make money at it? I believe you can.

Playing it safe and cozy, for example, you might sell any stock you own as soon as it gets into its resistance area. If it goes on through that area, you can buy it again. On Chart II, see Continental Motors. At any price over 13 it was obviously going to run into a generous supply.

In reverse, you might try buying stocks when they drop to their support areas—but only if there are signs that others are doing the same. Even at best, this is risky. I don't like buying stocks because they have gone down and look cheap. The reasons for the cheapness are often too good.

Sometimes a stock breaks through all its old highs and is said to be "free wheeling." Everybody who holds it has a profit. There is no automatic supply of stock through which it will have to force its way. Chrysler and Pan American World Airways have been in this enviable situation from time to time. See Charts III and IV.

A stock rises or falls to a certain level and then "moves sideways" for a considerable period, with nothing much in the way of volume. When volume picks up and the stock moves upward or downward, the move is often substantial. See Walgreen Company on Chart V.

CHART IV

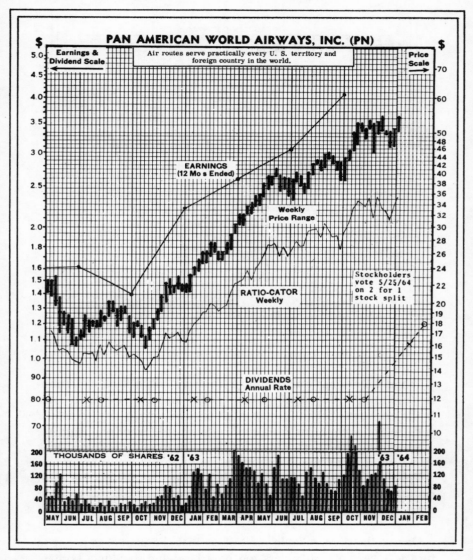

Courtesy of Securities Research Corporation, Boston

CHART V

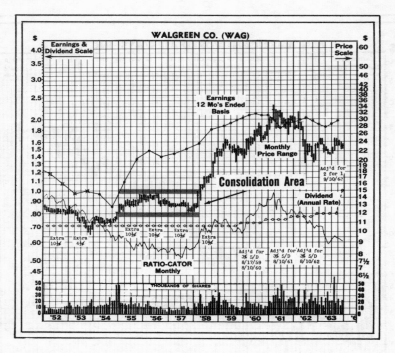

Courtesy of Securities Research Corporation, Boston

When a stock has burst through a supply area with a concentration of strength, that supply area somehow becomes a support area. If the price falls back to it, the stock may be a good buy—*provided* you are not alone in thinking so. See Stewart-Warner on Chart VI.

There are certain formations that help you recognize when a stock may have reached its top or bottom.

There are patterns that seem to tell us how far the market for a stock is going to go in its current directions. These seem to be right often enough to be worth our study.

One of the most reliable indications that the market is about to turn is a head-and-shoulders top or a head-and-shoulders bottom. You can see one illustrated on Chart VII, with Commercial Solvents.

First, there is an upward bulge on excellent volume. Then volume and price fall. The left shoulder has been formed.

CHART VI

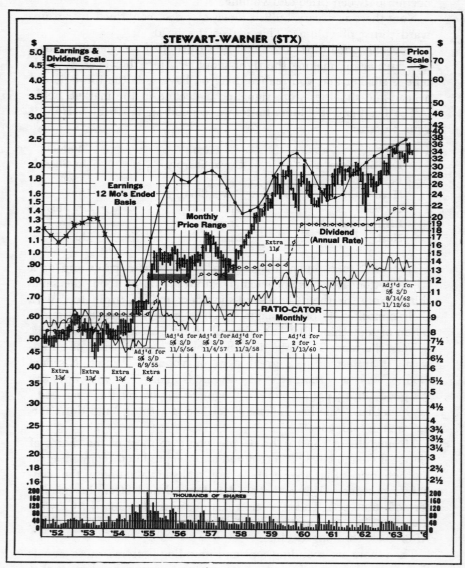

Courtesy of F. W. Stephens, New York

At this point remind yourself once again of the important connection between price and volume.

Now there is a very bullish move of price, confirmed by an upward thrust of volume. This makes the head.

Now the price dips—and don't be surprised if volume rises, too—and rises again, making the right shoulder. Here, however, the volume is smaller and you realize that you have seen the formation of a head-and-shoulders top, signaling a decline in the market. Sell!

The head-and-shoulders bottom is a good signal to buy. Here is your pattern:

	Price	Volume
Left Shoulder	Down Sharply	Up Sharply
Between	Up	Down
Head	Down Sharply	Up
Between	Up	Up Sharply
Right Shoulder	Down	Down
Next	Up	Up

It doesn't take much imagination to see that a triple top or a triple bottom is a less spectacular manifestation of about the same thing. None of them—head-and-shoulders top or triple top, with their opposites—is black magic. Each is merely a graphic presentation of something that has taken place time after time in markets.

Take the tops: The price is shoved up by a great wave of enthusiasm, manifested in a great deal of volume. "Watch National Guano," says a certain type of customer's man. "The wise boys say it's good for 15 points more." "Ought to hit 90 by the year end," says another. "Another Lukens Steel," cries a third, "and don't forget that I told you!"

Meanwhile, of course, the people who own most of the shares of National Guano have been tempted and tempted and tempted again by these prices that are far above any realistic valuation of the company's prospects. When the head is formed and after the head is formed, they sell. There is one reaction, possibly caused by "wise" investors "buying on the dips." That makes the right shoulder. After that, the long decline.

Then there are rounding tops and rounding bottoms, more signals that reversals have taken place. The thing to remember here is that you hardly ever "miss a market" by waiting around for a bit. Occasionally, it is true, a stock does come down and "make a V," but

CHART VII

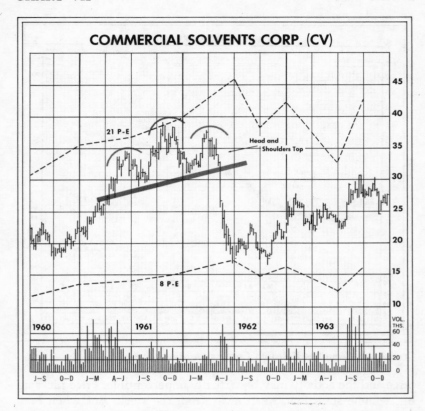

COMMERCIAL SOLVENTS CORP. (CV)

21 P-E

Head and
Shoulders Top

8 P-E

1960   1961   1962   1963

VOL.
THS.
60
40
20
0

J–S   O–D   J–M   A–J   J–S   O–D   J–M   A–J   J–S   O–D   J–M   A–J   J–S   O–D

Courtesy of *Current Market Perspectives,* a publication of Trendline Corp.

most reversals take a good deal of time to develop. The investor who tries to buy on "the bottom eighth" will be outsmarting himself more often than he will be making money.

If you wait for a time and make sure, you can count the points you miss as your insurance premium.

Let us examine the rounding bottom, which our friends the ancient Greeks might have described as *callipygean.* It is rather common among low-priced issues and often takes some *months* to develop.

Volume, says Harry Comer, follows the price trend—in other words, volume dries up as the price falls. At the bottom both the

CHART VIII

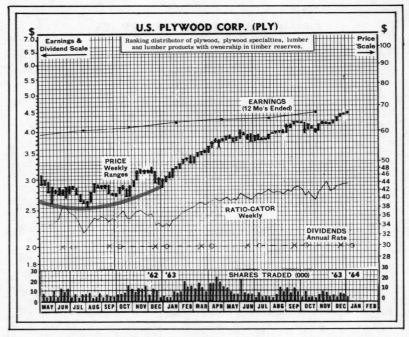

Courtesy of Securities Research Corporation, Boston

price and the activity may be virtually imperceptible. Price picks up but volume stays low. Keep away from the stock. But when both price and volume rise together, step in and buy. The turn has come. See U. S. Plywood on Chart VIII.

The key is obviously the number of shares traded.

Triangles are tricky affairs. Each one is the map of a battlefield. Over a number of days or weeks or months the price of a stock has pushed upward against a supply level or downward against support. In the first case, each time the bulls reach that level they are thrown back. Each time they rally their forces a little closer to the front line. In the end they are fighting in the trenches. If they push through the so-long-held line, and volume *rises,* the stock should shoot upward. If the volume *falls,* the defense has won. The stock will drop.

Now we come to a rather interesting point: Chart-readers say they can tell about how far the stock will rise or fall *by measuring the back of the triangle.* On Charts IX and X, Douglas Aircraft and Consolidated Electrodynamics make upward and downward triangles. Measure them for yourself.

Note before you leave them that triangles are usually intermediate affairs. They seldom mark the beginning or end of a wide movement.

We return to head-and-shoulder formations. Mr. Comer says that they also can be used for measuring. See Chart VII. You draw the "neckline" through the bottom fringe of the left shoulder formation. The distance from that line to the top of the "head" is the distance you can expect the stock to drop below the "neckline."

You will remember that we said something a little earlier about trends. The easiest forecast of market action simply assumes that what has been happening will continue to happen. In chart terms, you draw a trend line for a stock and watch for something to interrupt it.

The first interruption, at about the halfway point, is apt to be what is called a consolidation area. This is a kind of rectangular formation, like Walgreen on Chart V. The stock goes down a little, up a little, down a little, in what is called a sideways motion. If you break out as much as 3 per cent on either side with big volume, away you go!

Let us talk about gaps, which are up-and-down areas in which there is no trading. First, we should understand some things clearly:

On a monthly chart a gap means nothing.

On a weekly chart—that is, a chart using bars to show the high of the week and the low of the week with a little crossline for the close of the week—a gap means nothing.

Only daily charts will do.

The gap must be big enough to matter. For example, if a stock closes Tuesday at 23⅝ and opens Wednesday at 24 and does not thereafter sell below 24, you ignore it. All the other conditions are correct, but the gap must be bigger.

Volume must be heavy enough to support the reasoning that makes the gap important. Here is the reasoning: There has been

CHART IX

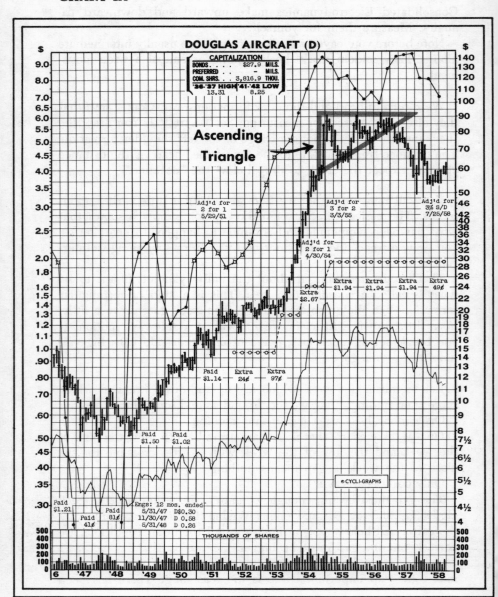

Courtesy of Securities Research Corporation, Boston

CHART X

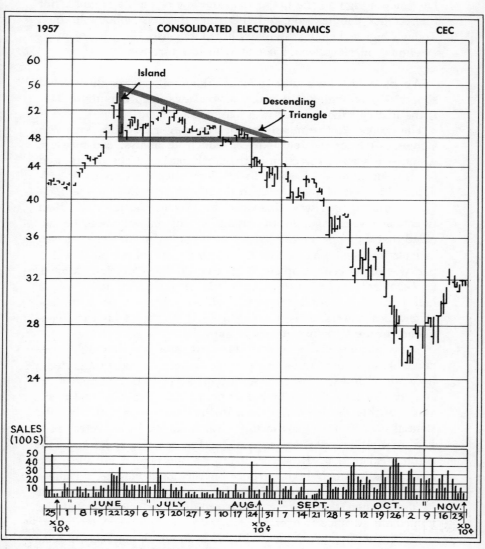

1957   CONSOLIDATED ELECTRODYNAMICS   CEC

Island

Descending
Triangle

SALES
(100S)

JUNE   JULY   AUG.   SEPT.   OCT.   NOV.

Courtesy of John Magee of Springfield, Mass.

overwhelming demand or supply. Let us say it is supply. Stock has been offered and the price has gone down and down and down, but always with a certain amount of resilience. Each day the stock has made a high a little better than the low of the day before. But then comes another sale and this time there is nobody to buy. Today's high is below yesterday's low. Obviously this idea of overwhelming offerings would not fit with low turnover.

We have just been describing the kind of volume that would support the reasoning that makes a breakaway gap important. This is the first gap that we see in a market movement.

The second is the measuring or runaway gap. This, says Mr. Comer, is one of the few tools by which an analyst can measure distance as well as direction in the stock market. (The others used for that purpose are head-and-shoulders, triangles and point-and-figure. The last of these will be described later in this chapter.) The measuring gap was discovered by Harold Gartley more than twenty-five years ago. As the result of long investigation, he decided that the appearance of this second gap—if it didn't get closed in later trading—signaled that the market move of which it was a part was 40 per cent complete. Robert D. Edwards and John Magee, in *Technical Analysis of Stock Trends,* estimate that the move is half finished. Today Mr. Magee, widely respected as a student of technical moves in the market, has lost a little of his early confidence in the signaling virtues of gaps.

"I am not anywhere near as sure that gaps are thoroughly dependable in an absolute sense as some technicians have suggested," he writes. "However, when a stock gaps away from a period of inactivity and stability, on high volume, it is probably a breakaway, and probably the beginning of a further move, very often a substantial one. Further gaps in the advance are to be expected. It is hard to say that a particular gap is the last one of a series and constitutes 'exhaustion.' However, if after a spectacular advance, the stock gaps into new high territory on very high volume, advances during the day to a new peak, and then closes near the bottom of its day's range, that is very strong presumptive evidence that the immediate advance is over."

Mr. Comer points out that, with stocks in which markets are relatively thin, there can be gaps in series. In each case, he says, the market analyst must make a new estimate, considering the distance from the original runaway gap to this new measuring gap to be 40 or 50 per cent of the distance to be traveled.

The action of American Metal Products, shown on Chart XI, illustrates one danger here:

Measuring gaps may be mistaken for exhaustion gaps. Either, of course, may come on smaller volume than brought the original breakaway gap, and therefore the analyst must be wary. It is not enough to check the daily closing prices. There is a possibility that an intra-day low (or high if the movement is downward) may close that gap. Then you will know that the suspected measuring gap was really an exhaustion gap. If you are long of the rising stock, this might be a good time to sell.

A word of warning: If you are going gap-hunting by yourself, watch out for ex-dividend days. There is a gap in American Telephone and Telegraph once every three months, when it pays its solid dividend and the price of the stock adjusts itself downward between days. Such gaps don't count.

Point-and-figure charting has many devoted followers. The most devoted claim for it is that it indicates not only the direction of the next move but its extent.

It is used mostly for individual stocks. It is a way, perhaps, of measuring the accumulation of selling around certain prices. You take a piece of chart paper, put a scale along the left-hand side and mark an "X" on a little square nearest to the present price. Each "X" may represent a point or a half-point or two points or anything else you wish. The choice depends on the volatility of the stocks and the time you have to give to this charting.

If the next change is upward you put your next "X" on top of the first one; if downward, you mark it in the next column. You then continue marking in that next column until there is another change of direction by as much as the unit you have chosen. Suppose you have a string of prices such as these: 62 63¼ 62½ 61⅞ 61 60¼ 59¾ 60⅛ 61¼. You ignore the fractions:

```
                    x
                   xx
                   xF
        60         xx
                    x
```

CHART XI

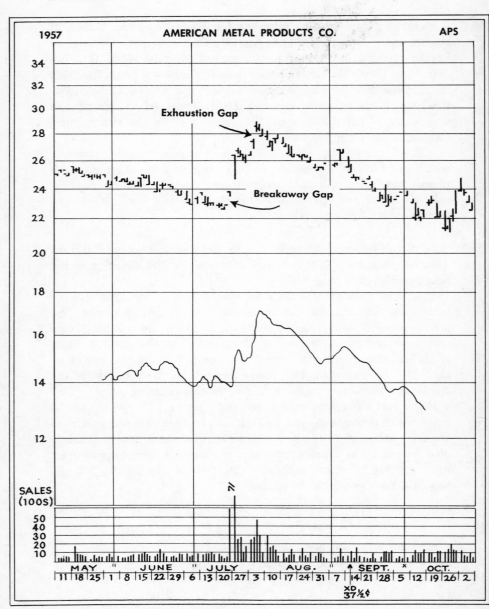

Courtesy of John Magee of Springfield, Mass.

CHART XII

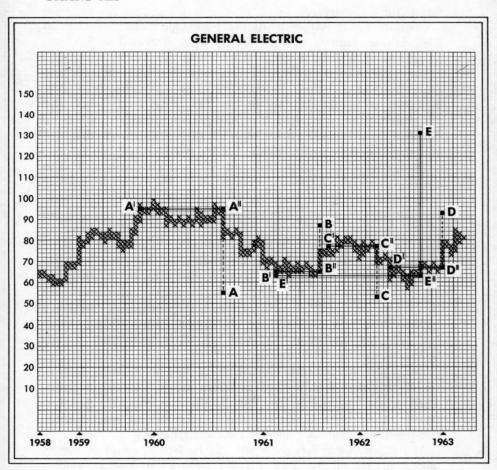

GENERAL ELECTRIC

Courtesy of Walston & Co., New York

There is, you will notice, no time scale on this chart. You keep some connection with the calendar by using the initial of the month you are in the first time you chart in that period. The "F" above stands for February.

Consider Chart XII, with its point-and-figure chart of General Electric from January 1958 to July 23, 1963, provided by Edmund W. Tabell of Walston & Co.

Some point-and-figure experts use a draftsman's dividers and draw circles all over their charts. One I know would cheerfully place one point of his dividers on the first "X" on 96 in the chart and the other on the 96 marked A". Then he would swing the first tip downward in a quarter-circle to cross 56 and announce that that was the level to which General Electric would drop.

Mr. Tabell and his son, Anthony W., use no dividers. This is because Mr. Tabell thinks you must have the "feel" in reading point-and-figure charts and that you can get this only by counting the "X's" with a pencil point. Chiefly, the point-and-figure chartist watches "congestion areas"—in which the "X's" move up and down, but mainly in a sidewise direction. Theoretically, these irregular horizontal bands are evidence that the stock is under accumulation by investors who think it will go up, or is being sold off by those who think it will go down. Eventually this pattern will be broken and the "X's" will start either up or down, forming a "wall." Then, says Anthony, the chartist can count from "wall to wall," and the number of "X's," wall to wall, is the number of units he can expect the stock to rise or fall.

The chart of General Electric is in two-point units—that is, an "X" was posted only when the stock moved upward or downward at least two points. The Tabells also post one-point and five-point unit charts for G.E., but have found in recent years that the two-point unit chart is generally the most reliable.

As Anthony interprets the chart, the horizontal count of twenty units along the 96 line from A' to A" (where you have a "wall" in a downward direction) indicated a possible drop of twenty units (forty points) to the level marked by A. The stock fell short of this dismal prediction by eight points (see E'). Again, in 1961, the count of 11 across the 66 line from B' to B" (a rising "wall") signaled a possible rise of 11 units to point B (88). The stock rose to 82. Another drop, to 54 (C), was predicted by counting 12 squares across the 78 line from C' to C", and a gain of 26 points was indicated by a count of 13 across the 68 line from D' to D".

All these projections were for relatively short terms. Anthony reaches back into 1961, to the wall marked E', for a long-term projection. Counting across the 64 line from E' to E" (the next wall that started upward from 64), he gets 34 units, indicating an eventual rise to 132 (E).

How do you decide which wall to choose, which "X" should be your starting point? It takes flair and, both Tabells emphasize, reference to other data and other types of charts to tell whether a congestion area represents a top or a base.

There are analysts, you see, who poohpooh the point-and-figure method. How, they ask, can the method combine time and distance indiscriminately? Left-to-right movement represents, after all, only the number of times that the price of a stock has changed direction. Why should that number suddenly become translatable into dollars?

My own feeling can be described as smiling reserve, expressive of the attitude I commonly adopt when everybody about me is talking one of the 700 or 800 languages I don't know.

Ordinary chart-reading I can follow. I can see the logical reasons behind the squiggles on the piece of paper. But about point-and-figure techniques I am doubtful. Sometimes I think I have the glimmerings of a logical explanation. It seems to fit into the concept of an "accumulation area" when a stock moves sideways for a time. But then I find myself questioning again: Of course a stock commonly makes a good run in one direction if it breaks out of an accumulation area on volume, but how can anyone tell how far it is going to go?

There are only two things about the point-and-figure method about which I am completely sure:

1. The experts on it never quite agree.
2. It seems to work more often than not.

Morris Goldstein of Francis I. du Pont & Co. uses a device based on the observed fact that markets move in the same direction more easily than they reverse themselves. This device is the 200-day moving average, which must be a lot of trouble for somebody to keep posted.

You understand how this is compiled. First you write down the closing prices for two hundred successive days, add them and divide by 200. The following day you drop the price for the first day—that is, you subtract it from the aggregate before division—and add to the aggregate the closing price for day 201. If the market as a whole (which we are considering here), or any particular stock being charted, is on the upgrade, it is evident that daily prices will be higher than the moving average price, and this is considered very bullish. Note on Chart XIII the steep rises which began in September 1953 and May 1958. But when the rate of gain starts to fall—that is, when the gain on days 201 to 210 is smaller than the gain on days 1 to 10, daily prices bend down toward the average line and give warning. And, of course, by the time daily prices have fallen below the average line the investor should realize that the time has come to sell.

(In actual practice, the firms that sell moving averages of individual stocks to their subscribers work by the week. Thus, a 200-day moving average will most probably be an average of thirty successive Tuesdays or Thursdays. This saves a lot of work.)

It is my feeling that moving averages expose the investor to the risk of being whipsawed. Suppose that he were to buy each time the price of his stock crossed the 200-day average line by as much as five points or 5 per cent. Or suppose that, while the average line fell, the price of the stock rose as much as five points in a day, in a week, or in some other period. Those would both be interpreted as buy signals. Suppose he were to sell when the stock price penetrated the average line on the downside, or continued to fall even though the average line was still rising. In some markets, as you and I have both noticed, our investing friend would find himself whipsawed—the movements would be small and the commissions and taxes would always be dead losses.

I find that there are others in Wall Street who agree with me. William L. Jiler, who has written a most valuable and readable book on charts (*How Charts Can Help You in the Stock Market,* Commodity Research Publications Corp., $10), and whose firm, Trendline Corporation, even puts out a 200-day moving average service, believes that it is too dangerous for general use. "It should be emphasized," he says, "that these guidelines should not be used as a 'system' for playing the market, but merely as another technical tool—a handy addition to the basic techniques of chart analysis. The daily price action should be given first consideration,

CHART XIII

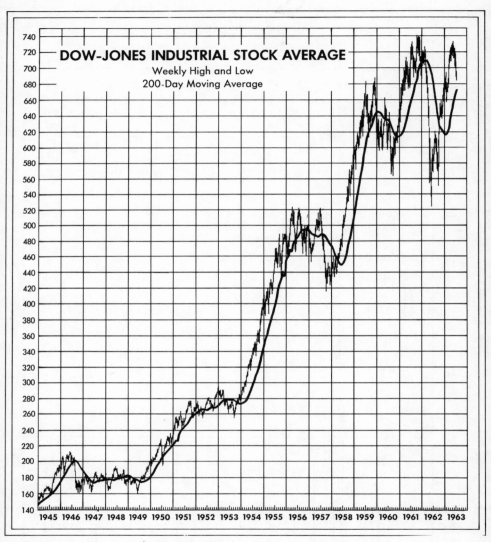

Courtesy of F. I. du Pont & Co., New York

CHART XIV

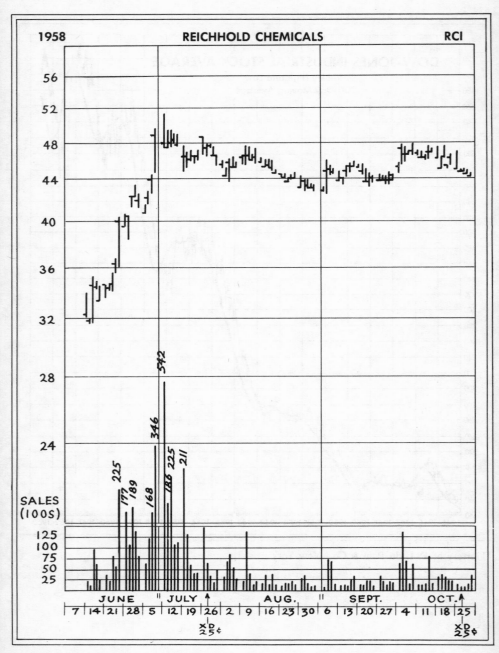

especially in timing market turns. The 200-day moving average is *not* a sensitive indicator, and trend reversals often are clearly outlined in the price action well before the moving average itself turns."

However, Curtiss Dahl, who wrote a book called *Consistent Profits in the Stock Market* back in 1951, based his entire approach on the moving average. He has instituted a weekly stock service from his offices at Box 401, Lafayette, Indiana, and has been experimenting with ten-week and five-week moving averages. These are said to be considerably more sensitive than those that run for a greater length of time.

Actually, I suppose that somebody some day will work out a system: so much penetration of the 200-day average line, so much for the ten-week average line, so much for the five-week average line—and will boast about it from the top of the Chase Manhattan Plaza Bank Building. I am afraid that his system is apt to suffer the same fate as the Clayton or "new high" system discussed some chapters back. If the market is a normal one, with most of the moves in one direction, he will make money. If, however, it simply fluctuates five or six points, first one way and then the other, he will find himself whipsawed and losing money.

Chart XIII (p. 139) shows the movement of the average and of the Dow-Jones Industrials. In the following table, using the monthly averages of Standard & Poor's industrial index, I have shown what might have happened. Our man would, of course, have done better if he had traded on the day after each crossing of the average line, but I do not believe that nonprofessional investors in real life ever move as promptly as that. I'll stick to the monthly averages.

USING THE 200-DAY MOVING AVERAGE

Bought		Sold		
Date	Price	Date	Price	Profit
June 1947	14.58	Sept. 1947	14.76	0.18
Oct. 1947	15.19	Dec. 1947	14.93	−0.22
Jan. 1948	14.60	Feb. 1948	13.88	−0.72
Apr. 1948	15.19	Aug. 1948	15.74	0.55
Sept. 1948	15.53	Oct. 1948	16.02	0.49
July 1949	14.55	July 1950	17.31	2.76
Aug. 1950	18.47	July 1951	22.31	3.84
Aug. 1951	22.35	Dec. 1951	23.83	1.48
Jan. 1952	24.61	Mar. 1952	24.04	−0.57

USING THE 200-DAY MOVING AVERAGE (*Cont.*)

| Bought | | | Sold | | |
Date	Price		Date	Price	Profit
Mar. 1952	24.04		Apr. 1952	23.96	−0.08
May 1952	23.94		Oct. 1952	24.48	0.54
Oct. 1952	24.48		May 1953	25.01	0.53
Nov. 1953	24.51		May 1956	49.64	25.13
June 1956	49.38		Sept. 1956	50.15	0.77
Dec. 1956	49.79		Jan. 1957	48.43	−1.36
May 1957	50.10		Aug. 1957	49.51	−0.59
Apr. 1958	45.09		Sept. 1959	61.21	16.12
Oct. 1959	61.04		Feb. 1960	59.60	−1.44
June 1960	61.06		July 1960	59.25	−1.81
Aug. 1960	59.96		Sept. 1960	57.96	−2.00
Nov. 1960	58.89		Jan. 1962	72.99	14.10
Feb. 1962	74.22		Mar. 1962	74.22	—

Figured this way, the operator made himself a net profit (before figuring commissions and taxes) of 57.70 points between June 1947 and March 1962. In that same period, of course, the market rose 59.64 for only one round-trip commission.

When I was collecting the original material for the chapter on traders, somebody suggested that Peter A. Shanaman of Dreyfus & Co. might be able to give me some information on tape-reading. I went after him and received a wad of fascinating stuff. It was not strictly confined to tape-reading. And it had the market-letter writer's failing of assuming that the future was limited to one day or one week.

The following example from Mr. Shanaman is as much chart-reading as tape-reading and illustrates vividly how the two arts may be combined for profit.

On August 5, 1958, he was writing his note to me. That day, he said, Reichhold Chemicals was selling upward from 46 to 47 but suddenly seemed to run into quite a bit of stock—what Mr. Shanaman called "a relatively excessive supply density." Once before Reichhold had tried to sell through this supply area and had failed.

Mr. Shanaman, writing for the hereafter in terms of tomorrow, suggested that this was the kind of situation that a tape-reader should watch. If Reichhold succeeded in getting through the 46-48 range it would be worth buying. Otherwise, it would sell off and, if held, should be sold.

Mr. Shanaman was quite right for that particular moment in space and time. Although the market rallied sharply on August 7 and 8, Reichhold Chemicals closed that week at 46⅜, the following week at 44⅝ and the month at 43. See Chart XIV. But it finally went on to close 1958 at 56⅝. The barrier at 47 was a Maginot Line rather than a Verdun.

QUESTIONS FOR REVIEW

1. Looking at a chart that shows prices rising after a long decline, how can you predict the price at which you could expect a large number of investors to sell?
2. What is the difference between a "supply area" and a "support area"?
3. What is generally indicated by a "head-and-shoulders" top?
4. Are rising prices alone enough to confirm a future big rise in a stock? Why?
5. What two scales, generally considered of prime importance, are ignored by point-and-figure chartists?
6. How do you compile a moving average? What would happen to an investor who used only this indicator in timing his moves?

CHAPTER XII

10 Ways to Multiply Profits—
or Losses

THE NEW YORK STOCK EXCHANGE publishes an attractive booklet called *The Language of Investing: A Glossary*, which contains the following definition:

> *Leverage:* The effect on the per share earnings of the common stock of a company when large sums must be paid for bond interest

or preferred stock dividends, or both, before the common stock is entitled to share in earnings.

There is an example, of course, but I prefer to use my own.

Suppose a company with invested capital of $20,000,000, divided among 2,000,000 shares. It makes 10 per cent of the capital or $1 a share.

Suppose the same company with the $20,000,000 divided into 1,000,000 shares of 5 per cent preferred stock and 1,000,000 common shares. This company earns the same $2,000,000 a year. Now, however, each $10 preferred share is paid only 50 cents or $500,000 in all, so that the 1,000,000 common shares have earned $1.50 each. That is leverage.

Double the earnings of the first example. Per share earnings on the common would rise to $2. Double the earnings of the second example. The preferred would still get its $500,000 and the common would earn $3.50 a share.

This is the only kind of leverage that most people ever consider. There are many other kinds, several of them in far more general use in security markets. The commonest is margin trading. While the Fulbright investigation was in progress in 1955, Dreyfus & Co. published an ingenious advertisement, showing how little leverage the modern stock trader enjoyed compared with the trader in 1929 and arguing from this that the collapse of 1929 could not be repeated. The advertisement assumed three traders, one on 10 per cent margin, one on 50 per cent and one on 70 per cent. Each man started with an equity of $1,000 and bought stock selling at $10 a share. Each time the stock gained $10 a share he pyramided, that is, bought as much more stock as he could. The stock went to $60 a share. The table on p. 145 shows what might have happened.

Jack Dreyfus, who worked out this table, apparently did not want to be too sensational. He had our boy pyramid each time the stock rose $10 a share. He could have made more progress if he had bought more stock on each 1-point appreciation. With 50 per cent margins, for example, he would have been holding 380—not 300—shares by the time the stock rose from 10 to 20.

The reader, of course, must remember that neither Mr. Dreyfus nor I have bothered to work out the commissions on these deals, a formality that would not be neglected were a Dreyfus & Co. customer to embark on them.

LEVERAGE OF MARGINS IN STOCK TRADING

Margin	Price of Stock	Appreciation on 10-Point Advance	Equity	Buying Power	Number of Shares Held
10%	$10		$1,000	$10,000	1,000
	20	$10,000	11,000	110,000	5,500
	30	55,000	66,000	660,000	22,000
	40	220,000	286,000	2,860,000	71,500
	50	715,000	1,001,000	10,010,000	200,200
	60	2,002,000	3,003,000	30,030,000	500,500
50%	$10		$1,000	$2,000	200
	20	$2,000	3,000	6,000	300
	30	3,000	6,000	12,000	400
	40	4,000	10,000	20,000	500
	50	5,000	15,000	30,000	600
	60	6,000	21,000	42,000	700
70%	$10		$1,000	$1,429	143
	20	$1,429	2,429	3,470	174
	30	1,735	4,164	5,948	198
	40	1,983	6,147	8,781	220
	50	2,195	8,342	11,917	238
	60	2,383	10,725	15,321	255

Any change in margin requirements—the "initial" margins at the start of a deal—brings a change in the direction of the market, sooner or later. "Sooner" may mean as few as 40 days, as it did in early 1958 on the plus side. "Later" may mean as many as 719 days, as it did in 1951–53 on the minus side.

Margins are changed because the money managers think markets would look better running in the opposite direction. At the end of World War II our Washington keepers jacked up margins from 40 to 50 to 75 to 100 per cent before they checked the rise. In 1955 the rise went from 50 to 60 to 70 per cent. Because they can keep pushing until things go as they prefer, the money managers have a little advantage over you, armed only with wishful thinking.

But even they can't time things infallibly. If a market really has the bit in its teeth, it can go cantering on for quite a while (and for quite a distance) before those chain-bit tactics begin to take effect. This is how changes in margin requirements have worked (and note that more than one change in margin and more than one change in credit have generally been necessary before the credit managers got their way) (see table on p. 147).

The "date of the next high or low" is the date when the market finally moved in the direction sought by the authorities. Counting only the lag from the first effort in each case, we find that the turn took an average of 277 days or approximately nine months.

When the money managers tried to check speculation, the market continued upward for an additional 30 per cent. When they tried to put brakes on a falling market, the slide continued for only a little more than 6 per cent.

Possibly the reason for the varying effect is that, when margins are raised, speculators have plenty of money from profits and don't need more buying power to keep on doing what they have been doing; but when things are sliding, the additional buying power from lowered margins is welcomed and used.

There are several other kinds of margin that can affect the market.

We have just discussed "initial margins." The Stock Exchanges themselves set "maintenance margins." These must not fall below 25 per cent of the market value of your securities.

Ten per cent margins are required on the "long" side when one security is convertible into another, if one is bought and the other sold. This is explained later in this chapter.

Five per cent margins on purchases of securities issued or guaranteed by the United States Government were explained in Chapter III.

When you exercise a right or a warrant to subscribe to securities, you may carry the securities at 25 per cent margin. You may continue opening such "special subscription accounts" with 25 per cent margin for six months. Then you must stop, unless you first pay off the indebtedness contracted more than six months ago.

"Over-the-counter" securities—that is, those not traded on registered stock exchanges—are not subject to the initial-margin rules that govern stocks on exchanges, *provided* you deal in them through non-member houses. Then you may borrow on them whatever your non-member broker or your bank will lend you. Exchange members, however, are required to set 100 per cent margins.

As you must have gathered from the above, regulation of the use

STOCK PRICES AND THE MONEY MANAGERS

Change in Margins Date	Margin Requirement %	Day Before S. & P. Industrials (Index)	Days to Next High or Low	Date of Next High or Low	Next High or Low (Index)
In effect	40	—	—	—	—
Feb. 5, 1945	50	13.36	478	May 29, 1946	18.53
July 5	75	14.44	328	May 29	18.53
Jan. 21, 1946	100	17.36	128	May 29	18.53
(In 1946)		(One push downward on credit)			
Feb. 1, 1947	75	15.15	105	May 17, 1947	13.40
(In 1948)		(Five pushes downward on credit)			
March 30, 1949	50	15.03	75	June 13, 1949	13.23
(In 1949)		(Five pushes upward on credit)			
(In 1950 and 1951)		(Two pushes downward on credit)			
Jan. 17, 1951	75	21.63	719	Jan. 5, 1953	26.99
(In 1951 and 1953)		(Two pushes downward on credit)			
Feb. 20, 1953	50	25.74	206	Sept. 14, 1953	22.70
(In 1953 and 1954)		(Four pushes upward on credit)			
Jan. 4, 1955	60	38.17	314	Nov. 14, 1955	49.54
(In 1955)		(One downward push on credit)			
Apr. 23, 1955	70	39.32	213	Nov. 14, 1955	49.54
(In 1955 to 1957)		(Six downward pushes on credit)			
(In 1957)		(One downward and one upward push on credit)			
Jan. 16, 1958	50	43.84	40	Feb. 25, 1958	43.26
(In 1958)		(Seven upward and two downward pushes on credit)			
Aug. 5, 1958	70	51.22	147	Dec. 31, 1958	58.97
Oct. 16, 1958	90	54.18	76	Dec. 31, 1958	58.97
(In 1959)		(Three downward pushes on credit)			
July 28, 1960)	70	57.40	89	Oct. 25, 1960	55.34
(In 1960)		(Four upward pushes on credit)			
July 10, 1962	50	59.11	329	June 4, 1963	74.25
Nov. 4, 1963	70	78.11	—	—	—
(In 1963)		(One downward push on credit)			

of credit in security markets is a thoroughly messy affair. A man with a good deal of money, playing in a large way, can get the leverage of low margins if he really wants it badly enough. Even the small player, it appears, can manage the same kind of thing in an even more round-about way.

Standard & Poor's magazine, *The Outlook*, on November 2, 1958, told of a specialized finance company that made loans against stock-market collateral. This one announced that it would lend $61 on a stock selling at $70, provided that the speculator would put in a stop-loss order to sell the stock if it dropped to $67 a share. The money was lent at a rate of 1 per cent a month and a one-month loan was the minimum.

I do not believe that an odd-lot trader could borrow in this way, but I shouldn't be surprised to find that the 100-share speculator could be financed. At first I was puzzled. How did the loan company get around the New York State usury laws? But Lewis L. Schellbach of S. & P. enlightened me. There is no legal limit in New York State on interest charged on loans of $5,000 or more against securities!

"Unregulated lending" by such companies—known in the Street as securities "factors"—was strongly attacked in 1963 in the Securities and Exchange Commission's special study of markets. Considering the effect of such lending upon the May 1962 market break in particular, the study could not produce any conclusive proof because there were, of course, no figures available on the amount of credit extended by those who do not come under Federal Reserve regulation. Nonetheless, the study concluded that "the dollar amount of unregulated lending appears to be substantial" and added that in the 1962 break such loans "were subject to the earliest margin calls," thus touching off further selling.

The S.E.C. expressly prohibits salesmen of registered stock exchange firms from arranging for their customers to obtain credit from factors "in excess of the amount of credit which registrant itself was permitted to extend . . . by the Federal Reserve Board."

Not all brokerage houses will let you buy all stocks on margin. Let me put that another way: All brokerage houses have rules against margin accounts in some stocks. Some will not margin stocks that sell below $3 a share. Some will not margin American Stock Exchange stocks that sell below $5 a share. Most have notably small approved lists of Canadian stocks.

These rules, of course, roughly reflect those of the Wall Street banks, for the brokers borrow from the banks on their customers' collateral. There is general agreement among Wall Street bank loan officers that, while applications for loans against stocks selling at $2 to $5 a share are not welcomed, there is no absolute bar against them. If stocks of that kind just happened to be included in a well-diversified list of higher-priced stocks, they would be accepted. What prejudice there is is due to the feeling that the $2 stock sells solely on expectations, the higher-priced issue on yield as well.

There are other considerations. "A broker's loan is no good," said the "Street loan" officer of a large bank, "if you can't sell the collateral in a hurry. I'd rather have a $4 stock that was selling 20,000 or 30,000 shares a day than an equal amount of International Business Machines. You'd almost have to have a secondary distribution to get rid of a good-sized block of that."

In former years there was a "loan desk" on the floor of the New York Stock Exchange and banks did their lending blindfold. That is, they would lend to anybody on the agreed rates if the stocks conformed to rules. For example, banks used to get an additional ½ per cent if all the stocks in a package were sold on the old New York Curb Exchange (now the American Stock Exchange). They used to take ½ per cent less if all the stocks in a package were rails.

"Nowadays," said one "Street loan" man, "we lend to our own customers, not to a bunch of strangers. Our so-called rules are designed to get us gracefully out of making loans we don't want to make. We can look over a handful of collateral and announce that we don't lend on a stock unless it is listed on the New York Stock Exchange, unless it sells between 17½ and 23⅞ a share and unless its name begins with an 'S.' It's a lot pleasanter to make up rules than to tell a customer frankly that you don't want to lend him the money he wants."

If you have strong ideas about the future of the market you can test them out and possibly make a penny or two without risking much of your own money. You do this by playing in the "put-and-call" market.

A put option is an agreement by somebody to buy such-and-such a stock from you at or before such-and-such future date at such-and-such a price. You buy such an option when you think a stock is going down.

A call option is an agreement committing somebody to sell you an agreed stock at an agreed price on or before an agreed date. You buy it when you think the market is going to rise.

A straddle option permits you either to put stock or to call stock at the same price on or before a given future date.

A spread option is the same as a straddle except that the prices

are different. You might buy the right, for example, to "put"
Chrysler at 53 but to "call" it at 57.

Puts, calls and straddles are usually sold at the current price, but
this is not invariably so. For example, as this passage was originally
written, Godnick & Son were advertising six-month calls on Royal
Dutch at 43, at 45 and at 47. They cost, respectively, $425, $325
and $237.50, plus tax, for 100 shares. (I am keeping this example
because, as this second edition is being prepared five years later, the
price of Royal Dutch—after 12 per cent in stock dividends—is about
the same.)

Say the market closed the night before at 44. You think it will go
to 50 before six months have run. In the light of your belief, you
examine the profitability of the three call options offered:

	Call at 43	Call at 45	Call at 47
Exercised at 50	$5,000	$5,000	$5,000
Cost of option	425	325	238
Cost at option price	4,300	4,500	4,700
Commissions and tax	89	90	91
Profit	186	85	−29

There is a rule in the put-and-call market that "the dividend goes
with the option." This doesn't mean quite what it says. In practice,
the dividend is not paid to you, the holder of a call option, but the
price at which you may call the stock is reduced by the amount of
the dividend. This is done automatically on the day the stock sells
ex-dividend (without the right to receive the dividend included in
its selling price). The same is true for put options.

If Royal Dutch paid 75 cents in dividends between your purchase
of the call option at 43 and your exercise of it at 50, your profit
would rise $75.50, the 50 cents representing a slight saving in com-
mission. Your actual profit on the $425 option—obviously the best
from the start, because on the others your cost fell a point or less
while the price for exercise rose two points—is thus $261.50. In other
words, while Royal Dutch rose about 13 per cent, you gained about
61 per cent.

How would you have made out if you had bought the stock itself
at 44, at which price it closed on the day before you read the ad?
You would have made the capital gain, net of commissions and
taxes, of $510.50, less than 17 per cent on your investment of $3,080

at 70 per cent margin. You would also have received dividends aggregating $75. That would bring the return up to 19 per cent.

If you exercised your option before the six-month period elapsed, all these gains would obviously be short term, taxed at your ordinary income rate. The same would be true if you took your profit on the stock you bought before the six months were up.

Suppose, however, that you waited. Suppose, also, that you are in the 40 per cent bracket.

On the actual stock you would pay 40 per cent on the dividend, reducing it to $45. On the long-term capital gain of $510.50 you would pay half your regular rate, or 20 per cent. Your after-tax income would thus be $453.40 or about 15 per cent on your original investment of $3,080.

How about your call option? At the end of the six-month holding period, *you do not exercise it.* You sell it. The New York Stock Exchange house that guaranteed it is quite willing to have this happen, because it collects two commissions anyway, even though no stock is bought or sold. And you certainly have a long-term capital gain on your call option, which was an asset held for more than six months.

Because you don't really get the dividend but merely a lower price for taking down the stock, all the profit becomes long-term capital gain. Your after-tax profit on the deal is $209.20, which works out at 49 per cent.

The literature of the put-and-call market is full of such passages as the following, written by Herbert Filer of Filer, Schmidt & Co. for the Encyclopaedia Britannica:

> A man owns 100 shares of XYZ which he bought at 70 and is now selling at 85. He sells his stock in the market at 85 and buys a Call Option Contract at 85 good for 90 days for $400. If after selling his stock XYZ continues to rise, he can in the 90 days recapture the stock at 85 through his Call Option. If on the other hand, however, the stock should decline again to 70, he is in a position to buy back at 70 the stock which he sold at 85.

The put-and-call brokers and dealers always talk in terms of the wide swings. You, as an investor or possible speculator in puts and calls, must consider the likelihood of a swing large enough to give you a profit. Stocks aren't always jumping up and down by fifteen points. Remember, I only assumed six points for that profitable example in Royal Dutch!

Following are a few offers of call options that were advertised in *The New York Times* on August 13, 1963, by Filer, Schmidt & Co., Thomas, Haab & Botts and Godnick & Son. In most cases among the six-month calls, the cost of the option was less than half the range in the stock for the year to date:

THE COST OF CALLS AND THE RANGE OF STOCKS

Stock	Call Price	Call Cost	Aug. 13 Close	7½-mo. Range 100 Shares
— Six Months —				
Cerro Corporation	29	$487.50	30⅞	$1,262.50
Reynolds Metal	33	387.50	33¼	1,362.50
Cinerama	14	237.50	13¼	450.00
Pure Oil	44⅝ *	450.00	44⅝	900.00
Brunswick	12¾ *	175.00	12¾	862.50
Western Union	29½	312.50	29½	762.50
Sperry Rand	14½	212.50	14⅝	362.50
American Motors	17¾	200.00	17⅞	700.00
Approximately 90 Days				
Texas Instruments	79.55	1,000.00	84⅛	3,250.00
Eastman Kodak	110	450.00	110½	1,625.00
Approximately 60 Days				
Standard Oil (Indiana)	59½	562.50	64⅞	1,825.00
RCA	71	400.00	71½	1,837.50

* Call price: "at the market."

Under a 1958 ruling (58–384) of the Internal Revenue Service a man with a profit on a call may protect it by selling the same stock short. There is only one important point to watch. He must do so at least a month after he bought the call option and at least a month before he exercises the call. If he did not, the Securities and Exchange Commission people might question him for making a "wash sale"—that is, buying and selling the same security (or almost the same security) at almost the same time.

Suppose, for example, you buy a six-month-ten-day call on a stock at 48 for $550. At least a month later, but not more than five months later, the stock is at 58 but you're getting afraid of the market. You decide to protect your profit by selling the stock short at 58.

Just to simplify the illustration, we'll suppose that your fears for the market were baseless. You finally close out your short sale at 58, the price at which you made it, and sell your call. Commissions and taxes cost $75.76 on the call and $97.92 on the short sale. Add the cost of your call and you have a net long-term capital gain of $276.32 on an original stake of $550. Your profit is about 50 per cent.

Could you work this from the start? Yes, but it wouldn't do you any good unless you were in a very high income-tax bracket. Suppose you buy a call at 48 and at the same time sell the stock short at 48. The stock drops to 38 and you cover. Your profit of $914.84 on the short sale is cut to $364.84 by the loss on your unexercised call. What you have net is a short-term capital gain. All profits on short sales are short-term gains, no matter how long you are in the deal.

Let us take it the other way: The stock goes to 58. Now the long-term capital gain on the call option is $374.24. The short-term capital loss on the short sale is $1,081.96. The short-term loss would naturally wipe out other short-term gains you had, but how high a bracket would you have to be in before you made any money on the deal? Chapter XVIII on taxes will explain how these things are figured. For the moment, the answer is that you would not make a profit even with that 10-point gain in the stock unless you were in an income-tax bracket higher than 67 per cent! (You will note, of course, that I simplified this illustration by picking out a stock that pays no dividend.)

There is another side to this business, of course. Somebody *sells* calls and puts and presumably makes money at it.

You own 100 shares of stock which is now selling at 56. Would you be willing to sell it at 58? Why not? You sell a call option, which your broker then endorses. Now, if the call is not exercised in sixty days, you have income of $200, income at the rate of $1,200 a year on your investment of $5,600.

You would naturally be most anxious to sell calls when you thought the market was going down, puts when you thought it likely to rise.

When you sell a put option you give its buyer the privilege of

delivering a stock to you at a given price. In his illustration of the
selling of puts, Herbert Filer assumes a man ready to buy a list of
stocks worth $52,700. Instead of buying outright, he accepts $3,000
for options permitting their buyers to "put" the stock he wants to
him. If the puts are exercised, he gets the stock he wanted at a net
cost of $49,700. If they are not, the money he didn't invest will have
earned him $3,000 in ninety days, which works out at a rate of 22
per cent a year on the $52,700 or—because he must put up only 25
per cent in margin with the guaranteeing broker—*88 per cent a year
on the money he actually has in use.*

A word of caution here: Puts are exercised from time to time, you
know, so that this 88 per cent is by no means guaranteed. Remember
that you don't *have* to sell a put just because somebody wants to buy
one. Sell puts *only* on stocks that you'd like to own.

Secondly, steer clear of selling puts on stocks that have just risen
rapidly on whoop-it-up campaigns. Why should *you* be the patsy?

I don't say that the following has ever happened, mind you, but it
could: That great European financier, Jean de la Forfanterie, working through a number of brokers here, picks out a stock with a
relatively thin market and starts buying it. The stock starts to rise
and the public is attracted to it. It goes from 10 to 12 to 14 to 16 to
18 to 20.

Jean sells some of his holdings, when he can do so without unduly
preventing the rise of the stock, but he still has stock and he is still
buying to keep the upward drive in motion. Now he stops selling.
Instead, he buys 60-day puts at 22, at 23, at 24. Each costs him
about $137.

The stock may stay up there without any help from Jean, in
which case he can sell out his holdings nicely and take his full
manipulated profit. But, by buying puts, he has fixed it so that he
can get out of the stock without actually selling it in the open
market.

I used my imaginary Frenchman in the illustration merely because Europeans or Americans working through numbered Swiss
bank accounts can still work this kind of manipulation in our
markets with little fear of the Securities and Exchange Commission.

Mr. Filer suggests that the person selling puts and calls does best
by staggering the dates and, presumably, the prices at which he
sells.

For those in income-tax brackets that force them into a search for long-term capital gains, Mr. Filer suggests this maneuver: You have held a stock for, let us say, three or four months. You have a profit of 10 points at 50, where you sell a call option. If the option is exercised after you have held the stock for six months or more, the premium you received ties right into the profit. In other words, you bought at 39 and sold at 50, so that you had a profit of $1,000 after taxes and commissions. But you had an additional profit of $200 or $300 or $400 which you received for selling the option! This is also long-term capital gain.

One bit of advice before we leave this subject: Don't play this game on margin with *all* your capital. Leverage works both ways.

Convertible bonds are another high-leverage proposition. Like other bonds, they are "senior" securities and are among the first to be paid off in the event of a company's liquidation. Furthermore, they may be converted into a stated number of shares of common stock before a given date. They are frequently described as "a long-term call on the common."

The "conversion value" of a convertible is simply derived from the number of shares of common stock you can get for it. If your $1,000 bond is convertible into 50 shares of stock, the "conversion value" is $20. Any time the market price of the common rises to $20, you know you can convert without loss.

When stocks are far away from their conversion prices, the matching convertible bonds move upward in gingerly fashion, if at all. As the stock price nears the conversion price, the two securities— debentures and stocks—begin to move more closely to their eventual percentage relationship. For example, here is a debenture that is convertible into stock at 50. This means 20 for every $1,000 bond or two for every $100 of par value. Thus, after the stock crosses $50 a share, the debenture should rise $2 for every dollar that the stock rises.

Moody's Bond Survey, to which you should certainly have reference if you are in bonds at all, regularly calculates conversion values in terms of the current prices of the convertibles and corresponding common stocks.

Charles J. Miller of D. H. Blair & Company provided for this revised edition a study his firm made in 1962, comparing the profits you might have made in a year by investing equivalent amounts in the common stock and in the convertible bonds of a dozen companies. Here are the results for six of the companies, to which I have added the conversion prices of the bonds, and the percentage of margin the investor would have put up for them.

The illustration "assumes purchase [on margin] of 100 shares and near equivalent of 70% [the margin requirement in 1961] of this amount as margin against convertible bonds of the same company. It does not include effect of commissions on either purchase. It does not include dividend income, interest income, or interest expense." Let the reader be again reminded that while bonds are in $1,000 denominations, they are quoted in hundreds.

COMMON STOCK

Issue	*Price Jan. 2, 1961*	*Price Jan. 2, 1962*	*Profit*	*Capital Invested*	*% Yield to Invested Capital*
A. T. & T.	104⅞	133⅝	$2,900	$7,350	39
Boeing	38⅜	50	1,150	2,695	43
W. R. Grace	39¾	81½	4,100	2,800	146
Lockheed	28	45¾	1,800	1,960	92
R. H. Macy	45⅝	70½	2,500	3,185	78
Burroughs	28¼	39⅞	1,150	1,960	58

CONVERTIBLE BONDS

Issue	*Price 1/2/61*	*Conv. Value 1/2/61*	*Price 1/2/62*	*Conv. Value 1/2/62*	*No. of Bonds Purch.*	*Capital Invested*	*Marg. (%)*	*Profit*	*% Yield to Invested Capital*
A. T. & T. cv 4¼s '73	275¼	137⅝	380¼	190⅛	14	$7,000	18	$13,300	190
Boeing cv 4½s '80	103½	51¾	119	59½	13	2,600	19.3	1,950	73
W. R. Grace cv 3½s '75	95	23¾	162½	40⅝	14	2,800	21	9,450	340
Lockheed cv 3¾s '80	121	24¼	188¾	37¾	10	2,000	16½	6,800	340
R. H. Macy cv 5s '77	141	47	223	74⅜	13	3,250	17.7	10,660	320
Burroughs cv 4½s '81	113	45¼	129¼	51¾	10	2,000	17.7	1,600	80

The big advantage in buying convertibles, as demonstrated by the above tables, is that the investor has the leverage of low margins. As D. H. Blair & Company explains it in a recent pamphlet:

"Bonds are not subject to the margin regulations of the Federal Reserve Board and therefore may be purchased for a considerably smaller cash investment than would be required if the normal margin rules were in effect, as in the case of the common stock. It is therefore apparent that for a specific amount of cash, significantly more convertibles can be purchased and *hence more stock controlled* than one could with the same equity investment purchase and finance the common stock." (The italics are mine.)

A few words of caution: The slogan that "a convertible gives you the safety of a bond and the profits of a common stock" might be true for the man who never bought such a debenture on small margin. But let me repeat that leverage works both ways. D. H. Blair cites the following example of how leverage worked against the convertible bond purchaser:

"If a customer purchased 250 shares of Burroughs stock at 42 during January 1962 and put up 70 per cent as dictated by the prevailing margin requirements he would have made an investment of $7,450. If, at the same time, he had purchased 10 Burroughs 4½s '81 (which are equal to approximately 250 shares of common) selling at 128, the customer would have had to invest $2,000 to carry the bonds.

"By the close of December 1962, the stock was selling at 28. The customer had a paper loss of 14 points. On the convertible debentures the price had dropped from 128 in January to 111 in December of the same year. This constituted a drop of 17 points. However, since the customer had invested only $2,000 of his own cash, the percentage loss was greater in the bond." The loss on the investment in the stock was 47 per cent. On the bonds it was 85 per cent.

Prices of convertibles and their corresponding stocks are kept at proper levels by a process called arbitrage. A trader buys a handful of bonds. Simultaneously, he makes an "exempt short sale" of the number of shares of stock he will get for the bonds. The exemption means that he may sell short at any price. He does not have to wait until he can do so at a price higher than the last different price.

Because there is virtually no risk involved in this transaction, the margin is only 10 per cent on the "long" side.

Here is an example I worked out in the spring of 1958: You notice that General American Transportation convertible 4s of 1981 are selling at 120 and that the stock is at 92. This interests you, because any time that there is a relationship larger than 3 for the stock and 4 for the bond you may be able to make money. The conversion price of the stock is $75.

On the New York Stock Exchange, you find, you can buy thirty bonds for $36,000 plus $75 in commissions. No taxes. Your broker also discovers that he can sell 400 shares of GAT for $36,800, less commissions, taxes and fees of $171.50 and interest on the borrowed $32,400 of not more than $30. You place both orders. Then you have the bonds converted into stock and deliver the stock in settlement of your short; that is, you return the stock you borrowed to make the short sale.

Your investment of equity has been $3,600. Your net profit in about a week has been $523.50.

You won't find too many such arbitrage deals, mostly because members of the New York Stock Exchange are constantly looking for them, too, and can work on much smaller differentials. However, there *are* some and, as you see, they are worth searching out.

Another kind of arbitrage concerns merger plans. Suppose Gulf Oil is actually about to absorb one of the dozens of companies that have been linked with it in merger rumors. Gulf, we shall say, is selling at 50. Its directors have voted to give one share of Gulf for three shares of Miasma Petroleum, but Miasma is selling at 15. The directors of Miasma and the shareholders of both companies still have to approve the merger.

I'm not going to work this deal out carefully, but let us say that you sell Gulf short (not an exempt short sale) at 50 and buy 300 shares of Miasma. This ties up $4,750, since you must put up the full margin on both sides until the deal is approved. Our illustration assumes margin at 50 per cent. You stand to make about $384, however, after taxes, fees and commissions, *if* the deal goes through. As a matter of fact, you have your profit in advance *if* the deal goes through.

Edwin H. Stern of Edwin H. Stern & Co. puts the game of arbitrage on a hard-boiled basis:

"A good company is going to absorb a bad company. I make a short sale of the shares of the good company and I buy enough of the shares of the bad company so I can deliver them to cover my short. I stand to make $2 per share if the deal goes through and to lose $10 if it doesn't. The odds are five to one against me.

"Why do I do it? My partners and I have made a careful examination of the circumstances and we feel there is a twenty-to-one chance that the deal will go through. So the odds translate into four to one in my favor, and that's the kind of deal I like."

Warrants should be bought when most of the hope has been squeezed out of them. They are wonderful speculations when the market has been depressed for a time and has just begun to rise. They are unwise speculations when everybody is being optimistic about the future of prices.

A warrant is a document that permits you to buy a share of stock at a certain price before a stipulated date. For example, when they were first issued, Atlas Corporation warrants allowed you to buy Atlas Corporation stock for $25 a share. (Stock and warrants since have been split 4 for 1 but this doesn't affect my illustration.) Henry J. Low of Gude, Winmill & Co. sends me a memo that shows Atlas stock selling in January 1955 at $41.62 and Atlas warrants at $16.50. This is about as close to the theoretical behavior of warrants as I have ever seen, for the option price was $25. If the stock goes up $1, the warrant must also rise $1. But while the stock will be rising 2.4 per cent, the warrant will be gaining 6.2 per cent. This is the charm of the warrant.

In September 1958, this charm was somewhat diminished. The option purchase price of Atlas stocks was down to $6.25 and the warrants were selling at $3.62. This made a combined price of $9.87 for stock then selling at $7.37. Each time the stock advanced $1 that would be 13.5 per cent. A similar gain for the warrant would be 27 per cent. The relative advantage had fallen even though the actual advantage had been raised by the stock split.

There are more than one hundred different warrants outstanding but only a few are easy to watch and to trade in—those that are listed on the American Stock Exchange. The rest are traded over-the-counter—that is, not on a registered Exchange—and few newspapers ever run the bid-and-asked quotations on them. There are unquestionably large amounts of money to be made in warrants by those situated so that they can watch the market in them without too much trouble. Sidney Fried's *The Speculative Merits of Common Stock Warrants* tells of $500 investments that turned into $250,000. But the warrants that most of my readers will have a chance to watch are these:

MARKET MOVEMENTS IN WARRANTS

	August 15, 1960			August 16, 1963		
	Stock Price	*Warrant Price*	*Option Price*	*Stock Price*	*Warrant Price*	*Option Price*
Alleghany Corp.	10	7⅛	6	10⅜	7½	6
Atlas Corp.	4½	2	6¼	2⅝	1	6¼
Tri-Continental Corp.	36⅛	23⅞	17.76	46½	37⅝	17.76
Above adjusted *		23⅞	22.56	59¼	37⅝	22.56
Hilton Hotels †	32½	6¾	42	19	4½	42
Textron	19¾	6⅜	25	39	15⅜	25

* One warrant permits the purchase of 1.27 Tri-Continental common shares.

† The 42 option price ran to October 15, 1963. Then it went to 46 until October 15, 1967, when it will be at 50 until the October 15, 1971, expiration date.

All of the above stocks are on the New York Stock Exchange and all the warrants on the American Stock Exchange.

Ask your broker about warrants when the market tone is depressed. Try to buy them when they are selling at a fourth or a fifth of the price of the stock, no matter how far away the option price may be. Then any upsurge in hope will give you a profit.

You should not buy just any old warrant. It's got to be a warrant for a stock you think ought to go up. I suggest searching out companies of the acquisition type, or the spin-off type. When they get going, they go!

The lower the price of the stock, the better your chances. You'll understand why when you read the Square Root Rule at the end of the next chapter.

Don't get cramped up against an expiration date. An unexercised warrant is worth nothing whatever when it expires. Of the five mentioned above, Hilton runs out in 1971, Textron in 1984. The others are perpetual.

Perhaps I shouldn't put this idea into your impressionable head, but warrants, when they go down, go down faster than the stock they stand for, and you *can* sell warrants short, on margin.

QUESTIONS FOR REVIEW

1. What is "leverage" as applied to margin trading securities?
2. What is a securities "factor"?

3. What is the difference between a put option and a call option? What are straddle and spread options?
4. What is a convertible bond?
5. What is arbitrage? How does it work in connection with merger plans?
6. What is a warrant? What is the difference between a warrant and a call option?

CHAPTER XIII

Technical Signals
to Watch For

ONE THING to remember about stock-market indicators is that the new ones always seem to work far better than the old ones.

This is because all stock-market indicators are tailored carefully to fit the idiosyncrasies of past booms and slumps. Little exceptions are built in that would have kept the followers they didn't have—because the indicators weren't yet invented—from losing the shirts they may or may not have had. This gives the new indicators almost perfect records. The old ones, suffering from the fact that no two market swings are exactly alike, look a little battered.

Another thing to remember is that nobody really believes and follows any one stock-market indicator with all his money. They are too uncertain. Even the most convinced technicians like to wait for "a little more confirmation." Thus, when a market falls out of bed—as in 1945–46—and the technicians can look back on the faultless signals of the breadth-of-market and quality-of-market indicators, those indicators get added prestige.

Most of the indicators described in this chapter arise from the feeling, often proved, that "the market interprets itself."

Fundamental market analysis is rather like seeing an old-fashioned movie hero tied to the railway tracks with the train thundering down on him. We think, The guy ought to be scared. Technical analysis is what is done by the hero's dog: "Master smells scared."

Here are a few of the methods that I am not going to describe in detail:

The "index of confidence" obtained by dividing Standard & Poor's index of high-grade common stocks into Standard & Poor's index of low-priced common stocks. This works now and again because the market turns to froth when whipped up by too much speculative activity. Low-priced stocks are favored. Thus, the index of confidence was 117.4 at the 1956 peak and 116.5 at the July 1957 peak, but only 102.2 at the October 1957 bottom. It had fallen to 96.4 by December 1957. Joseph E. Granville, author and publisher of a market service, feels that this indicator gives a "lead" of two to four months on major market turns. The index of confidence topped 200 before the 1946 and 1937 breaks. In 1928 it went to 467.3 ten full months before the collapse. However, at the December 1961 peak, the index was 80.4. In April 1962, the month before the break, it was 91.5 and at the June low it was 85.4.

The Lowry method measures market balance. It divides the aggregate gains of all stocks in a day by the aggregate volume in those stocks and then does the same for the aggregate losses. The idea is that the market is showing resistance to a trend when more volume is needed to move stocks in the direction of the trend.

When capital-goods stocks rise more rapidly than consumer-goods stocks, the speculative fever is supposed to be burning, so some analysts divide the S. & P. capital-goods stock index by the S. & P. consumer-goods stock price index. The ratio stood at 146 for the July 1956 peak and at 150 for the July 1957 peak. In June of 1958 it had fallen to 129. When November ended it again was at 129. But in December of 1961 it was at 108.5 and at the June 1962 low it was 102.3. In June 1963 it was 102.5.

Some analysts watch the relationship of the loans of member banks of the Federal Reserve System to their investments. The idea is that rising loans mean rising business activity. Banks invest in bonds when better uses for their money are missing.

Another indicator—also fundamental rather than technical— divides the loans of such banks by the monthly figure of checks drawn against the same banks. Debits (that is, checks drawn) move almost exactly with sales, and loans move with inventories, if we allow ninety days for loans to become inventory. This is another compass needle with neither end marked. The ratio can rise because (1) sales are going up faster than inventories or because (2) inventories are falling faster than sales. In either case, inventories will have to be replaced. In recent years this indicator has moved upward and downward as the Washington money managers have manipulated credit. It "signaled" the industrial recovery of September 1954 in May 1953, long before there was a noticeable slump from which to recover.

Various statisticians have invented various methods for plotting "normal" curves of stock prices. J. Eugene Banks of Brown Brothers Harriman & Co. derives a normal price by making a seasonal adjustment of the most recent quarterly earnings figure of the thirty stocks in the Dow-Jones industrial average and then relating it to the price-experience of the Dow-Jones industrial average over the preceding four quarters. Arthur Wiesenberger & Co. somehow relate their "normal price" to the cost of buying a dollar of income.

There are also, of course, statisticians who painstakingly divide industrial-stock yields by triple-A bond yields and then chart the results. This, I suspect, is a waste of time. Whenever the line falls below 1.00 the newspapers and financial magazines will raise such a yammer that you will know all about it. Then, in all likelihood, nothing will happen.

James F. Hughes of Auchincloss, Parker & Redpath tells an interesting story of the manner in which Leonard P. Ayres of the Cleveland Trust Company developed the so-called "breadth-climax method" of watching market movements.

One step was General Ayres's decision that the stock market has a forty-month cycle (or did between 1886 and 1923). The next was the discovery that a speculator could have made a good profit by holding stocks for twenty-three months, selling them and then waiting seventeen months before buying them again. This purely mechanical process, says Mr. Hughes, "would have been more profitable than purchases and sales that missed exact tops and bottoms by only two months."

In fact, he continues, the investor who caught the top and bottom month each time would have multiplied the original capital twenty-four times between 1886 and 1923 but the man who steadily missed the absolute highs and lows by as much as *one* month would have had a multiple of only ten times. Over the thirty-seven years this meant a drop from 9 per cent to 6.4 per cent in the rate at which the earnings were compounded (no income tax, of course).

To General Ayres, however, it meant that prices rose most rapidly just before they reached a peak and broke. They fell most rapidly just before touching bottom. In other words, we had "buying climaxes" and "selling climaxes." He set out to discover ways of recognizing them when they appeared. The result was the "breadth-climax index," which appeared first in 1926. It is based on that little table prepared by the Associated Press that appears nowadays in most newspapers serious enough to admit the existence of stocks:

	Issues Traded	Advances	Declines	New Highs	New Lows
Yesterday	1,261	570	405	25	35
Aug. 1	1,295	396	604	24	39
July 31	1,275	504	487	39	21

Mr. Hughes takes the difference between advances and declines as a percentage of the number of issues traded and then *cumulates* the percentages. Way back when, he started with 50 per cent plus. He has been minus more than 100 per cent from time to time.

The funny thing about a chart of this kind (see Chart XV on p. 167) is that it looks exactly like the chart of an industrial average or index. Much of the time the "breadth-climax index" parallels the Dow-Jones industrial average. When it breaks away this may mean something.

Mr. Hughes says that the breakaways are probably due to the fact that the "total issues" traded include quite a few preferred stocks and "money-rate stocks," which do not get excited when the cyclical issues are starting through the roof or through the cellar. Thus, when the cyclical issues are bringing higher and higher highs to the industrial average, the number of advances may be failing to exceed the number of declines at quite the old pace. In fact, there have been bull markets in which declines materially exceeded advances (in number) even while new highs were being made.

This was true, Mr. Hughes says, in July and August of 1929. The peak of that year was touched in the first week of September. In the first half of 1937 there was a similar downward swoop of the breadth index that would have saved a lot of money for anyone who had heeded it.

Then, from about May 1942, the breadth index rose reassuringly at a faster pace than the industrial average until halfway through 1946. In 1946 the charts show that the warning was there, but I personally doubt that anybody would have given it wholehearted credence.

In late 1952 and early 1953 the breadth index rose far less rapidly than the industrial average and should have given at least some warning of the market break to come in March. In 1957 it gave an even clearer indication, dropping steadily in May and June as stock prices pressed upward toward their peak.

Mr. Hughes says that the breadth index foreshadowed bull-market highs in November 1919 (before there was any breadth index), September 1929, March 1937, June 1948, and the triple top of April 1956, August 1956, and July 1957. Between February 15 and March 25, 1962, it gave a "major selling signal" foreshadowing the May 1962 market break—although other indexes continued to advance to new highs.

"If it had not been for various indications of short-term and inter-mediate trend reversals provided by the breadth index," he writes, "I doubt whether I should have continued its daily computation for the past 37 years. These minor trend indications have nowhere near the 100 per cent accuracy shown by the breadth index in forecast-ing major tops. Despite this fact, however, many important inter-mediate low points have been accurately pinpointed by various combinations of temporary selling climax indications which are by-products of the daily breadth computation. Also numerous reversals of minor and intermediate trading trends have been indicated by inability of price and breadth to keep in step while testing previous short-term and intermediate turning points."

My feeling about the breadth-climax index is that it makes pretty good sense. A man who likes to make a hobby of his investment activities could do worse than to keep a chart of the weekly high-low-and-close of his favorite stock-market industrial average or index and add to it a line showing the weekly percentage gain or loss in the breadth index. Suppose he had started on the week that ended with August 3, 1963. In that week 1,471 issues were traded and 726 or 49.3 per cent of these rose. Then, from his starting base of 50 points, he would subtract 0.7. He would be at 49.3. In the week ending August 10, 881 of the 1,470 issues rose—59.9 per cent. He would add 9.9 to 49.3 and plot 59.2. Or he might plot daily with a moving average.

And let not the investor forget that Mr. Hughes, like everybody else, uses other indicators. He doesn't put all his trust in breadth.

Joseph Granville's "Advance-Decline" line is a slight variation on the above and may be a little easier to plot because it does not involve the calculation of percentages:

TABLE OF ADVANCES AND DECLINES

	Advances	Declines	Cumulative Advances	Cumulative Declines	Cumulative Differential
Monday	600	400	600	400	+200
Tuesday	525	460	1,125	860	+265
Wednesday	470	510	1,595	1,370	+225

The Advance-Decline line is plotted from the figures in the last column.

Lucien O. Hooper of W. E. Hutton & Co. has what he calls an "indicator of market quality." It is based at not more than one remove on the idea that unsupportable overspeculation turns to the cheaper stocks.

Every day—or every week, if you want approximately the same result with less effort—you add up the prices of the ten most active stocks on the New York Stock Exchange and then divide by 10. After a time, your table might look something like this. When the market goes up, progressively cheaper stocks are providing the (possibly unhealthy) activity:

Week Ending		Down	Up	Index
February	7	47.75		48.23
	14		30.23	48.31
	21		31.04	48.45
	28		23.62	48.46
March	7	52.19		48.35
	14		22.02	48.51
	21		19.26	48.56
	28		18.36	48.72
April	4		17.96	48.80
	11	43.02		48.64

CHART XV

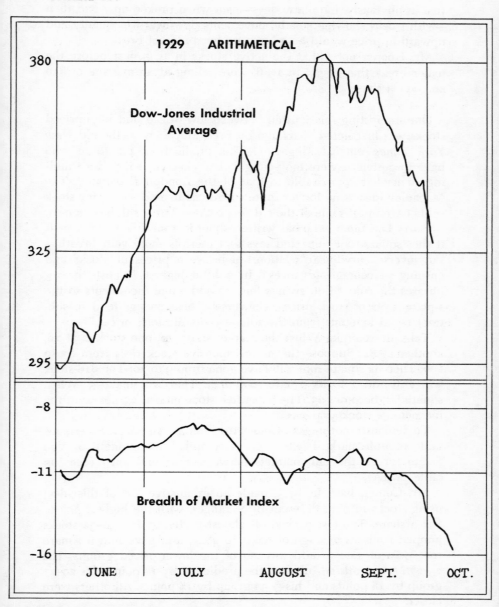

Courtesy of Auchincloss, Parker & Redpath

Obviously too many days in one direction would signal a reversal. Just as obviously, too many days—even when broken now and then —with stocks showing steady movements downward in quality and upward in price would be a build-up for a market break.

Mr. Hooper notes that the active stocks in 1945, just before the major break that began in 1946, were selling at an average of $10 and $11 a share.

One interesting relationship between low-priced and high-priced stocks was first noted years ago by Fred Macauley in the old *New York Times-Annalist Magazine*. This publication, for those who have forgotten or were too young to have known, enjoyed a standing somewhat comparable to that of the London *Economist*. The Macauley idea is no longer quite so true as it used to be, for stock splits have upset some of the old proportions, but it still has its uses.

Harry D. Comer, who has written about it from time to time, calls it the "square-root rule" and says that there is—hold your breath!— "an inverse curvilinear relationship between prices of stocks and ensuing percentage advances." In a little plainer English, he re-phrases the rule: "Bull swings tend to add equal increments to the square roots of stock prices. Conversely, bear swings tend to sub-tract equal amounts from the square roots of stock prices."

Take an example: When the market starts up, one stock is at 16, another at 81. Suppose the more expensive stock rises from 81 to 100. Then its square root will have gone from 9 to 10. The $16 stock will also add 1 to its square root of 4. That will make 5. When squared, 5 becomes 25. The expensive stock gained 23 per cent, the inexpensive stock 56 per cent.

To demonstrate this, Mr. Comer trots out an American experience table of bull markets, with figures compiled by Kenneth S. Van Strum for all the bull markets between 1897 and 1929 (see top table, p. 169).

Mr. Comer, back in 1945, made an exhaustive test of this idea, using stocks in nine different price ranges, with the highest $30 to $32 a share. The test clicked off almost perfectly. His 30–32 stocks jumped from an average of 30.93 to 48.43 and gave him a square root gain of 1.40 to add to each of the lower-priced groups. His 25–27½ group missed fulfilling the prediction by 1⅛ points, his 20–21 group by 1⅜ points and his 5–5½ group by 1¼ points. All others were closer.

Price Groups at Lows	Average Gain * %
0–5	241
5–10	146
10–15	127
15–20	106
20–30	94
30–40	79
40–55	73
55–70	73
70–100	43
Over 100	36

* After allowance for splits, etc.

Note once more that one of these dodges for playing the market—like the new-high method and the Clayton method—might have done considerably better with a little security analysis mixed in.

But it might be a good thing to note that, if you are using the new-high method and the Clayton method together, as Mr. Clayton now does, and have an otherwise equal choice between two stocks, the lower-priced one will probably give you the better play. As Mr. Comer observes, "There is much less market work necessary to move a $2 stock to $4 than to move a $20 stock to $40."

Morris Goldstein, chief of research of Francis I. du Pont & Co., ventures the assertion that industrial stocks are about 50 per cent

HOW THE SEASONS AFFECT STOCKS (1897–1962)

	Industrials		Rails	
	Years Up	Years Down	Years Up	Years Down
January	41	25	40	26
February	32	34	29	37
March	37	29	37	29
April	34	32	31	35
May	36	30	36	30
June	34	32	37	29
July	46	20	46	20
August	46	19	40	25
September	28	37	26	39
October	35	30	32	33
November	40	25	33	32
December	49	17	40	26

more likely to rise in December than they are in February or September.

To reach this conclusion, he has gone back over sixty-six years (1897–1962) of the Dow-Jones industrial and rail averages. In the preceding table some of the advances and declines total only 65 because the Exchange was closed for four months in 1914. The table shows the record, for what it is worth.

QUESTIONS FOR REVIEW

1. What is the breadth index, or Advance-Decline line?
2. Do you know what the "square-root rule" is?
3. On the past record, in what month are industrial stocks most likely to rise?

BOOK THREE

The Basic Issues

CHAPTER XIV

Our Own Little Crystal Ball

MY FAVORITE stock-market analyst is a man who says, "Look, if you were a customer I'd have to tell you what the market is going to do. Since you're not, I can confess that this market has had me buffaloed for the past three months."

He is my favorite because I so often feel that way myself.

Everyone who has ever been connected with the stock market has been wrong about it plenty of times. If any one person ever developed a 100 per cent sure-fire way of making money on every deal the market would probably go out of existence because that person and his followers would be marked men. If it were known that they always won, who would sell to them when they wanted to buy or buy from them when they wanted to sell?

It is a lot easier and safer to figure out what happened in a market than what is going to happen. That is why the ideas of Gerald M. Loeb of E. F. Hutton & Co. have such appeal. Mr. Loeb says that it is safer to take 10 per cent of your money, leaving the rest idle, and try to double it than it is to invest the lot for a normal investment return. This may be true, although I don't believe for a moment that Mr. Loeb keeps 90 per cent of his money idle. If it isn't in the stock market, he is using it to back half the shows on Broadway that look as if they had a chance.

But remember that point: *If you feel scared about the future, get out of the market. A minor speculative turn, later, can make up the income you lost. Unless timidity becomes a habit, there is nothing wrong with having only money.*

You will remember that in the first couple of chapters I mentioned that industrial production and industrial stocks rise and fall together only about half the time. The rest of the time one is rising and the other is falling. Since then, I believe, we have found ourselves leaning toward a number of decisions about the market. Perhaps I can summarize them this way:

In that 15 per cent of the time when both industrial production and industrial stocks are falling, it might be a good idea to be out of the market, to be in cash. Toward the end of the period, however, start watching for signs that the Washington money managers are going to make credit cheaper and more easily available. You may be able to buy bonds and money-rate stocks before they move.

When the market is merely uncertain, watch out for the "special situations" that you can pick up by the combined Clayton and new-high methods.

Because of their exceedingly high price-earnings ratios, *recognized* growth stocks fall about twice as fast as the averages when the market has a correction of 10 per cent or more. Ordinarily you will have a little warning—the other stocks will drop first and the growth stocks will hold fairly well—but get out promptly. And don't get back in unless you are convinced that the growth will be in the future as well as the past.

Buy growth stocks and buy cyclical stocks—those that move up and down with the business cycle—either *just when* or *just before* industrial production and industrial stocks start moving upward together. The best time, of course, is two or three months before.

This sounds as if I were recommending sorcery or at least second sight. In a way, I am. I believe that our economist-statisticians now know enough to predict fairly accurately that industrial production is about to turn upward or downward. So, if stocks are rising already and you can see that industrial production is about to rise, too, that could be a buy signal, a buy signal for growth stocks or cyclical stocks. That, of course, is what happened in May 1958. We are told that a slight upturn was signaled in February and that an investor might have known about it by April. A little later we shall go into this.

There is one big objection here: Is it advisable to buy growth and cyclical stocks at a time when we know that price-earnings ratios are all out of line, when we suspect that increased sales may be accompanied by smaller earnings; when, in fact, there is reason to believe that we are in the Indian summer of a bull market and that we'll be skating on the Hudson before long? A lot of Wall Street economists were asking such questions at various times in 1958 and in 1961. They were comparing the upward movement with that of the spring of 1930—when industrial production at least *seemed* to turn upward for three or four months.

My answer is, Yes. Get into the market with some of your funds. As General Ayres pointed out, the biggest profits are apt to come from the gains in the buying climaxes, when everybody emigrates to a never-never land in which the laws of economics and markets no longer govern. *But keep your stop-loss orders up to date!*

And watch for signs that the economy as a whole may bend downward and leave stocks up there in unsupported glory.

From time to time in the earlier chapters of this book I have mentioned some of the factors that Wall Street calls "the fundamentals." The cost of money is one. Naturally, inventories, retail sales, new orders, unemployment and the gross national product— the aggregate amounts spent or invested by governing bodies and individuals—are others. We have not been able to keep them completely out of our minds. Now we are going to concentrate on them for a little while, thinking of the 36 per cent of the time when business and the market rise together and the 15 per cent of the time when they fall together.

What we need, of course, are economic indicators that will move a little in advance of the main body of business. Are there any? In a work started by Wesley Clair Mitchell and Arthur F. Burns (the first chief of the Eisenhower Council of Economic Advisors) and carried on by Geoffrey H. Moore, the National Bureau of Economic Research staff has combed through more than eight hundred statistical series and come up with twelve * that anticipate the business conditions to follow. In fact, the records back to 1857 show that these "leading indicators" anticipate the peaks of business cycles by 7.9 months and the troughs by 5.1 months, on the average.

It is easy to see why some indicators should move ahead of business as a whole. Obviously contract awards for residential and nonresidential building have to precede the actual outlays for building. Again, new incorporations should be a good signal. A lot of companies are incorporated before they do anything at all. Then, the figure for new orders of durable goods is a "leader." The orders are to be filled in the months to come.

* When the first edition of this book was published, there were eight "Moore" indicators. Three have been dropped and seven added.

To make these figures usable, Dr. Moore and his staff correct them for *seasonal variation* and for *irregularity*.

Suppose the average length of the work week over the past three years had been 40.5 hours but that the average July work week had been 40.1 hours long. That would be 99 per cent of normal. Now, when July comes up with 39.4 hours you divide through by .99 and come up with 39.8. That is making a *seasonal adjustment*.

But how do you prevent a steel strike or the closing of the Suez Canal from upsetting all the data? First, you recognize that this irregularity is a brief, nonrecurring interruption of the normal flow. Over the year, the country will use just as much steel, because output will be at a heavier rate after the interruption. You adjust for irregularity by *averaging two to six months*. The nature of the statistical series governs the number of months you average.

If Dr. Moore received the June figure for a series he had decided to give a five-month average, he would add it to those for February, March, April and May and then plot his average for *April*. This gives up two months, in addition to the one month or two months that the Department of Commerce or the Department of Labor requires to calculate the most recent figure in the first place. That, it seems to me, is giving up too much of the possible advantage.

Leonard H. Lempert, director of Statistical Indicator Associates of North Egremont, Massachusetts, apparently feels the same way. In his weekly reports he fills in with estimates like these, which come from the July 10, 1963 number:

				1963		
Leading Indicators	Jan.	Feb.	Mar.	Apr.	May	Jun.
1. Average Hours Worked	402	403	404	403	405	
2. Accession Rate (Mfg.)	39	39	41	41	39 †	
3. Layoff Rate (Mfg.)	20	18	16	15	15 †	
4. Dur. Goods New Orders	167	171	175	179 *	177 *	
5. Housing Starts	122	126	151	162	169	
6. Com. & Ind. Bldg. Awds.	450	470	389	379	480	
7. Net New Businesses		10				
8. Failure Liabilities	1532	900	935	897	1223	
9. Corporate Profits (Net)		271				
10. Common Stock Prices	650	659	657	688	701	701
11. GNP Inventory Change		30			35 †	
12. Ind. Raw Materials Prices	85	85	84	85	85	84

* Revised since last week.   † Estimate.

These are merely indicators of ups and downs. No weights are involved. The failure-liabilities figure for January (and you must remember that a gain here is an actual loss) is $153,200,000. The number of hours in the average work week for January was 40.2. New orders are expressed in billions of dollars—$16,700,000,000 for January—and residential building contract awards in millions of square feet—83,600,000 for January. Only commodity and stock prices are expressed by index numbers.

Because these represent only ups and down, Mr. Lempert sometimes replaces them by plus or minus signs, and calculates what percentages are expanding. Like this, from his July 17, 1963 report:

THE LEADING INDICATORS SIMPLIFIED

	1962								1963				
	May	Jun.	Jul.	Aug.	Sep.	Oct.	Nov.	Dec.	Jan.	Feb.	Mar.	Apr.	May
Leaders	17%	21%	4%	29%	58%	75%	71%	54%	67%	67%	79%	75%*	58%
1. Avg. Hours Worked	0	—	—	0	—	+	—	+	—	+	+	+	0†
2. Accession Rate (Mfg.)	—	—	—	—	—	—	—	—	+	+	+	0*†	—†
3. Layoff Rate (Mfg.)	—	—	—	0	+	+	0	—	+	+	+	+	0†
4. Dur. Goods Orders	—	+	—	+	+	+	+	+	+	+	+	+	0†
5. Housing Starts	—	—	—	—	+	+	+	—	—	+	+	+	+†
6. Com. & Ind. Bldg.	—	—	—	—	+	—	+	+	+	—	—	+*	+†
7. Net New Businesses	0	—	—	—	—	—	—	+	+	+	+§	+§	+§
8. Failure Liabilities	—	+	—	—	—	+	+	—	+	—	+	—	—†
9. Corporate Profits	+	0	0	0	+	+	+	—	—	—	—§	—§	—§
10. Common Stock Prices	—	—	—	+	—	+	+	+	+	+	+	+	+
11. GNP Inventory Chge.	—	—	—	—	+	+	+	+	+	+	+†	+†	+†
12. Ind. Mat. Prices	—	—	—	—	+	+	+	0	—	—	0	0	0

Expanding (+); leveling-off (0), counts as ½ expanding; contracting (—). The directions of the monthly leaders are based on centered 3-month moving averages. † = estimate. § = latest figure extended. * = revised.

CHART XVI

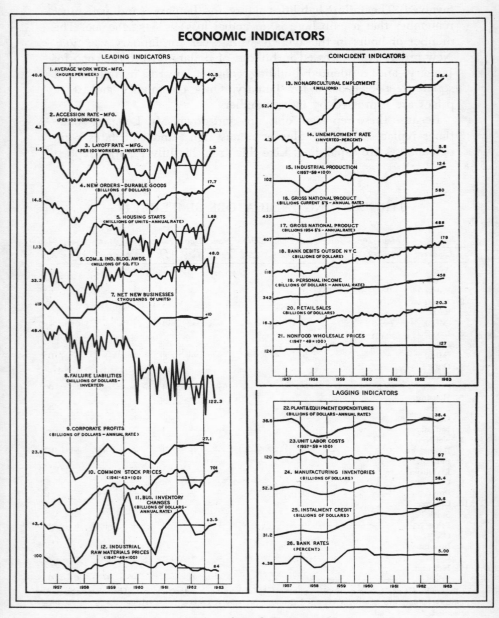

Courtesy of Statistical Indicator Associates of North Egremont, Mass.

If you wished, you could probably construct some leading indicators of your own on the Geoffrey Moore model. Dr. Moore tells how, in several papers published by the National Bureau of Economic Research, 261 Madison Avenue, New York 16, at $1 each. One was called *Measuring Recessions* and actually included all the seasonal adjustment factors you would need. Yes, you might have fun doing it, but the Lempert tables are so much more convenient! They cost $52 a year.

When the number of pluses drops to 0 or 1 you *know* that business is going to dip, regardless of what anybody tells you. When the number of pluses rises to 11 or 12 you *know* that industrial activity will keep rising for at least two or three more months.

Until the summer of 1958 I thought I knew how to foretell when the Federal Reserve System would start easing money rates. I thought this could be done by following two sets of statistics: the length of the average work week in manufacturing and the percentage of the civilian labor force out of work.

I had what was perhaps too strong an impression that the money managers, acting under the mandate of the Employment Act of 1946, would start propping up business whenever unemployment showed signs of topping 5 per cent and that they would definitely clamp down on industrial activity when unemployment fell below 3 per cent. We apparently need a certain amount of frictional unemployment. When we have too little, the job goes looking for the man, wages rise without corresponding increases in output, and we get inflation.

But in August 1958 I saw the Federal Reserve System start tightening money rates when unemployment (according to the most recent reports then available) was about 7½ per cent of the civilian labor force. The tightening continued in 1959, though unemployment generally remained above 5 per cent.

I see now that more data will be needed before we can formulate a new rule of thumb. I know—and you can see in the accompanying table and in the chart in the endpapers—that industrial production and the length of the average work week were both shooting upward when the Fed tightened money rates, but nobody could have had any assurance from past performance that unemployment would sink below 5 per cent. Perhaps our credit authorities thought control of overspeculation a more important job. Or perhaps they had made up their minds—like Armand Erpf of Carl M. Loeb, Rhoades & Co.—that conditions have so changed that the "full employment" of the future will overlook unemployment of 4,000,000 to 5,000,000 persons. Here is the table:

PRODUCTION, HOURS AND JOBLESS

	S. & P. Industrial Stocks	F. R. B. Industrial Production *	Average Hours Mfg. Work Week	Percentage Work Force Unemployed
January 1957	48.43	101	40.2	4.9
February	46.10	102	40.2	4.7
March	46.86	102	40.1	4.3
April	48.06	101	39.8	4.0
May	50.10	101	39.7	4.0
June	51.30	102	40.0	4.8
July	52.54	101	39.7	4.3
August	49.51	102	40.0	3.8
September	47.52	100	39.9	3.7
October	44.43	98	39.5	3.7
November	43.41	96	39.3	4.7
December	43.29	94	39.4	5.0
January 1958	43.98	92	38.7	6.7
February	44.01	89	38.4	7.7
March	44.97	88	38.6	7.7
April	45.09	87	38.3	7.5
May	46.51	89	38.7	7.1
June	47.62	92	39.2	7.7
July	48.96	93	39.2	7.5
August	51.00	95	39.6	6.7
September	52.40	95	39.9	6.0
October	54.55	96	39.8	5.5
November	56.11	99	39.9	5.6
December	57.09	100	40.2	6.0
January 1959	59.30	100	39.9	7.0
February	58.33	102	40.0	7.0
March	59.79	104	40.2	6.4
April	60.92	107	40.3	5.3
May	62.09	109	40.5	4.9
June	61.75	110	40.7	5.6
July	64.23	108	40.2	5.2
August	63.74	104	40.5	4.8
September	61.21	103	40.3	4.6

PRODUCTION, HOURS AND JOBLESS (*Cont.*)

	S. & P. Industrial Stocks	F. R. B. Industrial Production *	Average Hours Mfg. Work Week	Percentage Work Force Unemployed
October	61.04	102	40.3	4.7
November	61.46	103	39.9	5.3
December	63.56	109	40.6	5.2
January 1960	62.27	111	40.3	6.1
February	59.60	110	39.8	5.7
March	58.71	109	39.7	6.1
April	59.46	109	39.3	5.2
May	58.84	110	39.9	4.9
June	61.06	109	40.0	6.1
July	59.25	110	39.8	5.5
August	59.96	108	39.8	5.3
September	57.96	107	39.6	4.8
October	56.90	106	39.7	5.0
November	58.89	105	39.3	5.7
December	60.22	103	38.6	6.4

* 1957 = 100.

Only twice in that 48-month period did industrial production and industrial stocks run in the same direction long enough to do you any good. The first occasion was the movement downward that began in July or August 1957. The second was the upward drive that began in May 1958 and continued for a year. On the other occasions, you would hardly have been sure of the movement before it ended.

Following is a table showing how slowly money rates move downward following a slash in the discount rate of the Federal Reserve banks. Especially notice the rate charged member firms of the New York Stock Exchange, which in turn must charge their customers ½ per cent more on stocks and ¼ per cent more on bonds. And note the Treasury-bill rate. Banks buy Treasury bills when they can find no other profitable employment for their money.

Even when the movement is in the other direction, when the Federal Reserve wants to tighten money and check a boom, the response of the banks need not be immediate. Instead of calling loans,

MOVEMENT OF MONEY RATES*

	Discount Rate F. R. B. of N. Y.	Prime Comm'l Paper 4–6 Mos.	Call Loan Rates N. Y. S. E.	Treasury 3-Month Bills
			(in percentages)	
May 1960	4.00	4.25	5.11	3.392
June	3.50	3.81	5.00	2.641
July	3.50	3.39	5.00	2.396
August	3.00	3.34	4.85	2.286
September	3.00	3.39	4.50	2.489
October	3.00	3.30	4.50	2.426
November	3.00	3.28	4.50	2.384
December	3.00	3.23	4.50	2.272

* These are all monthly averages except the discount rates, which were changed on June 10 and August 12, 1960. The 3.00 per cent discount rate remained in effect for nearly three years, was raised to 3.50 per cent on July 16, 1963.

they will sell government bonds in order to get money to lend. If the pressure continues, they will even borrow from their Federal Reserve banks and so bring their reserves up to proper levels. Then the system must move again—selling Treasury obligations and raising reserve requirements and discount rates—until the cost of borrowing has checked the exuberance of business expansion.

The Sophisticated Investor will try to get into cyclical and growth stocks just as industrial stocks and industrial production begin moving upward together.

Often he can make his move two or three months beforehand by keeping an eye on the basic indicators which can forecast business upturns—and downturns.

QUESTIONS FOR REVIEW

1. What is a "leading indicator"?
2. How can the "leading indicators" warn you when to get into or out of cyclical stocks?

3. Can you depend on the Federal Reserve System to start easing money rates when unemployment tops 5 per cent?
4. Does money instantly become tighter when the Federal Reserve raises the discount rate?

CHAPTER XV

Formula Plans and

Investment Companies

FRAGMENTS OF our primitive naturism cling to us even today. We want the Magic Word that will make everything come right automatically. Why should we go to the trouble of thinking, of working out our own market tactics, when we can buy a book for a few dollars or hire a broker for a few commissions to do it for us?

Since I am absolutely certain that some of my readers bought this book with that idea in mind and since almost every barn in Brown County, Illinois, used to wear a sign that said "It Pays to Trade at Crane's," I am going to try to oblige. No customer will be sent away empty-headed.

Perhaps the easiest formula plan is the oldest. This involves keeping stocks and bonds equal. If you are interested primarily in income and want about 1 per cent more than you can get on a straight yield basis, this will appeal to you. It works best for a person who already has money and wants to put it to work without trouble or expense—someone who has just come into a legacy, for example.

You ask your broker for a list of fairly volatile but fairly sound stocks that happen to be yielding pretty well. Here, for example, is a "Sample $10,000 Portfolio" published in Standard & Poor's weekly *Outlook* for June 3, 1963:

No. Shares	Company	Approx. Cost	Annual Income	Approx. Yield (%)
25	Alabama Gas	$ 925	$42.50	4.6
45	American Investment	1,035	45.00	4.3
20	Borg-Warner	920	40.00	4.3
15	Cities Service	1,020	42.00	4.1
15	General Motors	1,095	52.50	4.8
20	Johns-Manville	980	40.00	4.1
20	May Department Stores	1,100	44.00	4.0
40	National Distillers	960	48.00	5.0
20	Niagara Mohawk Power	1,000	40.00	4.0
20	Sunshine Biscuits	1,060	45.60	4.3

You make a selection of these, or others—I am not recommending these particular stocks for indiscriminate investment at any time—and invest half your money. The other half of your funds you put into high-grade corporation bonds. At the end of June 1963, that part of your money would have yielded about 4 per cent. I figure your average yield on both stocks and bonds would be about 4 per cent.

But let us not talk about the end of June 1963. This is a formula for any time—or is supposed to be. At the end of six months you take a piece of paper and work out what your investment is worth. Let us say you started with $10,000 in stocks and $10,000 in bonds. The stocks are now worth $11,000, the bonds $9,800. The aggregate fund is $20,800 and half of that is $10,400. You sell $400 worth of stock and invest it in more of the bonds.

Six months later you even out the two funds again. And you keep on doing it. The effect of this is to make you take profits in stocks and bottle them up in bonds. That is good; that is safe; that is conservative; but you lose the cream of each milking. Between December 1953 and December 1961 Standard & Poor's industrial-stock average virtually tripled, going from 24.85 to 75.81. High-grade industrial bonds fell from 113.5 to 94.50. If you figure that one out for yourself, I believe you will discover that you end up with less than half the profit you'd have made by simply buying the stocks and bonds and holding on to them. Formula plans of this kind look best when the market falls. The bonds generally do pretty well, for the Federal Reserve officially and the money market unofficially are easing money. In any event, money can be taken from the bond account to buy more and more shares of stock. Then, when the market turns around, this greater number of shares of stock brings a greater and more rapid appreciation.

The formula outlined above can be changed in a number of ways. You may use common and preferred stocks, if you wish. That will bring a slightly higher yield basis. You may even use two kinds of common stocks, such as cyclical issues and sure-dividend issues. But all the plans make you take profits and add between 1 and 4 per cent to your ordinary investment income.

Some deep thinkers have worked out devices for changing the proportions of stocks and bonds according to the action of some market average or index. For example: For every 10 per cent that the Dow-Jones industrial average rises over the moving average of the last five (or ten or fifteen) years, you reduce the proportion in common stocks by 5 per cent.

If you remember the 200-day moving average we discussed a few pages back, you will realize that this kind of plan would lose most of any advance such as we had between 1949 and 1956.

Another variant would have you be conservative in choosing sound money-rate stocks but speculative in picking out convertible debentures priced fairly close to both par and their worth solely as bonds.

Dollar-cost averaging is a different kind of formula plan. It assumes that the investor is trying to put aside money to buy stocks, perhaps as a way of forcing himself to save.

Suppose that you bought ten shares of WHY at the end of every quarter and that the price went 20—15—10—5—5—10—15—20. You would have bought 80 shares for $1,000 and your average price would be $12.50.

Now change the signals. You invest $120 at the end of every quarter. The price moves the same way. This time you get 100 shares for $960 and the average price is $9.60.

The beauty of the dollar-cost-averaging approach is that a salesman can make a prospect believe that a falling market is a positive boon from heaven. Doesn't it give him a chance to buy more shares for the same money?

Most of the savings-investing plans you hear about assume that you will put in a little money each month of each quarter. I suggest that you sharpen a pencil before you go into any one of them.

The New York Stock Exchange has what it calls a Monthly Investment Plan. This will accept as little as $40 a quarter. Investors are given credit for shares and fractions of shares and the dividends declared on them are prorated. (For example, if you had 2.6 shares of General Motors and it declared a 50-cent dividend you'd be credited with $1.30.)

Monthly Investment Plan customers get a special deal on commissions. When they invest $100 or less at a crack, their commissions are 6 per cent. In other words, the commission on $40 would be $2.40. Ordinary customers, working outside the Monthly Investment Plan, would have to pay a minimum commission of $6.

Here is a table showing the commissions charged on the New York Stock Exchange and the American Stock Exchange as of January 1963:

MINIMUM COMMISSIONS ON ROUND LOTS
(100 SHARES)

Price per Share	Minimum Commission
Under $1	As mutually agreed.
From $1 to under $4	2% plus $3
From $4 to under $24	1% plus $7
From $24 to under $50	½% plus $19
From $50 up	1/10% plus $39

COMMISSIONS ON ODD LOTS
(FEWER THAN 100 SHARES)

Order Involving	Minimum Commission
Less than $100	As mutually agreed.
From $100 to $399	2% plus $1
From $400 to $2,399	1% plus $5
From $2,400 to $4,999	½% plus $17
From $5,000 up	1/10% plus $37

When the amount involved is $100 or more, the commission may not exceed $1.50 a share or $75 for a single transaction.

One more point: The price you pay for an odd lot "at the market" is the price of the first round lot to sell after receipt of your order, plus a "differential" that pays the odd-lot dealer for his trouble. This is 25 cents a share if the price is $40 or more, 12½ cents a share if it is less.

Suppose you bought three shares of a stock that crossed the tape at 40 right after your order. Your price would be 40¼, so you would pay $120.75. Your commission, as you can see above, would work out at $3.42 but the minimum commission is, after all, $6, so you would pay that. That is almost 5 per cent.

If you were buying twelve shares—$483—the commission would come down to about 2¼ per cent, which is more like it!

I am not blaming the brokers for these high commission rates on small deals. Even at such rates they probably lose money. Nor do I feel that small investors should be discouraged from buying stocks. I submit, however, that the small investor should be told exactly what he is doing when he pays his $40 a month.

The bigger the amount of the periodic payment the smaller the relative commission. Actually, a man who can save $40 a month would do a lot better to put the money in the savings bank for a year and then invest it in a lump. In that way the savings-bank interest would about equal his commissions. In the $40-a-month system commissions would cost him about $29 for the year.

Of course, the stock might rise more than that in the course of the year. True! And it might fall.

I have the same kind of prejudice against mutual funds. I feel that the people who buy them are definitely trying to buy income and that the loading charges, which run from 7½ to 8½ per cent, make income too expensive for those who need it most. (These charges, however, are usually only for investing. There is no charge for cashing in your mutual-fund shares and getting out, save in a few cases.) Especially I do not like heavy "front-end" loads, which have become more and more popular. These have followed the practice of the insurance companies which pay almost all the commission of the agent or sales representative in the first year, so that the insured has almost no loan value in his policy at the end of that first year.

In the mutual-funds segment of its special study of securities markets, published in 1963, the Securities and Exchange Commission's study group recommended that Congress amend the Investment Company Act of 1940 so that front-end loads might be abolished. The report added: "If it should be concluded that such abolition is not called for, such legislation should both substantially limit the amount and method of application of any such load and prohibit the offering of front-end load contractual plans by any mutual fund sales organization without the simultaneous offering of a level-load voluntary plan for shares of the same fund and (except for prepayment of selling charges) on substantially the same basis."

A customer's man in a brokerage house earns about three times as much for selling $10,000 worth of a mutual fund as he does for selling the same amount in an ordinary New York Stock Exchange stock. These charges seem exorbitant to me, as I can see no evidence that the customer is getting anything in particular for the extra money. Defenders of mutual funds point out that the investor *does* receive the benefit of expert advice from the investment counselors retained by the funds. On this point, here is a comment from *A Study of Mutual Funds,* prepared by the University of Pennsylvania's Wharton School of Finance and Commerce at the request of the Securities and Exchange Commission and published in August 1962:

"When the advisory fees were measured against the investment income of the mutual funds, the median per cent of such income paid out in advisory fees in fiscal 1960–61 by a representative group of mutual funds was 16.3 per cent. . . . Individual mutual fund shareholders do not pay higher management fee rates than they would incur through other institutional investment channels (which, however, normally do not involve a substantial sales charge). Nevertheless, they do not generally benefit from the lower charges that the volume of their pooled resources might be expected to make possible."

Investment methods of the investment companies are hardly to be envied. There is a feeling in the Street that the buying offices of these corporations mostly "go down the subway together," that is, they buy each other's choices and therefore push sections of the market higher at the same time. Again, they have a habit of running at the same time. Says the Wharton School study: "In connection with an analysis of fund activity in thirty individual securities which were mutual-fund favorites, the fund showed a definite tendency to buy on balance in the two months prior to cyclical upswings in the prices of such stocks and to sell on balance (or to have weaker purchase balances) in the two months prior to cyclical downswings. This lends some support to the hypothesis that fund activity may have been partially responsible for (and may have partially forecast) the major market movements in these issues. Mutual funds as a whole may to some extent have the ability to fulfill their own market predictions, and in particular, to validate their own appraisal of individual issues. There was more evidence of destabilizing behavior by mutual funds in individual issues than in the market as a whole, particularly within market declines."

However, during the stock-market crisis at the end of May 1962, the mutual funds actually functioned as a *stabilizing* influence. Fear that the funds would begin dumping large blocks of stock on the market as panicky investors began cashing in their shares was so great at the time that, according to some observers, "people didn't even talk about it." However, according to the New York Stock Exchange, the mutual funds on May 28—the start of the slump—bought 530,000 more Big Board shares than they sold. On May 29, also, they bought 467,000 shares on balance. But on May 31, when the scramble to buy stocks reached bargain-basement pitch, the funds *sold* 375,000 more shares than they bought. It seems clear enough that the funds on May 28 and 29 were snapping up bargains, and that on May 31 they were taking their profits. Thus, while the funds' actions may have caused wide fluctuations in individual issues, their effect on the market as a whole was a steadying one. In *Investment Companies 1963*, the current edition of their annual publication, Arthur Wiesenberger & Company remarks, "The experience of 1962 should go far to put to rest for all time the old bugaboo of 'what happens when mutual funds have to sell portfolio securities in a declining market to meet shareholder redemptions?' It didn't happen in 1962, in the worst stock market decline of this generation, despite the 'push-button' redemption privilege accorded every shareholder of a mutual fund.

"The behavior of investment company shareholders in 1962 proved a point often made but never before so forcefully demonstrated. That is the shield the investment company provides between the stock market and the investor's own emotions."

I suggest that mutual funds are probably all right for the man who feels he needs such a shield and who is perfectly sure that he can keep putting the money in, month after month, for five years or more. If he can't be sure or if he has a sneaky feeling that he's kidding himself, I think he should try to save up and buy at least $500 worth of stock at a time.

That would be a single company's stock, without diversification. If he wants diversification and all the benefits of professional guidance, he can get them by buying the shares of the closed-end investment trusts already listed on the various Exchanges.

Closed-end investment company shares are sold in the manner of industrial stock. Investors bet on the wisdom of the management and put in their money. The managers then invest the money, taking for themselves a management fee. As the values of the portfolios go up and down, so do the market prices of the stocks. But not dollar for dollar. The investing public tries to appraise past records of the managers, personality factors, the kinds of securities held. For example, Lehman Corporation is loaded with oils and sells at a premium when oils are on the upgrade. At other times it may be at a discount.

Here, for example, is Equity Corporation, which is a large holder of Bell Intercontinental Corporation. With the Bell holdings given their market value, the Equity Corporation portfolio had a value per common share of $4.98 at the end of 1962, but Equity's shares were selling at 3⅛, a discount of 49 per cent. Adams Express had a discount of 4 per cent and Alleghany Corporation either a discount of 3 per cent or a premium of 13 per cent, depending on how you figured the value of assets.

Of twenty-six closed-end investment funds listed by Arthur Wiesenberger & Co. at the end of 1962, five had premiums and twenty-one had discounts, five of 20 per cent or more.

Mutual funds, which are open-end investment companies, add the values in their portfolios each day, divide by the number of outstanding shares and then sell more shares at that price, *plus* a loading charge. Some of them have done exceptionally well. Some have done so poorly that you wonder how their managers keep out of homes for the feeble-minded.

Investment Companies 1963 examines 121 mutual funds that have been in business under the same management for ten years or more. It works out what would have happened to an original investment of $10,000 in a mutual fund made at the end of 1952. What would have happened, for example, if ordinary dividends had been taken by the shareholder but if he had agreed to have his capital-gain dividends—those from trading profits—reinvested in more stock? (Note that the profits are somewhat inflated by the fact that no allowance is made for income taxes on the capital-gain dividends received as stock.)

Using these methods, the mean figure at the end of 1962 seems to be about $19,000, meaning that the average investor added to his stake (before income tax on capital gains turned into stock) at the compounding rate of 8 per cent a year. (You will remember the remark by Samuel Lee Stedman and Armand Erpf of Loeb, Rhoades that less than 12 per cent a year is not worth planning for.) The mean-average ordinary dividend return over the years was around $4,500. Perhaps you could consider that as adding another 1 per cent.

There were actually eight companies that decreased the $10,000, though their dividend payments ranged from $3,000 to $5,500.

Loading charges ran as high as 8¾ per cent. In looking at these figures about mutual funds it is only fair that we consider what Arthur Wiesenberger & Co. consider "essential qualifications."

First, the firm reminds us, these results reflect the past, a 10-year period when stock prices were generally rising. You have to make up your own mind whether you can expect as good results in the future.

Second, it isn't always fair to compare the results of any two funds. One may have been after safety as a primary objective, another after growth and to hell with the risk. (After all, would you yourself always have chosen the big risk over the conservative play? If so, you're not like me.)

Third—and this qualification comes not from the firm itself but from Edson Gould, a partner—far-above-normal gains for any mutual fund usually result not from policy so much as from a few purchases that gave far-above-usual results. In other words, you can't bet that present holdings will give comparable results.

Another point is worth making: In every case the original investment is considered to be the invested amount *minus* the loading charge.

Shortly after I had completed the first edition of this book, I gave an informal talk on the stock market. The question of investment funds came up and I said about what you have just read.

But after the meeting a friend pushed me off into a corner. "You've got to tell me about the investment funds," he said.

"Why? Do you want to force yourself to save?"

"No. I don't have any trouble saving. But I want to rid myself of the job of supervision. How do I go about it?"

"A good broker should be able to help you. There are quite a few who will tell you when to sell as well as when to buy."

"In my experience," he said, "brokers are primarily interested in getting me to buy some new issue or some secondary distribution. When they aren't working at that, they're trying to get me to buy and sell and buy and sell again."

"That," I said, "is called 'churning' the account. If you know where you're going, it's easy to avoid. You simply say no."

"But I don't have *time* to get to *know* where I want to go!"

If you already have a chunk of money and can't spare the time for the fun of handling it yourself, make your broker lay out for you the facts about a number of closed-end and open-end investment trusts. *Don't consider a salesman who is able to offer you only one.*

Study carefully the relative advantages of buying perhaps $1,000 of assets for $800 (as you might be able to do with a closed-end fund selling at a discount on the New York Stock Exchange) or buying $1,000 of assets for $1,085, as you might if a mutual fund loading charge were added. The "cheap" assets might be earning at a rate too low to be worth while.

Regardless of the Wiesenberger "essential qualifications," past performances *do* count. But don't examine only the over-all record. See how much the value of the fund rose (or fell) in the last couple of years. It's the management *now* that matters. You can suffer if the brains have all been buried.

One interesting thing about loading charges is that the size of the charge doesn't seem to have any relationship to results. Neither does the lack of a charge. One fund with no loading charge came out well below the average, one almost on the average and one well above it. The last has virtually turned into a closed-end company. You pay commissions when you buy its shares.

I suggest, if you have enough money, that you buy into more than one fund. You might try a couple of closed-end funds selling at good discounts and a couple of mutual funds.

Make sure you understand the objectives of the fund. Remember, if you are told that *income* is the aim, that the pay-out value in half a dozen years might easily be less than what you put in. (This has happened with three such funds.) Funds that go out for capital appreciation are likely to give you the most income, too.

If you need encouragement to make you save, I suspect that the loading charge on a mutual fund is a slight fee to pay the encourager—*provided* you are not going to need the money for five years or more.

If you are apt to need the money sooner, give your wife permission to nag you about putting so much a month into the savings bank. (This will work two ways, for it will keep her watching the expenses, too.) Then, every six months or once a year, you can buy shares of a good closed-end fund selling at a discount in the New York Stock Exchange.

All these plans will give you diversification, which may or may not be what you want. *You may diversify out the profits as well as the risk.* The Monthly Investment Plan gives you no diversification. You have to use your head to pick out a stock. You may use the paragraph above to help you collect the money to buy such a stock.

One of these days, if you can keep away from fission, fusion and roller skates in hall closets, you *are* going to have the time to give to your investments. For that reason, I should not like to see you wrap yourself completely in the coddling comforters of the investment trusts. I think you should dress warmly but stride out into the Cold Hard World all by yourself now and then, if only to prove to yourself that you can do it.

The Sophisticated Investor does not need the discipline of a formula plan or an investment fund. He likes to think for himself.

QUESTIONS FOR REVIEW

1. Why is an investor generally better off saving his money and investing it in a lump sum at year end than putting a fixed amount into a monthly stock investment plan?
2. What is "front-end load"?
3. What is a "closed-end" investment company?

CHAPTER XVI

Are Good Common Stocks in Short Supply?

GEORGE KEITH FUNSTON, president of the New York Stock Exchange, takes pride in the phrase, "People's Capitalism," which he devised to describe our present American system. It is based on the idea that 170,000,000 Americans may and more than 17,000,000 do own shares in American business.

These are the direct shares alone. Indirectly, almost everybody in the country has some kind of stake in the profits of American corporations. In a very real and sometimes embarrassing way our investing habits have become socialized. Sometimes I suspect that our stock market isn't big enough to support the investment structure that the insurance companies, the unions and the investment trusts have tried to rear upon it.

According to a late 1963 study, institutional investors own about 20 per cent of the stock outstanding and do about 24 per cent of the trading on the New York Stock Exchange. Their importance is considerably greater than those figures indicate. Much of the trading on the Exchange is done by members going in and out for a small profit or loss. But what an institutional investor buys is apt to be a semipermanent holding. Except in highly unusual cases, it will not be sold next month or even next year. As the following table from the Exchange's *Fact Book, 1963* shows, the institutions tend to leave the individual investor less and less of the supply of common stock:

ESTIMATED HOLDINGS OF NYSE LISTED STOCKS BY FINANCIAL INSTITUTIONS

Type of Institution	Year End				
	1949	1956	1960	1961	1962
Insurance Companies:		(*Billions*)			
Life	$ 1.1	$ 2.3	$ 3.6	$ 4.5	$ 4.4
Non-Life	1.7	4.5	6.0	7.4	6.6
Investment Companies:					
Open-End	1.4	7.1	12.4	17.2	15.6
Closed-End	1.6	4.0	4.2	5.6	5.2
Nonprofit Institutions:					
College & University Endowments	1.1	2.4	2.9	3.7	3.2
Foundations	1.1	4.1	5.3	6.9	6.2
Other	1.0	3.1	4.4	5.6	5.0
Non-Insured Corporate Pension Funds	0.5	5.3	12.6	17.4	17.2
Common Trust Funds	—	1.0	1.4	1.9	1.7
Mutual Savings Banks	0.2	0.2	0.2	0.3	0.3
Total	$ 9.7	$ 34.0	$ 53.0	$ 70.5	$ 65.4
Market Value of All NYSE Listed Stocks	$76.3	$219.2	$307.0	$387.8	$345.8
Est. Per Cent Held by Institutions	12.7%	15.5%	17.3%	18.2%	18.9%

And what kind of stocks do the big investment trusts and the bank-managed trust accounts and pension funds buy? Why, exactly what you would expect: standard issues that no trustee could ever be criticized for buying; the securities of the biggest companies; the securities that are used in making up the principal market averages.

There is no criticism of this practice. When you have millions upon millions of dollars to invest, you parcel it out in pretty big chunks. You don't buy fifteen shares of American Telephone and Telegraph and twelve shares of Addressograph. This is another way of saying that institutional investors pretty well insist on the actively traded stocks of large companies. For example, almost all investment trust money is in a tight little list of about 120 companies. The bulk of that money goes into the fifty largest companies on the New York Stock Exchange.

Harold Clayton of the Stock Exchange house of Hemphill, Noyes & Co., whose investment methods we considered a few chapters back, ranks all active Big Board firms (1165 at the end of 1962) according to size by multiplying their outstanding shares by the price per share at the year end. Concerning the 1962 list, he had the following additional points to make:

1. Of total value of *all* issues, American Telephone & Telegraph
   alone equals 8.18%
2. A. T. & T. and General Motors together equal 12.96%
3. A. T. & T., General Motors and Standard Oil of New Jersey
   together equal 16.67%
4. A. T. & T., General Motors, Jersey Standard, du Pont and
   I.B.M. together equal 22.96%
5. The top 9 companies equal 30.32%
6. The top 12 companies equal 33.95%
7. The top 16 companies equal 37.65%
8. The top 22 companies equal 41.84%
9. The top 55 companies equal 54.20%
10. The top 200 companies equal 78.00%

In May 1963, Mr. Clayton also ranked the 200 largest corporations in order of percentage performance since the end of October 1962, the point at which the market began a determined upward climb. It is interesting to see how the ratings of the fifty largest corporations compare with the rankings of Vickers Associates, Inc., an investment advisory house that for some years has published a list of the "Favorite Fifty" stocks of the investment companies, compiled from its continuous service, "Guide to Investment Company Portfolios."

COMMON STOCKS OF THE FIFTY
BIGGEST COMPANIES

(End of 1962)

	Rank by Size	Vickers Rank	Rank by % Perf.† 10/23/62– 5/24/63	Percentage Performance 10/23/62– 5/24/63 (% Up)
American Telephone	1	5	42	22
General Motors	2	4	22	42
Standard Oil (N.J.)	3	3	30	34
du Pont	4	7	37	27
I.B.M.	5	1	22	42
Texaco	6	2	36	28
General Electric	7	11	36	28
Sears, Roebuck	8	24	25	39
Ford Motor	9	6	31	33
Standard Oil (Calif.)	10	9	38	26
Eastman Kodak	11	12	40	24
Gulf Oil	12	13	20	43
Royal Dutch Petroleum	13	8	28	36
Pacific Tel. & Tel.	14	n.i.*	39	25
Union Carbide	15	35	37	27
Procter & Gamble	16	n.i.	34	30
Socony Mobil Oil	17	20	24	40
Minnesota Mining & Mfg.	18	23	29	35
U.S. Steel	19	n.i.	41	23
Shell Oil Co.	20	n.i.	16	48
Shell Transport	21	n.i.	26	38
General Foods	22	34	41	23
International Nickel	23	10	42	22
Pacific Gas & Elect.	24	n.i.	41	23
Commonwealth Edison	25	n.i.	40	24
Standard Oil (Ind.)	26	38	22	42
General Telephone	27	n.i.	23	41
Phillips Petroleum	28	40	40	24
Reynolds Tobacco	29	36	32	32
Dow Chemical	30	n.i.	20	44
Amer. Elect. Power	31	21	38	26

COMMON STOCKS OF THE FIFTY
BIGGEST COMPANIES (*continued*)

(*End of 1962*)

	Rank by Size	Vickers Rank	Rank by % Perf.† 10/23/62– 5/24/63	Percentage Performance 10/23/62– 5/24/63 (% Up)
Monsanto Chemical	32	39	26	38
Con. Edison (N.Y.)	33	n.i.	39	25
Bethlehem Steel	34	n.i.	58	4
Texas Utilities	35	16	42	22
Amer. Home Products	36	n.i.	41	23
Southern Co.	37	14	47	17
Coca-Cola	38	n.i.	36	28
Allied Chemical	39	32	22	42
Continental Oil	40	17	32	32
Alcoa	41	n.i.	34	30
International Paper	42	29	23	41
Westinghouse Elect.	43	n.i.	19	45
Goodyear Tire & Rubber	44	28	14	50
Corn Products Refining	45	n.i.	28	36
New England Tel. & Tel.	46	n.i.	45	19
Corning Glass Works	47	n.i.	38	26
Campbell Soup	48	n.i.	39	25
J. C. Penney	49	n.i.	46	18
Public Service Elect. & Gas	50	n.i.	41	23

* n.i. means not included in Vickers Favorite Fifty.
† Naturally there are a number of ties.

Back in 1957, when all stocks were losing 14.3 per cent and the Favorite Fifty were dropping 16.95 per cent, another favored fifty, those of the Monthly Investment Plan of the New York Stock Exchange, were losing only 9.07 per cent.

Are the little odd-lot investors of the Monthly Investment Plan really almost twice as clever as the highly paid managers of the big investment trusts? No. We must remember that the little man got good professional advice, too, perhaps from the same experts who managed the trusts.

The fact seems to be that good security analysts are pretty seriously handicapped when working for investment trusts. They are limited to a relative handful of the existing securities. Then, once their funds are committed, they find that the market isn't big enough to allow them to change their minds. Where, for example, would you go to sell $165,000,000 worth of stock in Standard Oil Company (New Jersey)? The big investors in 1957 were locked in. The little investors were not. If they decided to get out of oils, they could do so. (Apparently they so decided, for the oil stock index dropped 24 per cent between its 1957 peak and the end of the year and 13 per cent for all 1957.)

Don't make the mistake of thinking that the trusts held most of Jersey Standard's stock. They didn't. At the end of 1956 they had only 1.43 per cent of it. But 107 of them owned 2,809,000 shares and that was more than 100 days of ordinary trading in the issue.

At the moment we are concerned with what happens to the standard issues when the market, having taken a dive, begins to climb. The downward pressure has been removed. The investment trusts' buying, although small, begins to exceed the selling of others. And what do the investment trusts, the pension funds and the trust funds buy? Why, the Favorite One Hundred Twenty, the Favorite Fifty. If the market is back on the upward track, these stocks will move with the least hesitation. Should prices fall back they would be met with new "buy orders" just below the market.

Again in May 1963, Harold Clayton observed that "while many hundreds of common stocks listed on the New York Stock Exchange [were] far below their all time highs, the ten *largest* companies on the Board (representing 32 per cent of the value of *all* listed common stocks) [had] performed as follows:

| | % of All Time High, |
Issue	as of May 16, 1963
American Telephone	89
General Motors	97
Standard Oil (N.J.)	96
du Pont	99
International Business Machines	78
Texaco	96
General Electric	82
Sears, Roebuck	92
Ford Motor	88
Standard Oil (Cal.)	98
	87% average

"It pays," he concluded, "to buy stock in the 'largest companies.'"

The reader may remember the action of the market in June 1958, when Lehman Brothers' One William Street Fund was doing its first buying. Market analysts were studying the favorite securities of Lehman Corporation, also managed by Lehman Brothers. Trading desks were putting together blocks of such securities. Each time such a block was bought by the fund or each time it expressed interest in such a block, the word flashed about Wall Street. The stock in question was then assumed to have "sponsorship." Other investors began to buy it, it went up, and One William Street, presumably, stopped buying it for a while.

Throughout each market slump investment trusts ordinarily "improve their liquid positions." As the little investors make their monthly payments, the trusts hold out the money or part of it. Instead of keeping 5 per cent of their assets in cash or short-term Treasury obligations, they are between 8 and 9 per cent liquid.

If the funds should invest 4 per cent of their aggregate assets over a limited period something like $500,000,000 or 12,000,000 shares would be involved. Added to the buy side of a dead-center market, this would be a considerable amount.

One other fact of life about the investment trusts may be of use: Many of them are impatient at the confining walls of the 120 stocks in which most of their investments are made. They struggle to get out and now and again buy a few thousand shares in something else. A studious person might keep track of such purchases and follow some of these stocks upward through the reports of Arthur Wiesenberger & Co. or some other Wall Street house that specializes in investment trusts. The more volume, the better the chance that other investment trusts will follow the first purchaser and drive the stock up to too high a price. It isn't so risky as it seems. When the hippopotamus puts a foot in the bath water to try the temperature, you jump in, too. Then, when the hippo climbs into the bathtub with you, up comes the water (price) level to cover you both comfortably. Vickers Associates, Arthur Wiesenberger and Capital Gains Research all report regularly when the dainty toes are being dunked. Standard & Poor's *Outlook* and *Barron's* report every quarter.

The Sophisticated Investor watches what the Big Boys are buying and selling.

QUESTIONS FOR REVIEW

1. What has been the effect of institutional buying on the supply of top-grade common stocks? On the prices of such stocks?
2. How can the small investor benefit from a knowledge of what the investment funds are buying?

CHAPTER XVII

We *Can* Have Another 1929

NEXT TO my wife's "Why don't we go home?" the question I hear most frequently at social affairs is, "Do you think, Mr. Crane, that there is any danger of another 1929?"

I hasten to be reassuring. "No danger whatever for the economy as a whole. The future may see deep declines in employment and production but I doubt that we'll ever again allow ourselves to go bankrupt so enthusiastically as we did in the early 1930s."

If my questioner looks happy, or even a little relieved, I add, "None of this, of course, applies to the stock market. That can drop even more violently than it did then."

When we talk about the economy, about jobs, about production, we are in the realm of almost absolute values. When we discuss the stock market, we deal primarily with the price to bid for a possibility.

There is, of course, no limit to possibility, any more than there is a limit to the power of man's imagination to conceive.

In the market we must always remember that what goes up *can* come down. We comfort ourselves by remembering that, after a climb almost to infinity, the drop can be no more than 100 per cent.

Once, when one of the Paris Rothschilds was asked how he made his money, he replied, "By selling too soon."

What makes this market vulnerable? How can we possibly have a collapse like the one which carried from 1929 into 1932, taking, between its high and its low, 86.13 per cent from the market value of the Standard & Poor's industrials, 88.81 per cent of the market value of the utility index and 92.13 per cent of the market value of the rail index?

The fact is that the auction market on the New York Stock Exchange is woefully thin, in spite of the measures taken by the authorities to fatten it out and give it muscles.

What do I mean by thin? Suppose we take an example: Between the December 1961 peak and the June 1962 bottom, common stocks on the New York Stock Exchange lost about $89,000,000,000, the equivalent of 6.3 years of dividends (*industrial* stocks lost the equivalent of 7.7 years of dividends).

That sounds like a general collapse but was not. In the six months aggregate sales on the Stock Exchange were 619,000,000 shares, about 8½ per cent of the total shares listed for trading.

What's this? Does our market value drop $144 for each share sold? It did in those six months. Between July and October 1957, the drop was $268 per share sold. And these were merely averages. On October 21, 1957, to give a more vivid example, 7,800 shares of du Pont were sold and the price dropped 6¼. Because there were 45,548,000 outstanding shares, the market value of all du Pont common shares fell $284,600,000. That is $36,487 for each share sold.

Another example? On September 23, 1963, General Motors slipped 75 cents or an aggregate of $212,976,300. On the same day General Electric fell 62½ cents. Down went the value of GE in the world's portfolios by $54,939,563.

Our trouble is that we have about 8,000,000,000 shares of 1,500-odd issues on the New York Stock Exchange, held by about 17,000,000 shareholders, most of whom never trade at all.

It was not always this way. Back in 1901 the 63,069,208 shares on the Stock Exchange were turned over 3.19 *times* or 319 per cent a year. In 1928, when we had 654,999,126 shares, they turned over 1.32 *times* or 132 per cent.

Since the passage of the Securities Exchange Act of 1934, which included a good many rules against practices that might or might not be manipulative, trading has topped 30 per cent only once, and in twenty-one of the twenty-eight years to the end of 1962 the figure was below 20 per cent. Since 1956 we have hovered between 12 and 15 per cent and the New York Stock Exchange reports that the turnover rate as of September 1963 is 13 per cent.

In other words, sales of fewer and fewer shares of stock, relatively, set the prices for all shares of stock.

Suppose that holders of just 1 per cent of the stock in the market should get scared and try to sell at the same time. How bad a market break would that bring about? As you can see, it would mean sales about one thirteenth as large as we ordinarily get in a whole year. Suppose we spread it out over a week? Then we should have five days with average sales of 16,000,000 shares. Our wildest recent break was May 28–31, 1962. Then 14,750,000 shares were traded in a single day—May 29—and if that hadn't been the rally day we should have been in serious trouble. Volume on May 28 was 9,350,000 shares and on May 31 it was 10,710,000. (There was, of course, no trading on Memorial Day, May 30.)

Let us try one other measure of thinness. At the peak of the 1929 excitement, daily turnover mounted to 1.8 per cent of all stocks listed. Today that would mean 144,000,000 shares, nearly ten times as many as on May 29, 1962.

Why is this market so thin? What is different about it? How has it changed from the "good old days"?

It isn't that volume is so much smaller than it used to be. Actually, only two years in history—1928 and 1929—had higher daily average volume than the years 1955 to 1960. Volume in 1961 and 1962 was exceeded only by that of 1929, and volume in 1963 broke all records. It is simply that our industrial plant, our business turnover and our total assets have grown so much bigger without any comparable expansion in our market for the stocks representing them.

Part of this is due to the fact that margins are higher. Before 1929 there were reputable Stock Exchange houses that asked the ordinary customer for "10 points or 10 per cent." It should be obvious that a man who could borrow 90 per cent for a speculation could make much more splash than a man limited to 10 or 30 or even 50 per cent. Smaller splashes seem to make smaller markets.

Suppose we look at the nature of the stock market and see how it can or may affect our trading. The most satisfactory way of doing this is the historical. It shows how today developed out of its yesterdays.

Apparently the selling of securities in this country started with the same auctioneers who used to dispose of the cargoes of merchant vessels. They sold shares in merchant (and possibly privateer) ventures and in insurance risks. Naturally, when United States Government "stock" became an object of speculation after the War of the Revolution, they took this on as well.

On May 17, 1792, under a buttonwood tree at 68 Wall Street, a group of merchants and auctioneers signed an agreement to charge the public minimum brokerage commissions of ¼ of 1 per cent and to deal on more favorable terms only with each other, thus shutting out rival auctioneers or merchants.

Today we romanticize these beginnings under the old sycamore or English plane tree, but we mustn't confuse them with the market as we know it today. According to R. I. Warshow's *The Story of Wall Street* (New York: Greenberg, 1929), only twenty-four issues were traded as late as 1815. One was a manufacturing company; the others government securities and bank stocks. A couple of years later only eight firms and nineteen individuals were engaged in the business. On one day in 1830 only thirty-one shares were traded.

Business was conducted by the system of "call-through." The Exchange president named each stock. The members called out their bids and offers. If a price was set it became the price for the day or the price until the next call-through, and anybody might trade at it. Just before the Civil War there were supposed to be two calls-through a day but the second was a formality. By 1862 there were four, plus two "open boards" in the street market that became known as the New York Curb Exchange and is now the (indoor) American Stock Exchange. By 1864 there were additional markets for substantially the same stocks in a room next door to the New York Stock Exchange, in the "Coal Hole" at 23 William Street and uptown at the Fifth Avenue Evening Stock Exchange.

The method of the call-through has not been abandoned in all parts of the world. Some European markets still use it. The biggest market to employ it recently was in Tokyo. General Douglas MacArthur's occupation of Japan abolished it and substituted the New York method, on the principle that American officials would have less trouble regulating a market system they understood.

In our country, before the War Between the States, most stock and bond trading was for future delivery. A trader might buy or sell stock for delivery in 30, 60 or 90 days. This method, still used in England, allowed speculation without undue complication. Today a man who sells stock that he does not have must borrow it and make delivery within four days. If a dividend is declared in the stock while he is "short" of it, he must make good that dividend. But when, in the last century, he merely sold a promise to deliver in 90 days, no actual stocks were involved and no dividends had to be made good.

By 1871 big changes had been made. The call-through was gone. The Stock Exchange had continuous trading. "Posts"—places where the last-sale prices of a stock were shown and where those interested in it might gather—were being set up. And the 30-60-90 day delivery system was almost dead.

The new system provided for four ways of trading:

1. There were deals for cash, which in those days probably meant cash on the spot, with immediate delivery of the securities involved. Today a cash sale before 2 P.M. must be settled by 2:30 of the same day; later deals within thirty minutes.

2. "Regular way" then meant that contracts must be settled by 2:15 P.M. of the following day. It meant this from 1817 until well into the 1930s. Then deliveries began to stretch out. They must now be made by the fourth business day after the sale, before noon.

3. and 4. Buyer's option and seller's option contracts were allowed and the latter are still extant. These permit the seller to deliver (and require the buyer to pay) at any time between five business days and sixty calendar days, as agreed, after the transaction. Buyer's option contracts, no longer permitted, would be the reverse of that. Under them, a buyer might wait until he had the cash ready and then ask for the securities to be delivered.

Naturally each delivery method can and generally does command a different price. What happened in the New York Stock Exchange was that most operators wanted to trade "regular way," so the market for that method became the best. This is true today, and other delivery methods usually crop up only at year ends, when special deals for income-tax purposes are being arranged.

In 1870, according to J. K. Medbery's *Men and Mysteries of Wall Street* (Boston: Fields, Osgood & Co., 1870), the regular list on the Stock Exchange contained 278 securities. Western Union was a great favorite. Others were Pacific Mail Steamship, Panama

Railroad, New York Central, Erie, Union Pacific, St. Paul, Toledo and Wabash and Rock Island.

Those were the years when the ticker was being introduced, when seats (memberships) were being made salable, when listing rules for securities were being applied for the first time. In 1878 telephones would begin to link brokerage houses and the floor of the Exchange. But the biggest change of all came in 1875, when a broker named Boyd broke his leg.

When Mr. Boyd returned to the Exchange floor he found his powers of locomotion sadly reduced. He could not dash madly from one trading post to the next, hoping to arrive in time to execute one of the orders he carried to buy or sell at this or that price. Under the old call-through system, a broker need never miss a market. If a customer had put in an order to buy 30 New York Central (the unit was 10 shares) at 73½ and the call-through had established a price of 74¼ at which trades were taking place, the broker might send off a smutty-faced little boy with a message for his customer: "Can buy at 74¼ or do you want to wait?" But with continuous trading the broker might be in another part of the floor when the desired price for Central was touched and abandoned.

Unable to get around, Mr. Boyd took a chair to the floor of the Exchange and announced that he would deal only in Western Union, then as popular as any other stock. If members wished to leave their "limit orders"—orders to buy or sell at fixed prices—with him, he would gladly execute them for a nominal charge.

This fee now ranges from $1.25 to $5 per 100 shares, depending upon the stock's price and is paid out of the commission the member firm receives from its customer. Incidentally, members who execute orders for other members on the floor are called "two-dollar brokers" because their fee used to be $2 for 100 shares.

Let us suppose that a firm such as Hemphill, Noyes & Co., which operates with a minimum of members on the floor, gets an order to buy New York Central at 19½ when the price is, say, 20. This order will be taken to a "specialist"—for that is what Mr. Boyd's successors are called—and left with him. When the price reaches 19½ he will execute the order and notify Hemphill, Noyes & Co.

About a quarter of all members of the New York Stock Exchange are specialists. In the course of a year they buy and sell for their own accounts, as dealers, about 15 per cent of all stocks bought and sold on the Exchange. If one includes all the shares they buy or sell as brokers for others, he finds that these 350 or 360 men have a finger in half the volume in stocks. Since the advent of Mr. Boyd and his chair, the Exchange has virtually delivered itself over to the specialist system.

On page 208 is an illustration (Chart XVII) of two facing pages from a specialist's book, a 4 x 11-inch affair specially made for the use of the calling. "Buy" orders are entered on the left side and "sell" orders on the right. All New York Stock Exchange specialists use such books, which they and their clerks keep in order. On the American Stock Exchange some specialists use books, and others tuck their order slips into the racks provided on the sides of the posts on the junior (but more modern) exchange.

The specialist has certain definite trading advantages. Orders have been left with him by other brokers. He may know, for example, of an order to sell 10,000 shares if a stock reaches 26, of another to buy 5,000 when it falls away to 24⅞. Because he "makes the market," he is able in normal times to guide it a little, to fail to hold it down when he is long of stock, to apply a tiny pressure on top when he has been obliged to sell stock that he did not own.

In return for these privileges, the Stock Exchange expects the specialist to maintain an orderly market. That means that he must "provide continuity of trading," narrowing the gaps between the last price and that of the next trade.

Suppose, for example, that the last trade, made at 43, exhausted all the stock at that or any other nearby price. The nearest bid is 100 shares at 39, the nearest offer 5,000 shares at 47. The Stock Exchange would not like today's Mr. Boyd to quote a market of 39 bid 47 asked. In fact, he must get special permission from a governor of the Exchange if he wants to make a trade at a price as much as 2 points away from the last sale. In this example, Mr. Boyd must be on both sides of the market; that is, both the bid-side and the offer-side must be his when someone asks for "the market."

What will he quote? A lot will depend on his own position—he may be long or short a good many shares—and on his opinion of the future. He can quote a "quarter-market" or a "half-market" or a "point-market" above or below or straddling the last sale. He may even open the gap wider. Always, however, he will be conscious that the governors of the Exchange have in their gift the assigning of stocks to specialists. Governors want close markets, with real continuity between prices.

This is the specialist's book in Safeway Stores as it might have looked one day in the fall of 1958. The abbreviations, of course, are the names of firms. It is easy to spot CML as Carl M. Loeb, Rhoades & Co., B as Bache & Co., DW as Dean Witter & Co., LFR as L. F. Rothschild & Co. and DOM as Dominick & Dominick. The numbers to the left of the abbreviations stand for hundreds of shares and where there is a total too big for the eye to add quickly it is written in.

This example of a specialist's book was prepared by James Crane Kellogg III, former chairman of the New York Stock Exchange and senior partner of Spear, Leeds & Kellogg. At the moment at which we catch our glimpse of the book, the market is 33¾ bid, 33⅞ asked and the "size" is 2,500 on the bid side, 2,400 on the asked side. In other words, if a broker came in with 2,500 shares to sell "at the market"—which means at the best price available—the book could take it all without the specialist's doing any buying of his own.

A "market order" to buy 3,000 shares would "clean up the book" at 33⅞ and take some of the stock waiting to be sold at 34. That, we can see, would touch off a "stop order" to buy 1,000 shares, another to buy 200 shares, in the event that the price of Safeway got as high as 34. We presume that these are speculators who went short of the stock and want to limit their losses.

What is the meaning of the 200-share "stop" at 34, with the "limit" at 34¼? This is an attempt by somebody to make sure that he buys this stock and liquidates his short position. In other words, when stock is sold as high as 34, the "stop" is activated. When that happens, the speculator wants to insure that his order will be executed first. Instead of having a bid of 34 in the market, his "limit" makes the bid 34¼ or less. This improves his chances.

There is another unusual order, this on the sell side, where Bache & Co. would sell at 34 or at 33⅝ "stop." Somebody wants to have it both ways, without the need to enter another order. Then, at 34½ on the "sell" side, there is the McK (Thomson & McKinnon) order to sell "stop limit." The sale can be made only at this price.

See page 208 for example of specialist's book.

CHART XVII

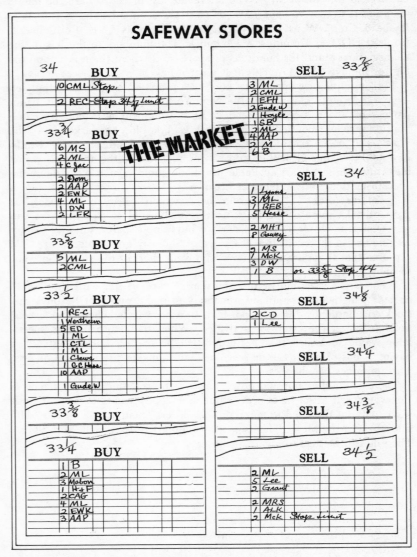

Courtesy of Spear, Leeds & Kellogg, New York

When Ford Motors was going on the Big Board for the first time, the governors labored long over the problem of assigning a specialist firm. It had to be a firm with plenty of resources. That narrowed the field down to twelve or fifteen. It had to be a firm with members who both could and would make a good, tight market. That narrowed the field to five. Finally, almost on the toss of a coin, the choice went to M. J. Meehan & Co. In July 1958, Ford cut its dividend and the price broke 2⅝ in a couple of hours. The Meehan firm justified its choice by Ford. At no time did the stock drop more than ⅛ between sales. The specialists were forced to take 9,000 shares. On the next two market days the stock rose.

More important, perhaps, than continuity of trading is the compulsion the specialist feels to keep the stock active and interesting. There are plenty of dead stocks on the New York Stock Exchange— those that trade fewer than 1,000 shares a week, as you can verify from your Sunday newspaper—and nobody enjoys owning them or being a specialist in them. If the specialist is ready to buy when anybody wants to sell and sell when anybody wants to buy he may be able to create an appearance of activity in his stock.

Specialists at the eighteen posts where active stocks are traded— 200 to 250 inactive stocks are traded at Post 30 by two specialists, in 10-share units—are required to be able to buy 400 shares of each stock in which they specialize. Most specialists are banded together in firms, a couple of which handle fifty stocks each. Individual specialists commonly work in joint-account arrangements with others, so that if they are ill or take a vacation the entire market will not be upset. At the high prices of recent years, the average specialist seems to need, as minimum, between $60,000 and $80,000 of capital, in addition to his membership on the New York Stock Exchange. This membership, which has varied in value from $4,000 to $625,000 since 1868, sold at $205,000 in mid-1963 and hit a recent low of $115,000 after the 1962 market break.

Does the average specialist have this kind of money? In a few cases, yes. In most, no. He raises it, plus a good deal more, by what are called subordinated loans. In other words, the lender's claim is subordinated to (comes after) claims of any security-market creditor of the specialist. Lenders are willing because, if they lend cash, they get 8 per cent interest—this is the maximum, but it also seems to act as a minimum in most cases—and "may share in organization profits to a reasonable extent," provided they belong to the firm or family of the borrower. They get the interest even if they are outsiders.

There is also a way in which a brokerage house customer may pledge the equities in his brokerage account to finance a specialist. The customer would continue to get the yield from stocks or bonds but in addition would be paid 4 per cent of their value as interest. However, such borrowings against customers' securities may not constitute more than a quarter of the specialist firm's capital, and that stricture does not hold against subordinated loans made in cash.

Specialists, naturally, do not like to take unnecessary risks. If a firm has twenty stocks, its members will try to be long of ten and short of ten. That is, if they have to sell stock they do not have in order to provide a continuous market, they will borrow it. But they will manage some other account so that they accumulate stock. Then the profits or losses from a general lunge upward or downward in the market will wipe each other out, theoretically, at least.

According to *The Stock Market* (New York: Ronald Press, 1957), in which George L. Leffler gives the best current description of practices, functions and rules, New York Stock Exchange specialists on September 23, 1955, had an aggregate inventory of 1,651,000 shares worth almost $50,000,000. That was a Friday. The next day President Eisenhower had his heart attack. When the market opened on Monday, September 26, there was a great wave of selling. To keep prices from dropping through the cellar, the specialists personally bought 23 per cent of the stock offered. At the end of the day they had accumulated 1,099,000 shares more at a cost of $49,100,000 and, by buying, had been forced to close out almost their entire short position.

The average specialist at the close of that 7,716,650-share day was holding about $280,000 worth of stock. All specialists together held about $100,000,000 worth. The aggregate was just a bit more than $\frac{1}{20}$ of 1 per cent of the value of all stocks listed on the New York Stock Exchange.

It was a frail prop but it did the job. On Tuesday, as specialists dared to breathe once more—for they couldn't have absorbed many more shares—the market recovered. After a rocky October, it continued its climb and all the specialists were off the hook before November was half ended.

In the first edition of this book, I asked the question: "What would have happened if the market had continued its slide on Tuesday?" and theorized on the situation as it might have affected a single imaginary stock. We now have something of an answer, for on another Tuesday, May 29, 1962, the market *did* prolong the slide begun on Monday. A midday turn-around in prices, however, prevented disaster.

It seems that the "heart-attack market" was a dress rehearsal for the May 1962 break, but there has been a sharp difference of opinion regarding the role of the specialist as a stabilizer in 1962. The New York Stock Exchange, in its own study of the break, makes a hero of the specialist. The Securities and Exchange Commission's study, released in 1963, insists that the trading of some specialists in certain key stocks (notably A.T.&T., I.B.M. and Korvette) "tended to be passive at best and possibly destabilizing in nature." Granting that specialists' activities in the "heart-attack market" "probably had a discernible market impact," the S.E.C.'s study group stated, "the same cannot be said of May 28, 1962."

On that day, the Exchange reports, specialists bought and sold 3,093,220 shares and had a net purchase balance of 206,400 shares. (Compare this with the 1,099,000 shares they bought in the "heart-attack market.") This is 6.7 per cent of their total purchases and sales—not significantly above the percentage figure in normal periods, the S.E.C. study notes.

The Exchange insists: "The degree to which specialists' purchases and sales for their own accounts tend to maintain price continuity normally is extremely high. It is noteworthy that the effectiveness of specialists' over-all performance in this regard was even greater than usual in the May 28-31 market, despite the handicap of unusually difficult operating conditions:

"1. STABILIZATION—About 93 per cent of all specialists' transactions were purchased at declining prices or sales at rising prices. This compared with a stabilization ratio of about 83 per cent for all of 1962.

"2. CONTINUITY—87 per cent of all transactions in 50 stock issues selected for detailed analysis were made at price variations of a quarter-point, and eighth-point or no change at all from the previous transaction—compared with about 86 per cent for all issues studied in 1962."

Regarding the above, the S.E.C. study retorts: "As a public relations matter the Exchange has sought to project the image of the specialist as a stabilizer, but the problems in this area are too deep for any confusion to exist in the public mind between the specialist's basic function of maintaining price continuity and market stabilization." The study group found that the Exchange's test of stabilization, based on an analysis of particular sales in relation to the sales which immediately preceded them, was inadequate because it took little account of long-range trends. While some specialists on May 28 did undertake to "cushion the public's selling by giving depth to the markets, [others] confined their activity to providing technical price continuity and a few specialists seemed to contribute to the 'pounding' down of prices by their selling."

Observing that some specialists seemed to lack enough capital to deal with large blocks of stock put on the market, the study recommended that each specialist should be required to have "capital ability to carry at least 1,200 shares and preferably a higher amount such as 2,000 shares" in each stock in which he is registered.

The S.E.C. study group also wanted the Stock Exchange to tighten its surveillance over specialists, to eliminate conflict of interest between their function as brokers for other brokers and dealers for their own accounts. "In the last twenty-five years," said the report, "the specialist's dealer function has become as important as, if not more important than, the brokerage function. . . . The conflicts of interest inherent in any simultaneous combination of dealer and broker function have been intensified."

Whatever the eventual fate of the specialist, whatever the additional regulations that may be imposed upon him, we can still get a good idea how a typical specialist will function in a "selling climax."

If a shock comes after the market for a stock has opened, there is seldom much of a problem. After the opening, orders on a specialist's book have priorities. They don't all hit him at once. If the man has done his best to support a stock and asking him to do much more would be unreasonable, Exchange governors will permit him to let the price break a point or two or three between sales. That may bring in bargain-hunters eventually and check the declines.

The big problem is in opening markets, for thousands of orders—virtually all to buy or all to sell, depending on the news—pile into the market at one time, and at the opening there are no priorities.

Your frightened order to sell 100 shares "at the market" ranks evenly with every other "market" order, no matter how big or important the seller.

At the start of World War I, the Exchange closed down for some months. Since then it has adopted the idea that it must open what stocks it can. The others will remain unopened until they find new market levels.

We shall examine the situation as it affects a single imaginary stock, POW, and from the viewpoint of the imaginary specialist firm that handles it, Joshua Murray & Relatives. Yesterday the whole market dropped about 7 per cent and POW declined from 66 to 60 despite the purchase of 15,000 shares by Murray at a cost of about $950,000. (Three or four important stocks were supported by their specialists on September 26, 1955, to the extent of more than $1,000,000.)

Today the news is still bad. Orders to sell have been accumulating overnight in the brokerage houses. Now, before the opening, Murray, his partners and his clerks are adding them up. Perhaps the Stock Exchange is also lending a clerk or two, for this is one of the key stocks.

Open market orders to sell aggregate 45,000 shares. There are open market orders to buy, but only for 5,000 shares. The book in POW, thanks to cancellations, shows 300 shares to buy at 59, 700 to buy at 58 and 4,000 at 55. After that, nothing. The specialist firm could open the stock at 55 only if it were able itself to buy 35,000 shares. This it cannot do.

There are a half-dozen firms in Wall Street that have active trading desks. They are ordinarily quite happy to pick up stocks at unusual prices. Murray or one of the Exchange governors concerned in the opening starts making calls to Goldman, Sachs & Co., Bear, Stearns Co., J. & W. Seligman, Wertheim & Co., Blyth & Co., Carl M. Loeb, Rhoades & Co., Lehman Brothers and the others. But there are dozens of other specialists in the same kind of trouble and even such resources have a limit. In the end, the combined trading desks have pledged themselves to take only 15,000 shares, at 55 or less.

Now—and by this time some stocks have opened and to take a measure of the collapse seems possible—brokers of the commission houses who brought in the mass of selling orders are notified that the opening will have to be below 55 and possibly as low as 50.

Do any of their customers want to cancel? A few cancellations come in; not enough. The situation is advertised on the tape. This, and a worsening in the general market, bring in more sell orders. The day rolls by and the stock doesn't open. At one time it might have opened if Joshua Murray & Relatives had been able to buy 10,000 more shares at 50, but they weren't.

While POW and a dozen other key issues have been having these troubles and the market as a whole has been losing ground, leaders in finance and government have been discussing remedies. Everybody makes statements to the effect that business is sound and the newspapers print a lot of them. Some of the banks form a consortium or pool to buy stock or lend more money to the already overextended specialists.

After the close of the market, New York Stock Exchange members are allowed to trade in its listed stocks in the over-the-counter market. Some of their customers are actually desperate to get out of POW. There is no question of priority of orders now. The question is to find a buyer. Here is a man who will take 1,000 shares at 40, another who will bid 39 for 5,000. Gradually, as the phone calls multiply, a price is set and becomes part of the consciousness of Wall Street before the market opens the following day. Let us say it is 46, down 20 points since the market break began.

Perhaps POW can open on that next day. Perhaps it will have to wait. Sooner or later, of course, the market will rally. It always has. There will be more public buyers than sellers and the price will rise. Murray will have to supply some stock "to provide continuity of market" but he will not be any more generous than he has to be. After all, if he sold all his 15,000 shares between 46 and 52½ he'd probably lose about $150,000. But if he can work slowly, he can get back much of his apparent loss even though POW never does return to 66.

This is how it works: At 46 he seems to have lost $260,000. Now, as the market rises to 52, he sells 60,000 shares at an average of 50. The market falls to 48 and he buys 60,000 shares at an average of 49. His loss has been cut to $170,000.

This chapter has borne two main messages for the investor: The market is thin and sensitive, and too large a structure has been reared on the frail capital of the specialist; it can break sharply and unexpectedly. Therefore it is not wise to commit yourself in such a way that you can be *forced* to sell too much too quickly in such a market.

Play within your means.

Also, a sharp drop in the market does not mean the end of the world. There are always rallies. Try not to panic. Between the market peak on September 4, 1929, and the year's low on November 13, industrial prices fell 44 per cent. Of the 55 trading days, however, 22 showed gains.

Between the 1937 peak on March 6 and the year's low on November 24 industrial stock prices fell 47 per cent. Of the 216 business days, 98 showed gains.

The time to sell is when stocks are rising.

QUESTIONS FOR REVIEW

1. Why do we say the present stock market is "thin" compared to that of 1901 or 1928?
2. Can the "market break" of May 28, 1962, properly be compared to that of October 29, 1929? Why?
3. What is a specialist?
4. What does a stock exchange expect of its specialists?

CHAPTER XVIII

There *Are* Things You Can Do About Taxes

It is all very well for me to say, as I did in an early chapter, that 90 per cent of my readers should concentrate on profits rather than on taxes. There is still something to be said for knowing something about taxes.

Example A: You bought 100 shares of Slythy Toves, Ltd., at 10.

Now, three months later, you can sell with a profit, after all commissions, taxes and fees, of $400. The market looks queasy. You're afraid of it. And you're only in the 30 per cent income-tax bracket.

If you sell now, you will have a short-term capital gain and your tax will be, at your ordinary tax rate, 30 per cent of the profit of $400, or $120. You will have $280 of the profit left.

If you waited until the six-month holding period was up, you would pay a long-term capital-gains tax at half your ordinary rate, in this case, 15 per cent, or $60. That would leave you with $340.

But if the stock should drop only ¾ of a point, you would make less at long-term than at short-term.

Example B: We have the same situation, a $400 profit after three months, but now you are in the 85 per cent bracket. If you take your profit now, with the ordinary income rates applying, you will have an after-tax profit of only $60. Not unless the stock drops by 3¼ points will you do as poorly at long-term capital gains, taxed at the maximum of 25 per cent.

For some years I have been writing a great deal about taxes but I have done so only as a reporter, not as an authority. Dozens of accountants and lawyers have called my attention to legislation, decisions and interpretations, have held my hand or my brow while I wrote the stuff and have painstakingly gone over the stories before they achieved publication. Those who have been most helpful—because they have seemed to sense what makes a good newspaper story—have been J. S. Seidman of Seidman & Seidman, Henry Oppenheim and Arthur J. Dixon of Oppenheim, Appel, Payson & Co., William J. Casey and John D. Cunnion of Business Reports, Inc., and V. Henry Rothschild. Mr. Rothschild and Mr. Casey are lawyers, the others accountants.

All of what follows I have written about before, but with Arthur Dixon's permission I am here following the general outline of his paper "Taxation of Securities Transactions," delivered before the 1958 Tulane University Tax Institute. Mr. Dixon, Mr. Seidman and Mr. Oppenheim have helped me to bring it up to date, including the applicable parts of the "Technical Amendments Act of 1958."

It might help us to recall to mind how capital-gains taxes are figured. First we add long-term capital gains (on deals that took more than six months to complete) to long-term capital losses. We get a net figure that is either plus or minus. Let us say that you, in the 30 per cent bracket, have a long-term capital gain of $1,200 and a long-term capital loss of $1,000. Your net long-term capital gain is $200.

Now you do the same with a $900 short-term capital gain and a $1,000 short-term capital loss. The net figure is minus $100, which you subtract from your $200 long-term capital gain. You end up by paying your 15 per cent tax on $100. This is half your regular rate.

This, of course, is what you have been doing year after year. There is nothing new about it. There is nothing new about it because you are thinking in 1964 about figuring the tax for deals in 1963, or you are thinking in 1965 about filling out the return for 1964. That is the wrong time to do the thinking.

You can do yourself a great deal of good by looking over your securities before the end of each year, I'd say in October, before the usual tax selling commences. But let us say the time is December in this example:

A.	You have already taken a long-term gain of	$1,200
B.	You have a short-term paper gain of	$1,200
C.	You have a long-term paper loss of	$1,200

If you close out Deals B and C this year, what happens? C wipes out A and leaves you with B, the short-term gain. On this you pay at your ordinary income-tax rates. Say you are in the 30 per cent bracket. It costs you $360.

Let us try it another way. You wait until January (next year) with B and C. Then they will wipe each other out. That leaves you with the long-term gain you've already taken. The tax on that is $180, still assuming that your next dollar of income will be taxed at 30 per cent.

The rule here is simple: *If you can avoid it, don't use any loss to reduce a long-term gain.* Save the loss. It will be more valuable if used to offset a short-term gain. All you risk is the chance that you may never again have a short-term gain. This could happen if you died.

Before we go on to more complicated matters, let us note a few matters that occasionally evade the memory:

If you end up with a net capital loss, you may deduct up to $1,000 of it from the ordinary income of the year in which the loss was incurred and in each of the next five years. But in the carry-over period the loss must be applied first to offset capital gains.

If you buy on a Stock Exchange, your minimum holding period to qualify for long-term capital gains starts *on the contract date* and ends *six months and one day later.*

Most of us are "cash basis" taxpayers, that is, we don't figure accrued income or obligations when we make out our tax returns. If you, a "cash basis" taxpayer, sell stock in one year that will not be delivered until the following year—due to the fact that regular-way deliveries now take place in four business days—you have a strange rule. Any loss may be deducted this year but any profit is not taxable until next year.

If you have a long-term gain and have decided to sell the stock, never wait for one more dividend. *Sell just before the ex-dividend date, not just after it.* Why? Because ordinary dividends are taxed at the full rate for ordinary income. Ordinarily, the amount of the dividend is included in the price just before it is paid. Why not pay taxes on the dividend at long-term capital gain rates?

You have 100 shares of Steel bought in January and another 100 shares bought in April. Neither lot has been transferred into your name. You have left them in the custody of your broker. If you decide to sell 100 shares in August, make sure you write your broker a letter—and keep a copy—telling him which lot to sell. Ordinarily, the Internal Revenue Service would rule first-in-first-out but that may not be the way you want it. You might have a long-term gain on the first lot and a short-term loss on the second. Write your broker: "Sell the Steel I bought April 3," and get a written acknowledgment.

You have a big gain in Hullabaloo Oil but are afraid that the market is going to go all to pieces. Moreover, you do not want to take your gain in it this year. You protect yourself by going short in Hullabaloo—if your gain is already a long-term gain—or in a substantially similar oil—if your gain is still short-term. Then, if the market falls, you will lose on your Hullabaloo but make on your short sale. The law says that a short sale does not exist for tax purposes until it is closed out. That can be next year.

With substantially identical securities and the market in a highly volatile and nervous condition, you might go short of one and long of the other. Then, depending on how they moved, you could close out one this year and the other next year. If your gain came on the short side, both plays would be for short term. If your gain came on the long side, you might let that one run for six months and one day after you close the short sale.

You are not allowed to turn a short-term gain into a long-term gain by making a short sale in the same security and so "freezing" the gain until the holding period has stretched to six months and a day. That is why, above, I stipulated "substantially similar" stocks.

The Internal Revenue Service has ruled that, if a taxpayer has a short position in a stock and a dividend is paid on it, the so-called "short dividend" is an ordinary deduction. Out of this ruling has come a flock of ingenious tax-saving schemes. Unfortunately for my average reader—the man in the 30 per cent bracket—they are of far more value to the big fellows than they are to him.

We start out by assuming that your ordinary net taxable income is $12,000, on which your tax will be $2,720.

In addition, here near the end of a year, you find yourself with a net long-term capital gain of $1,500 and a net short-term capital loss of $1,300. Do you remember that I suggested above that a net short-term loss should not, if avoidable, be used to wipe out a net long-term gain? If you do it in this case, you will be left with a net long-term gain of $200 on which you, a 30 per cent bracket man, will pay $30. Your whole tax bill will be $2,750.

Now you pick out a stock selling for, say, somewhere between $50 and $70 a share that is about to declare a dividend of, say, $5 a share. You go short of 300 shares. After taxes, fees and a round-trip commission—it no longer saves money to close out a deal in fourteen days or fewer—this might net you a short-term capital gain of $1,300. We assume that the stock will fall by about the amount of the dividend. That short-term gain will wipe out the short-term loss you started with. Then will the "short dividend" of $1,500 wipe out the long-term capital gain you had at the beginning? No, fortunately. The short dividend *is subtracted from the ordinary income* on which you pay taxes at your full rate. The long-term gain is taxed at half that rate.

We'll suppose you were lucky and that the drop in the stock was at least as large as the dividend. Then you'd come out of this enterprise with a profit of $25 to $50. If, however, you were in the 78 per cent bracket and the amounts involved (other than taxes) were multiplied by 10, you'd increase your take-home pay by $6,000, actually more than 11 per cent.

Until about a decade ago the New York Stock Exchange would let you sell short "for cash" right after an ex-dividend date and simultaneously cover "regular way," so that you knew what your profit would be. Now that is not allowed. You have to take the risks of the market.

There used to be a wonderful way of turning a short-term capital gain into a long-term gain that worked just the opposite of the deal described above. Congress in 1958 put a crimp in it. I believe it can still be made to work but the risk is a bit greater.

In former days a man who had a short-term capital gain might turn it into a long-term capital gain by "buying the dividend" of a regulated investment trust. A capital-gain dividend—that is, a dividend declared from the trading profits of such a trust—is considered a long-term capital gain for the recipient. So our man with, let us say, a short-term capital gain of $1,300 might buy $1,500 of such long-term capital-gain dividends. This would be another of those simultaneous deals, buying the stock "dividend-on" and selling it "ex-dividend." The stock without the dividend would ordinarily drop by the amount of the dividend. There would have been no market risk for the 1956 or 1957 investor.

Now, however, he must take such a market risk by holding the investment trust stock for thirty-one days. Because of commissions, fees and taxes, his short-term capital loss on the deal will be $1,700. This will leave him with a net short-term capital loss of $400, to be applied against his long-term capital gain (from the dividend) of $1,500. In the 30 per cent bracket our man actually comes out with a profit of only $25. In the 78 per cent bracket the deal would increase his take-home pay from $286 to $825—*if* the market didn't move against him.

I could write a good deal more about this subject but it doesn't seem worth while. As you can see, most of the more amusing gimmicks are designed for the heavy-money taxpayer, not for my average reader. Again, Congress has almost *got* to stop flinching from the job of a thorough tax reorganization. The Kennedy-Johnson Administration's new tax law will probably be in effect for returns on 1964 income.* And, of course, I prefer to write for the ages.

* As this book goes to press, the new tax law is already in effect.

The Sophisticated Investor prepares for this year's tax return this year, not next April 15.

QUESTIONS FOR REVIEW

1. When should you try to avoid using any loss, long-term or short-term, to reduce a long-term capital gain?
2. Why should you sell just before the ex-dividend date when taking a long-term capital gain in a stock?
3. When does a short sale become taxable?

CHAPTER XIX

A Final Word to the Wise

CRANE'S LAW OF MARKETS and J. P. Morgan's Law of Stocks—"They will fluctuate"—are possibly the only consistently infallible laws in this field of human activity. Crane's Law of Markets reads:

> *Sooner or later you will hear somebody say just what you've been saying about the market. Since you will know that the opinionated onionhead hasn't been right since nine months before he was born, you will go and do the opposite.*

This is why markets go up just when everybody seems to have agreed that they've got to go down.

In other words, the dynamics of the market are constantly changing. People do different things for the same reasons or the same things for different reasons. Sometimes the reasons are economic; more often they are psychological.

You can be sure of a lot of things but you can't be *damn* sure.

We saw one abrupt change in market dynamics take place in June 1958. Congress had been gaily voting to spend more money than the administration wanted, and had been doing nothing about higher taxes. It assumed that the money would be borrowed. Stock-market people, trying to keep the recovery boom going, filled the air with loose talk about the coming inflation, just as if the United States were going to go chasing after the Russia and Germany of the Twenties or the Japan and China of the Forties.

This alarmist chatter proved highly embarrassing to the Treasury Department, which had been slinking around corners whenever anyone mentioned long-term financing of the Federal debt. (In 1956 it had refinanced $67 billions of maturing obligations with short-term stuff. Out of $68.5 billions of marketable debt refinanced in 1957, only one billion was in long-term bonds.)

Just when the market analysts were beginning to comment on the speed of the apparent business recovery and were remarking that the Federal Reserve Board would shortly be raising money rates to keep the incipient boom from going too far, the Treasury came out with a bundle of long-term obligations. The Treasury-bond market had its most abrupt collapse on record.

It is obviously good sense to buy bonds when the Federal Reserve Banks start lowering interest rates. It is just as obviously bad sense to buy them at any time when, two or three or four months hence, the Fed is certain to start raising money rates and lowering the prices of outstanding bonds.

There will be other changes in market dynamics and some of them may invalidate temporarily some of the things I have said in these chapters. For example, the imposition of an excess-profits tax would play hob once more with the relative earning powers and market values of stocks.

Again, we'd see some changes made if Congress restored to the Federal Reserve System its former control over installment and mortgage credit or—as I heartily recommend—gave it new powers to turn certain taxes and depreciation allowances on and off. The time has come when we must recognize that mere controls over the bulk of credit and money are not delicate enough for our economic system. The moves of our central bankers should not be as easy to forecast as I showed them to be in the first three chapters.

Here are some of the things that *might* happen, things you should keep in mind and give the good, searching, long view if they appear:

Really cheap thermofusion as a source of power for electric generating might play hob with the coal and natural-gas companies.

A couple of big cities might go "on strike" against the ever-bigger automobiles, refusing to allow the two-lane car street room. That would mean a big cut in gasoline consumption and, by chopping the resale value of the used car, would reduce new car purchases.

Our failure to conserve natural resources—we actually subsidize their waste—is making us more and more dependent on foreign supplies. Think what a Communist *coup d'état* might do.

The next *big* move on the national economic front may, as Armand Erpf suggests, include 4,000,000 to 5,000,000 unemployed in the formula for "full employment." I think we realize by now that we cannot come within 3 per cent of actual full employment without having inflation. The sloppier definition of "full employment" would remove the pressure on wages and prices. That would be deflationary. So would the higher taxes to take care of our new army of jobless. I am not advocating this, but I think you should be warned that it may turn up.

So much for the changing dynamics of the market. The time has come for a summary. What have I said? Here are some high points:

There are ways to profit when the economy is turning downward, because government actions can be anticipated. Put some of your money in Treasury bonds at small margins. Put more of it into "sure-dividend" stocks, also on margin.

If you are the average reader of this book, be mighty easy to scare when you have a profit. In other words, don't hang around waiting out the six-month holding period so you can get a long-term capital gain and pay a lower tax. If you are my average reader, you can get out whenever you feel queasy, for you are in or below the 30 per cent income-tax bracket.

Play the market like a professional. Cut your losses and let your profits run.

Buy stocks when they are making new highs and attracting attention, not when they are down at the bottom and nobody loves them.

Never buy on the news that a stock is to be split or pay a big dividend or that a company is to merge or has received a big contract— unless you can see from the past action of the stock that this news was completely unexpected by the investing public. Generally the only time you can make money on such news is to buy long before the rumor is confirmed.

If you are trading, follow a trend until you can see for sure that it has reversed itself. Then run like a thief.

On the long side or the short side, don't get aboard a stock that isn't moving. Wait until somebody else has started it; then hop aboard.

Most stocks aren't any better than the market in which they trade. Now and again, however, you will find a stock that can run against its market. It is not too hard to discover these after they have moved up for quite a way; you can see them making new highs while the rest of the market is going down. Your problem is to learn to analyze their prospects so that you can decide whether there is any profit left in them.

Most of the so-called signals given by too-high price-earnings ratios and too-low yields should do nothing more than put you on your toes. The biggest gains seem to come *after* these two indicators have gone noticeably out of line.

There are ways to test the "growth" in growth stocks and if it isn't as much as 12 per cent a year they are not the stocks to put away and forget. Most so-called "growth stocks" are too thoroughly wedded to the business cycle or already on the way down.

There are certain stocks in which "growth" is induced by company policy. Perhaps a company with a big tax-loss credit is absorbed so that the first company's profits, for a time, become tax-free. Or perhaps good earners with low price-earnings ratios are acquired, so that the new earnings will have a bigger market value. Keep your eyes open for this kind of opportunity. Men in the upper income-tax brackets like such companies and bid them up.

Operating with a fraction of your money (this kind of thing is naturally a bit risky) look for ways of increasing your leverage in such situations as I have described in the paragraph above. Perhaps there is a convertible debenture on which you can get better than the regular Stock Exchange margin. Perhaps you can pick up a warrant at an attractive price. And always remember the Square-Root Rule: The cheaper the stock the faster its percentage gain— or loss.

Well, that's the story. Now, if you'll excuse me, I'll get back to my telephoning.

Maybe somebody downtown has a good tip!

QUESTION FOR REVIEW

1. Cite J. P. Morgan's Law of Stocks.

Glossary

Dear Barbara Brythwyte: *If you are truly a beginner, I suggest that you read the following definitions before you tackle Chapter I:* STOCKS, PREFERRED STOCK, BONDS, YIELD, EARNINGS REPORT, CAPITAL GAINS, MARGIN, BALANCE SHEET.

If I use a term that puzzles you and you cannot find it in the Glossary, turn to the Index. The definition may be in the main text up forward or buried inside the definition of another term here in the Glossary. Words defined are listed in SMALL CAPITALS *in the Index.*

Good luck!

ARBITRAGE: Buying and selling the same security simultaneously in different markets, or buying and selling equivalent securities simultaneously. If a bond convertible into 40 shares of stock can be bought for $1,000 while the stock can be sold for $27 a share, you have a deal. This is described at length in Chapter 12, starting on page 155.

AT THE MARKET: This phrase distinguishes an order that is to be executed at the best possible price from an order that can be executed only at a designated price. When markets are thin, or stocks inactive, investors are well advised to use the "limit order" (see page 232).

You hear that a stock is 38 bid, 38⅝ asked. You put in an order "at the market" to buy. Before your order can reach the floor, two more orders are executed and you find yourself paying 39. This was more than you wanted to pay. If, however, you had bid 38⅛ or 38¼, you might have bought the stock before the day was over. If you didn't get it after a reasonable time, you could raise your bid.

AVERAGES: Once upon a time Dow, Jones & Co. added up the prices of five representative stocks and divided the total by 5. This was the first market average that ever made a dent in investing consciousness in this country.

This average was expanded several times. Others—notably *The New York Times,* New York *Herald Tribune* and Associated Press averages—were started, and various devices were worked out for making adjustments when stocks were split. Mathematicians can find things wrong with all four of these averages but the ordinary investor continues to watch them. Most "systems" of playing the market use the Dow-Jones average of thirty industrial stocks.

BLUE CHIP: Jacques Coe of Jacques Coe & Co. defines a blue chip as "a stock priced so high and yielding so little that it is not worth owning." Actually, the word has no exact meaning. It is used as a label to help sell stocks.

Theoretically, it should mean a stock of such assured position that its dividend is safe and its future growth is assured. It should mean a stock so well established that no trustee could be criticized for buying it (even if it *did* immediately lose half its market value). If you insist on using the term, I suggest you understand it to mean those of the 120 stocks most popular with the investment companies that are not too closely bound to the business cycle.

BALANCE SHEET: Accountants show the condition of a company by *balancing* its assets on one side against its capital and liabilities on the other. ASSETS are what a company holds. LIABILITIES are what it owes or must pay. Its CAPITAL or NET ASSET figure is obtained by subtracting liabilities from assets. A balance sheet might look like this:

Assets

Quick or Current Assets		$ 280,000
Cash	$ 20,000	
Tax anticipation notes	30,000	
Accounts receivable (sums owed us)	50,000	
Inventories of raw materials	60,000	
Inventories of finished goods	120,000	
Fixed Assets		550,000
Land	50,000	
Buildings (less depreciation)	200,000	
Machinery and equipment (less depreciation)	300,000	
Investments		169,999
Goodwill		1
Total Assets		$1,000,000

Liabilities

Current Liabilities		$ 140,000
Bills payable (owed for supplies and services)	$ 40,000	
Accrued taxes	30,000	
Owed to banks	70,000	
Long-term Debt (mortgage on plant)		300,000
Capital Account		560,000
Preferred stock (4,000 shares of $50 par value each)	200,000	
Common stock (10,000 shares of $20 par value each)	200,000	
Earned Surplus	160,000	
Total Liabilities		$1,000,000

BID-AND-ASKED: When you are buying or selling a security, your first step is to "ask the market." What is being bid for the stock? What is being asked? You ask your broker to get you the current "bid-and-asked." By dialing a number on a special telephone instrument he can receive the current bid-and-asked quotations of any New York Stock Exchange or American Stock Exchange stock. At the end of the day, if a stock has not traded, newspapers collect and print the bid-and-asked quotations.

In the securities market that exists off the registered exchanges there is no way of telling which was the last sale, so the newspapers print the bid-and-asked quotations as a guide to investors.

BONDS: A bond is merely an evidence of debt, an IOU issued by a governmental body or a corporation. It promises to pay rent (INTEREST) for the money, generally twice a year. It promises to pay back the face amount (PRINCIPAL) at the end of a certain period. Sometimes the contract under which it is issued (the INDENTURE) promises that a certain amount will be set aside each year or on each interest date for the purchase of these bonds in the open market or by calling them in by lot. These amounts are called a sinking fund.

There are many kinds of bonds.

DEBENTURES or DEBENTURE BONDS, like the bonds of governmental bodies, are secured by the general credit of the borrower. The interest on MUNICIPAL BONDS, those issued by states, cities and other taxing authorities within the states, is exempt from Federal income taxes, but capital gains realized on such bonds are not exempt.

Some bonds are secured by mortgages on particular properties, some by mortgages on all of a company's property (GENERAL MORTGAGE BONDS), some by liens on batches of the stocks and bonds of subsidiaries (COLLATERAL, TRUST BONDS). There are also INCOME BONDS, which only pay interest when it is earned and give the investor less protection than a cumulative preferred stock.

BOOK VALUE: Wall Street over the years has been paying less and less attention to book value of a stock; it is more interested in its earning power.

Assume a company with no capital stock other than common shares outstanding. You subtract all liabilities from all assets and then divide the remaining assets by the number of common shares. What you get is book value for each share.

Now assume a company with 1,000 preferred shares, each of which will be entitled to $110 if the company is ever liquidated. Assume 10,000 common shares. Now, if assets are $500,000 and liabilities are $170,000, we are left with NET ASSETS of $330,000. We subtract $110,000 for the preferred shares and are left with $220,000 for the common shares. Dividing that figure by the 10,000 common shares, we find ourselves with a book value of $22 a share.

CALL LOAN: A loan, made to finance the purchase of the securities, that may be called for payment at any time. For the most part, banks make such loans to brokers in units of $100,000. Brokers then lend to their customers in smaller pieces and at slightly higher interest rates.

CAPITAL GAINS: The Federal and state tax laws distinguish between two kinds of income: ordinary income and capital-gains income. If you earn money at your trade or profession or receive it as interest or dividends on investments, that is ordinary income. If you make money by buying something as an investment or a speculation and then selling it at a profit, that is a capital gain. (However, if your regular business is buying and selling things, the profits you make are considered ordinary income.)

There are two kinds of capital gains, according to our tax laws. A short-term capital gain is a profit made in not more than six months. It is taxed at the same rate as ordinary income. A long-term gain is a profit made after holding the asset for more than six months. It is taxed at half the rate you pay in taxes on ordinary income, up to a maximum of 25 per cent. You will find a full explanation in Chapter 18, starting on page 215.

CASH FLOW: This is a relatively new concept in securities markets. You will find it discussed at some length in Chapter 9, starting with page 101. Briefly, you add to the net income of a corporation all the amounts charged off but not necessarily paid out. Among these are bookkeeping items such as depreciation, depletion and special reserves. Cash flow gives a measure of the ability of a company to pay dividends and (after deducting for the dividends) its power to invest in expansion.

CASH SALE: "Regular way" deliveries on the New York Stock Exchange are made on the fourth business day after the transaction. Sometimes an investor wants to get possession of a security on the same day. Then he enters a cash sale.

Reasons for such a desire on his part are discussed on pages 219 and 220. See also Ex-DIVIDEND.

COLLATERAL: Property pledged to assure the repayment of a loan. It may be any property, but today we usually think of collateral as stocks and bonds.

COMMISSION: In the security markets, a commission is what a broker charges for buying or selling for another person. The stock commission rates on the New York Stock Exchange and the American Stock Exchange are set forth on page 186 of Chapter 15. Bond commission rates are mentioned on page 37 of Chapter 3. The commissions one broker charges another are on page 205 of Chapter 17.

CONVERTIBLE: An adjective used to describe a security that can be converted into—that is, exchanged for—another kind of security. Most generally, debentures, preferred stock or other senior kinds of stock can be converted into the most junior kind of stock. This is cagey language, isn't it? The reason is that the most junior kind of stock can be called capital stock, common stock, Class B common, ordinary shares and possibly one or two things more.

One company not too long ago got permission to make its Class B common, which paid no dividends, convertible into Class A common, which did. I believe that the Internal Revenue boys are not likely to grant any more permissions of this kind.

CORNER: Theoretically, a corner exists when so little stock is available that those who sold short "are forced to do business at an arbitrarily high price with those who engineered the corner." This comes from the New York Stock Exchange's own definition, but when Artloom was driven up from 3¾ to 27⅝ in spring and summer of 1958, the Exchange declined to rule that

a corner existed. The American Stock Exchange also dodged the issue when E. L. Bruce was forced from 16⅞ to 77 on the Exchange and then was traded over-the-counter at 192. These prices, it appears, were *not* arbitrarily high because there was evidence that *some* shares existed outside the groups that had done the main buying.

In practice, then, there is no such thing as a corner, because neither Exchange will enforce its rule against corners. If you sell short and the price is driven through the roof, you are on your own.

CUMULATIVE PREFERRED: If a stock labeled "cum pf" is unable to pay its dividend this time, the amount is added to what the company will owe on the next dividend date. The arrearages pile up if the company is not prosperous. Some day, the story goes, the company will make a lot of money and all those nice arrearages of dividends will be paid off. That is the theory. It seldom happens that way. Almost always the piled-up back dividends on the cumulative preferred stock—and often the preferred stock itself—are paid off with more shares of common stock.

CURRENT ASSETS AND LIABILITIES: The former are holdings that are either in cash or could presumably be turned into cash within a year. They include bills that other concerns owe the company, Treasury bills and notes (including tax anticipation notes) and inventories of crude and finished goods. Current liabilities are debts that must be paid within a year. They include bills payable, accrued taxes, bank loans and funded debt maturing within a year. See also BALANCE SHEET.

CUSTOMER'S BROKER or REGISTERED REPRESENTATIVE or CUSTOMER'S MAN: This is "your broker" nine times out of ten, for there are five or six times as many customer's brokers as there are office partners of New York Stock Exchange member firms.

About 19,000 men and 1,000 women have either taken the Stock Exchange's examinations or the courses of the New York Institute of Finance (37 Wall Street, New York 5), which take eight months and cost $135 in person and $125 by mail. The courses exempt those who take them from the examination. Incidentally, anybody who wants to learn all about the stock market in ten easy lessons had better steer clear of those NYIF courses. They are meant for professionals, people who want to make a career of finance, and they are pretty hard work. However, according to the Institute, many high-ranking Army and Navy officers—men who have learned how to study—are taking the courses in preparation for retirement and are not finding the going too heavy.

The average age of the customer's broker is fifty-four. He is not supposed to be paid on a commission basis but his salary somehow or other adjusts itself almost miraculously to what he produces.

DEALER: The opposite of "broker." A *broker* buys or sells *for* you and gets a commission. A *dealer* buys or sells *to* you (directly or through your broker) and makes a profit.

Odd lots are handled by dealers, who buy round lots and break them up into smaller pieces as you require them. Specialists are dealers much of the time. They buy and sell stock for their own accounts to keep the market orderly. Your own broker may become a dealer without the formality of donning a mask. He does this when he is helping to market a new issue of a security or to make a secondary distribution. And if you should want to buy or sell a stock that is not listed on one of the major exchanges, so that he has to deal in the over-the-counter market (which really means that he buys or sells over the telephone) he may act either as a dealer or a broker. When he sends you a confirmation of your trade, he must tell you which he was.

DEBENTURE: A bond—or, if you prefer, a promissory note—backed solely by the credit of the issuing corporation and junior to its other bonds; that is, paid off later if the company goes bust and is wound up.

DEPLETION: A bookkeeping device intended to compensate for the exhaustion of the natural resources owned by a company. For example, if a company thinks it has reserves of 20,000,000 tons of iron ore and it mines 2,000,000 tons in one year, it makes a bookkeeping entry to represent this. Theoretically the sums set aside for depletion are used to acquire new ore-bearing lands.

DEPRECIATION: Another bookkeeping device, intended originally to keep a company from paying taxes on nonexistent plant values. In late years it has been used as a device to encourage the construction of surplus capacity.

In STRAIGHT-LINE DEPRECIATION, if a building had a life of twenty years, a company might deduct 5 per cent of its original cost each year before paying taxes on profits. Machinery might be depreciated in ten years or in five years.

Since World War II, the government has allowed accelerated depreciation to persuade industrialists to build more plant. That doesn't seem to have been fast enough, however, so now almost anybody can double the rate of normal depreciation on a brand-new asset. In the DECLINING BALANCE method of depreciation, for example, a property normally depreciable in ten years—or 10 per cent a year—is allowed 20 per cent on 100 per cent of the cost in the first year, 20 per cent of the remaining cost—80 per cent—or 16 per cent in the second year, and so forth.

DIVIDENDS: A corporation makes a profit. Three or four weeks after the end of the accounting period (generally a quarter-year) the directors meet and decide what to do with the money. Suppose the company has 1,000,000 shares and the profit for the quarter has been $1,800,000. A reasonable amount to pay to the holder of each share would be $1. Such a payment would be called a "dividend."

EARNED SURPLUS: Accumulated earnings, which may be drawn upon to pay dividends when they have not been earned in the most recent quarter.

EARNINGS REPORT: A statement of a company's operating success for a period of a year or less. Ordinarily you see it as a brief statement of sales, net profit and net profit for each common share. Each of these figures is compared with the figure for the same period a year earlier.

Be watchful where earnings reports are concerned, for they can be highly misleading. Sometimes a company includes nonrecurrent items, such as profits on the sale of property, with profits from ordinary operations. Sometimes it changes its accounting methods from year to year. For example, a company can make an appreciable difference in its apparent earnings by adopting one of the "accelerated depreciation" methods now permitted or by changing its accounting for inventories from first-in-first-out (FIFO) to last-in-first-out (LIFO).

In 1958 United States Steel altered the accounting on its pension fund and adopted "sliding scale" methods of handling depreciation. In other words, it wrote off less for depreciation because gross income was smaller. For the first nine months of 1958 it was able thus to report net income of $3.57 a share. If it had used the 1957 accounting methods the figure would have been something like $2.20 a share. With United States Steel selling at 66, this changed the price-earnings ratio from 30 to 18.4.

As the years go by, investors forget the special circumstances modifying the published figures. They take them as gospel and even build investing systems on them. I feel that some authority—perhaps the Stock Exchanges—should insist on uniform accounting for shareholders. Let the companies keep another set of books for the tax collectors!

EQUITY: An amount owned over and above a debt. If you borrow $5,000 to buy $10,000 worth of stock, the $5,000 that you put up is your initial equity. It rises and falls as the market price of the stock fluctuates.

EXCHANGE ACQUISITION OR DISTRIBUTION: These are methods of filling big buy orders or executing big sell orders on the floor of the New York Stock Exchange by offering extra inducements to what seems to be the wrong side of the deal. A principal who wanted to buy 15,000 shares at 60 might authorize his broker to offer special commissions to other brokers to persuade their customers to sell to him. Such customers would usually pay no commissions.

The Exchange Distribution works in reverse, for the man who wants to sell offers extra commissions to brokers to persuade their customers to buy.

EX-DIVIDEND is one of the least understood expressions in Wall Street. It means that, from the day a stock sells "ex"—without—its dividend, the buyer does not get the dividend. You undoubtedly have seen the table reporting dividends in your daily paper. It may look like this:

Company	Rate	Period	Payable	Holders of Record
Drainpipe Trousers, Inc.	25c	Q	2-16	2-6

This means that the directors of Drainpipe Trousers, Inc., have declared a quarterly dividend of 25 cents a share, payable on February 16 to shareholders whose names are on the books of the company at the close of business on February 6.

But note this: "Regular way" delivery on the New York Stock Exchange is now delivery on the *fourth* business day *after* the sale. If February 6 is a Friday, then Monday, February 2, is the last day on which an investor could buy for "regular way" delivery and still get the stock in time to have it registered in his name. (Actually, he doesn't have to have it registered; he'll get the dividend without doing this, but he must have been able to do so.) Therefore, under the Stock Exchange rule, the stock goes "ex-dividend" on Tuesday, February 3.

If you happen to have open "stop orders" either to buy or sell, it is a good idea to check up on them when the stock goes ex-dividend. Stop orders to sell are automatically reduced by the amount of the dividend; stop orders to buy are reduced if the customer so orders.

FUNDED DEBT: Long-term debt of a company, with repayment terms arranged and interest rates settled.

GIVE-UP: In midtown Manhattan there is a hotel brokerage office into which transients flow in a ceaseless stream. They watch the illuminated tape for a half hour, an hour. Sometimes they drift out. Sometimes they move to the side of the room to speak to a customer's broker, for a large sign says: "GIVE-UPS WELCOMED."

This means that the brokerage house in the hotel will happily see that your orders are executed, even though your account may be in another brokerage house. Perhaps it will wire your home broker and tell him to do the job. Perhaps, after verifying your account, it will execute the order but "give up" the name of your home broker. In either case, you will pay only the one commission and in either case the two brokerage houses will divide the commission.

GROWTH STOCK: There is a whole chapter devoted to this subject. Let us note here that almost anything can be (and has been) described as a growth stock, if somebody is trying to sell it.

Actually, there are two reasons for growth. The industry may be expanding at a rapid enough rate to make an investment in it worth while. With industrial companies the minimum annual "worthwhile" growth rate is about 12 per cent. Since the aluminum industry is increasing its annual sales by an average of 12 per cent, this industry qualifies. Your job is then to pick out a stock in the industry for which future growth has not been overdiscounted. (This may be something of a job. In mid-October 1958, Alcoa was selling at 32.4 times estimated 1958 earnings, 26.4 times reported 1957 earnings. The comparable ratios for Aluminium, Ltd., were 39.4 and 25.4; for Kaiser Aluminum 39.5 and 27.3; and for Reynolds Metals 23.4 and 20.3.)

The second reason for growth is Company policy. An ordinary company can be turned into a growth company. If it is profitable but not noticeably so, it can merge with a company that has a great tax-loss credit. Actual earnings may stay the same but reported earnings may double because taxes do not have to be paid. Or a company with a stock given a high price-earnings ratio (say, 24 times) may acquire a profitable company with a low ratio (say 8 times). An extra dollar formerly earned by the smaller company meant only $8 in the price of its stock. Now it means $24.

HEDGE is a word borrowed from the commodity markets. Suppose a miller buys actual wheat to grind into flour. He does not want to gamble that the price of wheat will fall during his manufacturing operation and reduce the price that he can get for his flour. Therefore he "hedges" his risk by selling his promise to deliver the same amount of wheat at some future date. If the price of wheat should rise, he would lose on this short-sale future contract but at the same time his actual wheat would become worth more. For the cost of the commissions, which are small in the commodity market, he has protected himself against a possibly serious loss. When he sells the actual flour, he buys to cover the short futures contract in wheat.

In the stock market one often hears that investors are "hedging against inflation," which means that they are trying to buy stocks that will rise as much as living costs will rise.

INTEREST: Interest is the rent that people pay for the use of money. Bonds and mortgages are mostly figured at "straight interest"; that is, the interest money is collected after the use. DISCOUNTS are used for most commercial loans and installment loans; that is, the amount of the interest for the whole period is subtracted in advance. In COMPOUND INTEREST the amount earned in interest is added to the original amount, the "principal," and goes on earning at the same rate. If $100 is lent at 6 per cent interest, compounded annually, then it amounts to $106 at the end of the first year. At the end of the second year this $106 is multiplied by 1.06 and

comes out $112.36. Then the $112.36 is multiplied by 1.06 and becomes $119.10. If you were compounding semiannually, you would multiply $100 by 1.03 after six months, $103 by 1.03 after a year, and so on. But if you buy bonds in the market, you pay the accumulated interest in addition to the contract price. This is true when interest is accumulating. When bonds are in default and paying no interest, they are traded "flat." Then you pay no accumulated interest when you buy.

LEVERAGE may be described as a financial arrangement that increases the possible profit (or possible loss) from an investment or speculation, just as Archimedes increased the lift of a lever by moving the fulcrum.

Suppose that you had a warrant, entitling you to buy one share of Jennings Jigsaws, Inc., selling at $40, for $20 plus one warrant. Today the warrant is worth $20. Now, if the price of the actual stock rises from $40 to $42, that is a gain of $2 or 5 per cent. At the same time, the price of the warrant must rise from $20 to $22, which is 10 per cent. That is leverage.

LIMIT ORDER: An order to buy or sell at a certain price *or better*. You might tell your broker: "Buy 100 Sperry Rand at 20⅛." If he could, he might buy at 20 or lower, but not at 20¼. When markets are thin and disturbed, limit orders make pretty good sense. They prevent you from getting a worse deal than you expected, simply because yours was the only order "at the market" in a given situation.

LIQUIDATION has several applications. It can mean winding up a company. It can mean turning securities into cash. In the argot of the market, it sometimes is merely a strong word for selling.

LOADING CHARGE: An additional fee added to the net asset value behind each share of a mutual fund in order to compensate the salesmen and the fund managers for selling the share to you. A few open-end investment funds have no loading charges. Most of them have charges running between 7½ and 8¾ per cent. There is ordinarily no charge for turning in and liquidating your mutual-fund shares.

MANIPULATION: Suppose you and I have an option to buy 100,000 shares of stock at $10 a share. It is now selling at 6, interest in it is low and volume is pretty small.

In the old days, before the Securities and Exchange Commission, we might start out our operation by "closing her on the up-tick." Every night, just before the close of the market, we'd keep buying stock until the price showed a modest gain for the day. If we were operating on a shoestring, we'd sell back most of this stock the next morning to the investors who had been attracted by the constant rise in price. At night we'd push her up again.

People begin to wonder what great secret is sending our stock—let's call it CQD—up beyond 7½. The company officers tell the simple truth: "We haven't any explanation for the rise. All we can tell you is that we are drilling four wells in the Friendless Child Lake region of Manitoba."

This gets into a newspaper and a couple of market letters. Suddenly the Friendless Child Lake region begins to seem synonymous with the Williston Basin or Spindletop.

Now is a good time for "wash sales." I put in an order to sell 2,000 shares at 8. You, working through a different broker, put in an order to buy 3,000 shares "at the market." You get my 2,000, and a little more from other sources. I make you reach. I sell you some more at 9. The public begins to nibble. Word gets around that one of the wells must have come in. Before

the day is over there are people in Wall Street who can tell you that it was flowing 52,000 barrels a day. The company, of course, merely reports (perhaps truthfully) that four wells are being drilled and the signs are not bad. We continue with our wash sales until the public takes the play away from us. Then, at 12 or 13 or 14, we take down our optioned stock and let the dear public have it.

Dodges such as this are illegal today in this country. My spectacles would be rosy indeed if I suggested that they are no longer practiced. They are. Where a stock is also traded on another exchange, such as Toronto or Montreal or London or Milan or Amsterdam, at least half of the monkey business may take place outside this country, making it almost impossible for American (or Canadian or British or Italian or Dutch) authorities to trace.

Participants are usually members of exchanges, because "wash sales" can be awfully expensive for non-members of an exchange, but this is not entirely necessary. The eventual profit may be big enough to carry quite a load. The main necessity is that activity be scattered, so that the authorities can't pinpoint it too easily.

If those in control of a company have an interest in sending its stock higher (perhaps to facilitate new financing) they have recourse to all kinds of legal dodges. They can raise apparent profits by reducing depreciation. They can arouse investor excitement by mergers and splits. They can adopt a policy of buying properties and then "spinning off"—distributing as dividends —some of them, which is always popular with taxpayers in the stratospheric brackets.

In my job I watch the stock market every day. There is seldom a time when I am not conscious that manipulation of a sort is going on in at least half a dozen stocks. Some of them make quite profitable speculations for the man who figures on getting out in a hurry whenever they turn. See Chapter 10.

MARGIN: The amount *you* pay when you buy or sell securities with the use of credit, or the amount of your equity in the securities after you have entered into the deal. Many of the uses of margin are described in Chapter 12. Brokers have both cash accounts and margin accounts, for which you sign different agreements.

MATURITY: The date when, if all goes well, the principal of a bond or debenture will be repaid.

ODD LOT: Fewer than 100 shares of a stock for which the unit of trading is 100 shares, or fewer than ten shares for a stock for which the unit of trading is ten shares. The ten-share-unit stocks are the inactive ones handled by two specialists at Post 30.

There are two ODD-LOT DEALER firms on the Exchange. These agree to sell you (or buy from you) an odd lot of any size, whenever you wish. The price is governed by the first round-lot trade to appear on the ticker tape after the receipt of your order on the floor. The odd-lot dealer is paid for his trouble by a DIFFERENTIAL. This is 25 cents a share for stocks selling at $40 a share or more, 12½ cents a share for stocks selling at less than $40. Thus, if you *sell* 40 shares of stock at 30, an odd-lot differential of 12½ cents a share or $5 in all will be subtracted from your proceeds of $1,200, along with the commission, the transfer taxes and the fee charged by the Securities and Exchange Commission.

OPTION: A right to buy or sell a security at a specified price and often within a specified period. A RIGHT usually expires rather promptly. PUT OPTIONS and CALL OPTIONS are commonly sold for periods ranging from thirty days to six months and ten days. The former give the right to deliver stock at agreed prices. WARRANTS are sometimes issued in perpetuity. More commonly they have expiration dates and sometimes changing values as they grow older. All are explained at length in Chapter 12.

OVER THE COUNTER is a boundaryless area policed by the National Association of Securities Dealers, Inc. Actually it is an over-the-telephone market for securities that are not traded on a registered stock exchange and for dealers who are not members of registered stock exchanges. Neither part of that definition above is exclusive. Non-members of exchanges deal happily in listed securities—and members do, too, after the exchanges have closed for the day. Again, some of the best over-the-counter markets for individual stocks are made by members of registered exchanges.

Almost all trading in United States Treasury obligations is done over the counter.

There are three main reasons why stocks are traded over the counter. The first is a definite dislike for the publicity given price movements in an auction market. Several big New York City banks were once traded on the New York Stock Exchange but they took themselves off to the relative quiet of a market that never reports a sale, merely a bid price and a mechanically marked-up "asked price."

Secondly, some companies can't be bothered with making all the reports required by the Securities Exchange Act of 1934, or don't feel the need for the greater public interest that comes with listing. Among these are Anheuser Busch and Christiana Securities, the latter the great private investment trust that holds large quantities of E. I. du Pont de Nemours & Co.

The third reason is that it provides a market for the stock of the little companies, the new companies, the unseasoned stocks that are just beginning to come to the fore. Among these stocks are almost certainly some excellent buys. Unfortunately the newspapers that print lists of over-the-counter stocks and their quotations are forced by space considerations to concentrate on the well-known and stodgy issues, not on the exciting newcomers.

One last point: Banks and over-the-counter houses may lend as much as they wish against over-the-counter securities. They are not covered by either Regulations T or U of the Federal Reserve Board. New York Stock Exchange firms may *not* lend against over-the-counter securities.

PAR once meant $100 in every case. It is still assumed to mean that in the case of bonds. If you want to set a limit on your bid for a bond at, say, 100½, you may tell your broker, "Pay up to par and a half."

With stocks, par values have been messed up pretty thoroughly by the exigencies of company financial policy. Safeway Stores and General Motors have par values of $1.66⅔ a share, E. I. du Pont de Nemours and Co. $5, Superior Oil of California (which sells above $1,500 a share as often as not) $10, Kaiser Aluminum 33⅓ cents, Allied Chemical $18, General Tire and Rubber 83⅓ cents and Hercules Powder $2.82½. And there are some, mostly preferred stocks, at par value of $100 a share and some—fewer than in the past—with no par value. In the latter case the stated value is obtained by dividing the number of common shares into the capital account after deducting the aggregate liquidating values of all preferred shares.

PREFERRED STOCK: When we mention stock without a descriptive adjective, we almost always mean common stock.

Suppose you and I and Johnny down the street have founded a little company to make solar batteries. Each one of us puts in $10,000 and we issue ourselves 1,000 shares of stock apiece. Our little company does well. In fact, it is worth almost $100,000 when it is offered a terrific deal. If it can raise $100,000 more it can take over the plant that has been making most of the battery parts. This will cut our costs in half and make our output much more profitable.

Now, you and I and Johnny haven't been taking any dividends. We've been hoeing all the profits back into the company. We haven't any more money to invest. Do we want to let other people—nonworkers—share in all the limitless possibilities of this wonderfully good thing? Not on your life. We'll sell no shares of common stock if we can help it.

Instead, we sell preferred stock. We undertake that each $100 share of preferred stock will pay a dividend of $1.50 every three months. The preferred stock will get its dividend, we promise, before any money is paid to us, the common stockholders. If the company goes bust, the preferred shareholders will be paid off first from the liquidation of the assets. We may promise other things. For example, we may agree that all dividends must be paid on the preferred before the common stock gets any. Unpaid dividends may pile up. In other words, the preferred dividends are to be "cumulative."

Instead of this or in addition to this, we may make the preferred stock "participating." That is, after the preferred stock has received such-and-such a dividend and the common stock has received such-and-such a dividend, any further dividends shall be in such-and-such a proportion. For instance, after the preferred has received $6 a share and the common $8 a share, the preferred and the common shall participate share-for-share in any further profits distributed as dividends. (There are 3,000 shares of common and only 1,000 of preferred.)

When such generous provisions are granted, preferred stock almost invariably has provisions for calling it in and retiring it. For example, this cumulative participating preferred we have been talking about might be called at $110 a share at any time up to 1965 and at $105 a share thereafter.

Most preferred stock does not vote in the affairs of the company unless dividends are in default.

PUTS AND CALLS: See OPTIONS. See also the description of the use of Puts and Calls starting on page 149.

Briefly, a PUT OPTION gives you the right to sell 100 shares of stock to the maker of the option at an agreed price on or before an agreed date. Suppose you thought the market was going down and bought the right to "put" General Motors at, say, 50. If the stock fell to 40, you might then buy the stock at that price and the seller of the put would be forced to buy it from you at 50. A CALL OPTION is the same thing in reverse. It is bought by a man who thinks the market is going to rise.

QUOTATION: The "bid-and-asked" for a security. It is often shortened to "quote." The ticker tape prints "quotes" from time to time, generally when the market is slow and the tape must be kept moving.

Unless you happen to be watching a tape, you are well advised to have your broker "get you a quote" on anything you wish to buy or sell. He does this over a special telephone line to the Stock Exchange concerned. When he dials the number of the stock, he is connected with a girl who tells him (for example) "General Telephone 53 bid a quarter asked." That means 53 bid 53¼ asked. You can then decide what bid or offer you want to make.

RALLY: A rise following a decline in the market or in a particular stock.

In the market as a whole, it is sometimes handy to be able to spot the *quality* of a rally. If most of the stocks affected are those with large short interests, we may guess that the shorts are taking their profits and that underlying sentiment has shown no sign of changing. This is technical.

If, however, stocks with real values to offer—and relatively small short interests—are the ones to gain, we may add that fact to what we know about the quality of the market. A technical rally means little. The genuine rally, however, *may* mean that strength is developing.

REGISTERED REPRESENTATIVE: Another name for Customer's Broker, q.v.

RIGHTS: A company needs to raise more money and wants to give its present shareholders—often because it is required by law to do so—the first crack at the new stock (or debentures). Since these securities are going to its own shareholders, the company can price them well under the current market price. It might, for example, offer a shareholder a piece of paper that conveys the right to buy one share of common stock at $50 (when the market for it was $75) provided he also presented ten *rights*. In other words, he would be permitted to buy one share for each ten shares he held. Such rights generally expire rather promptly. If you are not in position to put up the money to exercise your rights—and you can carry the stock on 25 per cent margin—you may sell the rights.

If you are not a shareholder to start with, you may buy the rights in the market, buy the new stock and carry it on 25 per cent margin.

S.E.C.: The Securities and Exchange Commission was established by the

Securities Exchange Act of 1934 to regulate securities markets. The S.E.C. administers the act named above, the Securities Act of 1933 and several other laws intended to protect the investor. But if you think a Stock Exchange firm has gypped you, you'll get faster and more definite action by complaining to the Exchange, which is mighty proud of its reputation for fair play. And if you have been treated unfairly, you'll get your money back. I don't think I've ever heard of an investor getting his money back as the result of a complaint to the S.E.C.

SECONDARY DISTRIBUTION: The sale of a large block of already-issued stock by the methods used for marketing new issues. It is done off the Stock Exchange, usually by telephone.

Here is a big block of stock. Perhaps an estate is being settled. Perhaps a large shareholder needs his money for something else. Perhaps he thinks the stock is going to fall and he wants to get out. Or perhaps he has just grown tired of seeing it around. The present market is around $70 a share. But he knows that selling 100,000 shares in the auction market would probably drive the price down to $60 or below, for this is not an especailly active stock. He goes to an underwriting house, which offers him, say, $66 or $67 a share. It then organizes a selling syndicate. Stock Exchange members get the permission of the Exchange to participate. Then the customer's brokers go to work persuading their customers to buy the stock. There is an extra persuasiveness in their voices. Selling secondary distributions is about twice as profitable as selling stocks at regular Exchange commissions.

SHORT SALE: If you sell stock that you have borrowed—naturally, in the hope of being able to replace it at a lower price—that is a short sale.

The whole business is explained in Chapter 7.

SPONSOR: This is a fuzzy word. The New York Stock Exchange glossary doesn't even include it, which may be rank cowardice but is probably oversight. The Webster's New World Dictionary definition is "a person or agency that gives endorsement to or vouches for some person or thing."

On the Stock Exchange, I suppose that originally the sponsor was the chief underwriter for the stock of a new company. Jay Cooke & Co. were the original *sponsors* of the Northern Pacific Railroad Company. More recently, F. Eberstadt & Co. *sponsored* the first public offering of the common stock of Chock Full O'Nuts Corporation, until then held solely by its founder.

Nowadays the "sponsor" may not have had anything to do with the underwriting of an issue. The research department of a brokerage house may make a careful study of a company and decide (1) that there are hidden values in it that will make money for the firm's customers; (2) that certain changes can be made in the company's way of doing business that will provide either genuine growth or tax advantages for high-bracket holders; (3) that this is so good a proposition that the firm itself should take a position, i.e., buy some of the stock.

By any of these three methods, the brokerage firm becomes close to the company or is presumed to have become close to the company. Thus when the firm suggests that customers buy more shares and the shares go up, and the company then takes action making the shares worth their new high price, the firm is recognized as a "good sponsor."

Any brokerage house that puts out a lengthy study of a company does not automatically become the sponsor of that company. McDonnell & Co. and David J. Greene & Co. both did that for American Telephone and Telegraph Company and neither can be called its sponsor.

SPECIALIST: A member of a stock exchange who fulfills a double function. First, he is a broker, executing LIMIT ORDERS—that is, orders to buy or sell at stipulated prices—that are left with him by other members of the Exchange. Secondly, he is a dealer, buying and selling these stocks for his own account.

Because this double function gives him an advantage, the Stock Exchanges have heaped responsibilities on him. He is made to maintain an orderly market, with proper CONTINUITY of prices. In other words, stocks must not be allowed to jump a point or so between sales, simply because there is no public bid or offer. In that case, he must make a bid or offer himself. Sometimes, strangely enough, the market is so thin that both the offer to buy and the offer to sell are his.

A lengthy description of the specialist's functions starts on page 205.

SPLIT: This is a debatable word. It *should* mean a division of the shares of a company into a greater number of shares by dividing the par value of the authorized shares. For example, a company with 2,000,000 shares of $10 par value might *split* its stock into 4,000,000 shares of $5 par value. If, on the other hand, that same company had an earned surplus of $33,000,000 and the directors voted to declare a 100 per cent STOCK DIVIDEND of 2,000,000 shares without changing the par value, that *should* be described as a stock dividend and not a split.

In practice, however, Wall Street generally uses the Stock Exchange definition: any issue of new stock as big as 25 per cent is called a split— that is, we talk of a 5-for-4 split;

but anything smaller—even though it may result from a change in the par value—is called a stock dividend.

From the investor's point of view the distinction I should like to make is a valid one. The directors of a company may almost always vote a 100 per cent stock dividend (if the surplus is available) without putting it to a vote of the shareholders. But the shareholders must vote to change the par value.

STOCK: Heaven only knows how we came to use this word for corporation shares. It originally meant government bonds. I suspect that it changed its meaning because we named our market places "Stock Exchanges." Then shares became so much more important than bonds that they gradually took over the word "stock."

"Shares" are not hard to understand. Our ancient Venetian ancestors—Bernard Shaw once said that, going sixteen generations back, each of us is descended from everybody then alive in Europe—sold shares in merchant ventures in Erzerum and Trebizond. In fact, the whole capitalistic system is built on the share. The rewards of a partnership go to the men who do the work. When additional capital is needed, shares are sold for money to men who take no part in the work. In "limited" companies their risk is limited to the amount they have already invested. In this country incorporation provides the same limitation. General partners in partnerships have no such immunity.

STOCK DIVIDEND: Additional shares of stock distributed to existing shareholders. See SPLIT.

STOP ORDER: An order to buy or sell a stock "at the market" when it reaches a certain price. You buy at 20 but are nervous, so you try to limit your possible loss by putting in a STOP-LOSS ORDER at 18. As soon as the stop price is reached, this becomes a market order. That is, the broker must sell at the best price he can get. If the market were dropping rapidly, you might find you had been sold out at 17½ or 17 or 16.

A STOP-LIMIT ORDER tells the broker to buy or sell at a fixed price or better after the order is "elected" by having another lot sell at the given price. Suppose you had gone short of General Motors at 50 and wanted to limit your loss in case the stock rose. You might put in a stop-limit order at 53. When the stock sold at 53 your order would be elected. But the specialist handling the deal for your broker might not be able to buy at 53, because the market might have run right on up to 53½. In fact, with only a stop-limit order, you wouldn't get out at all unless the stock later fell back to your limit price.

For this reason the stop-limit order used alone is not common. On specialists' books you will find it in this form: STOP 53 LIMIT 54. This means that your order will be "elected" when the stock sells at 53 but that the specialist may now bid up to 54 in order to get you out of your short contract. This, you can see, greatly enlarges your chances of getting out and cutting your loss.

TRANSFER TAX: Both the Federal Government and New York State charge transfer taxes on stocks. That of the Federal Government is now four cents on each $100 (or fraction thereof) involved in a sale. The tax may not exceed eight cents a share. New York State's tax ranges from one cent a share, on stock selling under $5 a share, to four cents a share, on stocks selling at $20 or more. Florida, South Carolina and Texas have transfer taxes of ten cents, four cents and 3.3 cents for each $100 of par value or four each

share of a no-par-value stock.

TRANSACTION FEES: The Securities and Exchange Commission charges a fee of one cent for each $500 (or fraction thereof) involved in any deal on a registered exchange.

TURNOVER: Ordinarily, the number of shares bought (or sold; only one side is counted) in round-lot trading on a stock exchange.

Odd-lot deals are calculated separately. Why? It is conceivable but not likely that every share bought from odd-lot dealers in a day could be matched by a share sold to them, so that they would not buy or sell any shares in the round-lot market. It is also conceivable that all the persons selling odd lots were selling steels and chemicals and all the persons buying odd lots were buying oils and drugs, so that the odd-lot dealers had to keep trading in round lots in order to keep even.

There is a discussion of Stock Exchange turnover starting on page 201.

UNLISTED: A security not listed on a registered stock exchange. See OVER THE COUNTER. Some stocks are not listed but—by a special quirk in the law—are "admitted to unlisted trading" on exchanges other than the New York Stock Exchange.

WARRANT: This is like a right but it usually has little demonstrable value when issued and therefore runs for a longer period. The holder of a warrant is given the right to buy a share of stock within a stipulated period and at a stipulated price. A discussion of warrants starts on page 159.

WHEN ISSUED: The shareholders of a corporation vote today to authorize an issue of, let us say, rights. A little time must pass before the printer delivers the actual certificates and they are mailed to the shareholders. That does not stop the market from dealing in them.

They are traded on a "when, as and if issued" basis. Naturally, deliveries do not have to be made until the Stock Exchange or the National Association of Securities Dealers so rules.

WIRE HOUSE: A member firm of the New York Stock Exchange with many branches or correspondent firms linked by a great leased-wire system.

YIELD: Dividends or interest calculated as a percentage of the purchase price. With stocks, you divide the annual dividend by the price. Thus, a stock selling at 80 and paying $4 a share yields 5 per cent.

The *current* return on a bond is figured in the same way but the yield to maturity is harder to calculate. If you need to know it your broker—who almost certainly can't figure it, either—will look it up for you in a bond basis book.

Index

SMALL CAPITALS indicate terms that are defined in the glossary and the text.

241